The Institute of Chartered Accountants in England and Wales

TAX COMPLIANCE
FA2013

For exams in 2014

Question Bank

www.icaew.com

Tax Compliance
The Institute of Chartered Accountants in England and Wales

ISBN: 978-0-85760-850-5
Previous ISBN: 978-0-85760-849-9

Second edition 2013

British Library Cataloguing-in-Publication Data
A catalogue record for this book is available from the British Library

Printed in the United Kingdom by Polestar Wheatons

Polestar Wheatons
Hennock Road
Marsh Barton
Exeter
EX2 8RP

Your learning materials are printed on paper obtained from traceable,
sustainable sources.

Contents

The headings in this index indicate the main topics of questions, but questions often cover several different topics.

Preparation questions provide you with a firm foundation before you attempt the exam standard questions.

Questions with dates beside them are past exam questions from the old syllabus. Where appropriate, they have been amended to reflect the format and style of this exam.

The real exam will contain four questions.

ICAEW

Question Bank

Your exam will consist of four questions. The second sample paper exam is as follows:

Sample paper 2	Question 1 – Ethics, IHT, CGT	31 Marks
	Question 2 – Sole trader, IT, NIC	25 Marks
	Question 3 – CT for company with long period	25 Marks
	Question 4 – Partnership and VAT	19 Marks

The first sitting of the new syllabus exam in September 2013 is as follows:

September 2013	Question 1 – Adj to profits, SDLT, CGS	27 Marks
	Question 2 – CAs, IT, NIC, IHT incl DTR	36 Marks
	Question 3 – Ethics, CGT	21 Marks
	Question 4 – Employment income	16 Marks

| Time available | 2.5 hours |

1 Preparation question: chargeable gains

Pravin supplied the following information in order that his accountant could compute his capital gains tax liability for 2013/14.

(1) He sold a painting on 1 August 2013 for £31,800 which he had purchased for £10,000 on 10 May 1980. It was worth £16,800 on 31 March 1982.

(2) He sold part of a plot of land on 5 July 2013 for £108,000. He had purchased the land as an investment on 6 December 1983 for £200,000. Incidental costs of sale were £1,970. The market value of the remaining part on 5 July 2013 was £612,000.

(3) He sold 24,000 shares in Book plc (a quoted company) on 1 July 2013 for £84,000. He had acquired shares in the company on the following dates.

Purchases	Number of shares	Cost
		£
1 May 1986	20,000	18,000
1 March 1989	4,000	4,000
1 May 2002	4,000	10,628

(4) On 10 September 2013 he sold a property for £120,000, which he had purchased for £50,000 on 1 February 1984.

Pravin has taxable income of £27,010 for 2013/14.

Requirement

Compute Pravin's capital gains tax liability for 2013/14.

Guidance notes

1 This question involves a number of separate disposals. They should be dealt with one at a time, and then the gains combined at the end.

2 The painting is a chattel (tangible movable property). Special rules apply to non-wasting chattels, based on their value. What are the value-based rules, and how (if at all) do they affect this case?

2 Preparation question: chargeable gains

John and Norma Major, who have been married for many years, carried out the following capital transactions in January 2014.

(1) John sold for £10,700 a cricket bat, signed by the 1978 England Test Team, which he had bought at an auction in May 1982 for £1,300.

(2) Norma sold her sister a bronze statue by Henry Moore for £10,000. Norma had inherited the statue on the death of her mother in August 1984, when its value was £16,300. Norma's mother had bought it in May 1982 for £13,000. The market value in January 2014 was £48,000.

(3) John sold £20,000 13¾% Treasury stock for £27,400. He had acquired the stock in September 1987 at par.

(4) John sold to his son-in-law a one third interest in a plot of land for £15,500. John had acquired the entire plot of land in June 1984 for £16,000. The value of the one third interest in January 2014 was £13,500, and the value of the remaining two thirds was £28,000.

In addition, during 2013/14 Norma had the following transactions in securities.

(i) Sold 2,250 quoted ordinary shares of Nero plc (a 0.1% holding) for £23,350 in March 2014. Before making the sale she owned 6,750 shares, of which 4,500 were purchased in December 1987 for £4,599, and 2,250 were acquired in August 1998 on the occasion of the company's rights issue of 1 for 2 at 160p per share.

(ii) Sold 3,800 quoted shares of Livia plc (a 0.5% holding) for £18,430 in June 2013. Her previous transactions in these shares had been as follows.

January 1980	Purchased	1,500	Cost	£3,300
April 1987	Purchased	2,400	Cost	£5,793
May 1992	Bonus issue	1 for 2		

The market value on 31 March 1982 of the shares purchased in January 1980 was £2.50 per share.

(iii) Gave her brother 12,000 quoted shares in Augustus plc out of her holding of 40,000 shares in March 2014. She had originally purchased the shares in January 1998 at a cost of £61,875. The shares were valued at £1.60 each in March 2014. The holding never exceeded 0.7% of the company's share capital.

John and Norma are both higher rate taxpayers.

Requirement

Compute the CGT payable by the Majors for 2013/14 and state when it is payable.

3   Preparation question: PPR relief

(a) Sebastian sold his home on 6 February 2014 after ten years of ownership for £200,000. Sebastian bought the house for £46,000 and was away from the house for four years from 6 September 2004 to travel with his girlfriend. While he was away Sebastian allowed his cousin to use the house rent free. In May 2009 Sebastian added an extension which cost £18,000.

Sebastian is a higher rate taxpayer.

Requirement

Calculate the capital gains tax payable by Sebastian.

(b) Amy sold her home on 31 July 2014 for £350,000. She purchased it on 1 June 2003 for £500,000 and installed a new kitchen on 1 July 2004 for £12,000.

Amy lived in the house from 1 June 2003 to 31 May 2007. She was then employed abroad from 1 June 2007 to 31 January 2009. Amy lived in her house again from 1 February 2009 to 31 December 2009. Amy then moved into her boyfriend, Harry's house in January 2010 which is where she currently still lives. Whilst abroad and since living with Harry, Amy's house has been unoccupied.

Requirement

Calculate the capital gain/loss on the sale of the house.

4 Preparation question: inheritance tax

Birket is a divorced man aged 80. He has a daughter Victoria, his only child, and grandchildren who were born in 1986. The following information is extracted from your files.

Lifetime gifts

(1) The only gifts made by Birket before 1 April 2010 were as follows.

26 June 2001	to his cousin Rudolf	Cash	£74,300
10 January 2008	to a discretionary trust	Gross chargeable amount	£140,500

No lifetime tax was paid on the gift into the discretionary trust as it was covered by the nil rate band in January 2008.

(2) On 1 April 2010 he gave £43,000 to his nephew Chad in consideration of Chad's marriage, which took place on that date.

(3) On 15 August 2011 he transferred a 3% holding of quoted investments valued at £205,000 to the discretionary trust created in January 2008 with his nephews and nieces as beneficiaries.

Provisions of Birket's will

By his will Birket made bequests totalling £285,000 to various charities. He left his shares in Kariba plc to his nephew Chad; his personal possessions and £500,000 to Victoria; and the residue of his estate to be held in trust for his grandchildren.

Birket had been a sole practitioner of his own investment business since 1974. His interest in the firm is valued at £524,000 for inheritance tax purposes.

He also owns 450,000 quoted ordinary shares in Kariba plc. He has owned these shares since 1985 and they are valued at 230 pence per share for inheritance tax purposes.

Birket's other assets comprise a minority investment in quoted shares, personal possessions and bank balances with likely values totalling £886,350. Debts are £37,300 and funeral expenses estimated at £2,450.

Requirement

Calculate the inheritance tax payable assuming Birket were to die in December 2014, stating who would pay the tax and the due date of payment.

Note: Assume the FA 2013 rates continue in the future.

5 Dahlia Simmons

Dahlia Simmons died, age 61, on 1 November 2013. She was domiciled in France but had been resident in the UK for 15 out of the 20 years prior to her death.

Dahlia was survived by her husband, Dan, and her daughter, Violet, age 30, and her estate at death consisted of:

- A house in London, value £600,000
- A flat in Paris, value £300,000
- £15,000 in an account in the Paris branch of Barclays Bank
- £25,000 in an account in a London branch of Barclays Bank
- A shareholding in a UK unquoted investment company, value £20,000
- A shareholding in a Canadian quoted company, value £50,000

On 1 October 2011 she settled cash of £1 million (from her London branch bank account) into a discretionary trust for the benefit of her nieces and nephews. The trustees paid the inheritance tax due. The cash settled was used to buy a portfolio of quoted securities, which now have a value of £3 million. This had been her only lifetime gift.

In her will she left £10,000 to a UK charity, her London house to Dan, and the rest of her estate to Violet.

Requirements

(a) Calculate the total inheritance tax liability, with brief explanation of Dahlia's domicile.   **(14 marks)**

(b) State who is liable to pay the tax on the lifetime gift and the death estate and when.   **(3 marks)**

(17 marks)

6 Nicola Jones

Nicola Jones, a higher rate taxpayer, made the following disposals during 2013/14:

- Sale of a vase for £16,000 on 16 May 2013. The vase was one of a set of four vases which had cost Nicola £30,000 in June 2000. The remaining three vases were valued at £45,000.

- Sale of 5,000 shares in Pomme SA, a French company, on 12 September 2013. The shares were valued at €34,450 on the date of sale, when the exchange rate was €1.25 : £1. Nicola had purchased the shares for €5,000 in July 2003 when the exchange rate was €1.46 : £1. She keeps the proceeds of sale in her French bank account.

Requirements

Calculate Nicola's capital gains tax liability for 2013/14 assuming that:

(a) She is UK resident and domiciled.   **(5 marks)**

(b) She has been UK resident for ten years but is not domiciled in the UK, and that she claims to use the remittance basis.   **(4 marks)**

(9 marks)

7 Nicolette Paulson

Nicolette Paulson died on 1 March 2014. Her estate comprised the following:

	Market value at 1 March 2014 £
House in Sussex (owned outright, jointly with her husband, Ray) 50% value:	625,000
20,000 shares in Matthews plc	See note (1)
8,000 Paulson Investments Ltd shares	See note (2)
Life interest in a trust	See note (3)
Cash and chattels	225,220
Outstanding liabilities (including income tax and capital gains tax)	23,655

Notes:

(1) The shares in Matthews plc were quoted at 380 – 396p on 1 March 2014, with daily bargains of 382p, 385p, 390p and 396p. Nicolette had inherited the shares on the death of her grandmother on 30 September 2010 when they had been valued at £50,000. The value of her grandmother's chargeable estate on death was £515,000 and the executors of her estate had paid IHT of £14,500 in respect of the shares.

(2) Nicolette owned 8,000 shares in Paulson Investments Ltd, an unquoted investment company, and her husband owned the remaining 2,000 shares. The relevant values on 1 March 2014 were as follows:

	Per share £
100% holding	350
75% – 99%	310
50% – 74%	290
25% – 49%	250
0% – 24%	220

(3) Nicolette was the life tenant of the Paulson Trust set up by her grandfather. The Paulson Trust is a qualifying interest in possession trust. The trust assets were valued at £250,000 at 1 March 2014.

During her lifetime Nicolette had only made one gift, a cash gift of £105,000 to her daughter, Janet, on the occasion of her wedding on 12 August 2009.

In Nicolette's will she left the following:

- £500,000 to the British Heart Foundation, her favourite charity,
- The house in Sussex to Ray, and
- The balance split equally between Janet and her son, Bruce.

Requirements

(a) Calculate the inheritance tax payable as a result of Nicolette's death. **(14 marks)**

(b) State who is liable to pay the tax, how much and by when. **(5 marks)**

(19 marks)

8 The O'Donnell Trust

The trustees of the O'Donnell Trust made the following disposals during the year ended 5 April 2014:

- Sale of a painting at auction on 12 June 2013 for £25,000. The painting had a base cost of £5,000 and the trustees had to pay auctioneer fees of 5% of the proceeds.

- Sale of £25,000 8% Treasury stock for £32,500 on 17 August 2013. The trustees had acquired the stock in April 2008 at par.

- Sale of a residential property on 31 October 2013 for £425,000. The property, which had a base cost of £250,000, had been owned by the trust since 1 September 2001 and had been used by Toni, a beneficiary, as follows:

Dates	Number of months	Use of property
01.9.01 – 31.10.05	50	Occupied by Toni whilst at university.
01.11.05 – 30.04.07	18	Let to tenants while Toni took time out after university to travel around the USA.
01.05.07 – 31.10.07	6	Occupied by Toni while interning at a UK company.
01.11.07 – 31.07.09	21	Let when Toni moved out to live with her boyfriend.
01.08.09 – 31.10.09	3	Occupied by Toni after she split up from her boyfriend.
01.11.09 – 31.07.10	9	Empty after Toni was sent to the USA by her new employer on 1 November 2009.
01.08.10 – 31.10.13	39	Let until the date of sale.

Requirements

(a) Calculate the trustees' capital gains tax liability for 2013/14 assuming all possible reliefs are claimed. **(13 marks)**

(b) State the due date for the trustees' self assessment tax return and payment of any CGT liability. **(3 marks)**

(16 marks)

9   Joanne Cohen (J09)

Joanne Cohen died on 1 June 2014. Joanne sold her principal private residence for £980,500 on 30 April 2013 in order to move into a residential care home. She had purchased the property on 1 April 1980 for £120,000 and its market value at 31 March 1982 was £150,000. She used her property as follows:

Dates	Number of months	Use of property
01.04.80 – 31.01.91	130	Occupied as Joanne's home.
01.02.91 – 31.07.94	42	Empty while Joanne was studying in Canada.
01.08.94 – 30.11.10	196	Let to tenants while Joanne was working elsewhere in the UK.
01.12.10 – 30.04.13	29	Empty while Joanne was required by her employer to relocate to Canada on 1 December 2010. She did not move back into the property.

Joanne transferred £345,000 to a discretionary trust for her son, Mitchell, on 1 February 2013, having received a substantial inheritance on the death of her husband, Neil, in July 2011. This was her only lifetime gift. Neil's chargeable estate on death was worth £350,000 and he left it all to Joanne. Neil had made no lifetime gifts and had always lived with Joanne, wherever she was.

When Joanne died on 1 June 2014, her estate comprised the following:

- 100,000 shares in KD plc, a quoted trading company, representing a less than 1% stake. On 31 May 2014 the shares were valued at 318 – 322p with marked bargains on that day of 317p, 320p and 327p.

- Land held as an investment. In May 2014 Joanne received an offer from a property developer to purchase her land for £430,000.

- Cash and personal chattels worth a total of £412,000.

Joanne's outstanding income tax liability at 1 June 2014 is estimated to be £12,910. Joanne made no other disposals in 2013/14, other than the sale of her home. Joanne was a higher rate taxpayer in 2013/14. Joanne's entire estate was left to her son, Mitchell.

Requirements

(a) Calculate the capital gains tax payable on the sale of Joanne's home.   **(8 marks)**

(b) Calculate the inheritance tax payable as a result of Joanne's death. State the due date(s) for the payment of the inheritance tax on Joanne's estate, assuming all beneficial elections are made.

(13 marks)

(21 marks)

10 Pearl (D09)

Pearl has made the following disposals during 2013/14:

- Gift of £100,000 in cash to her daughter, Emily, on the occasion of her marriage on 15 May 2013.

- Gift of an oil painting worth £45,000 to Oxfam, a registered charity, on 1 August 2013.

- Sale of 100,000 shares in Table Ltd, an unquoted investment company, to her son, Ben, on 15 August 2013 for their market value. The shares were valued at £2.45 per share at the time of the gift. Pearl originally paid £0.15 per share in January 1994.

- Sale of 50,000 shares in Sofa plc to Ben on 1 October 2013 for £119,000. On 1 October 2013, Sofa plc shares were quoted at 330-338p with marked bargains of 331p, 337p and 338p. Pearl purchased the Sofa plc shares in October 1975 for £0.63 per share. On 31 March 1982 the Sofa plc shares were valued at £0.80 per share.

Pearl's only previous lifetime transfer was in June 2007 when she gifted £308,000 to a discretionary trust for the benefit of her children. In the event of her death, Pearl's remaining estate (estimated to be approximately £2 million) will be gifted to Save the Children, a registered charity.

Requirements

(a) Calculate Pearl's capital gains tax liability for 2013/14.   **(6 marks)**

(b) Calculate the inheritance tax due, if any, which would arise as a result of Pearl's death assuming she were to die on 1 April 2014.   **(11 marks)**

(17 marks)

11 Todd Lovett (M10)

Todd Lovett died on 12 January 2014. His entire estate was left to his daughter Lucy and comprised the following:

	Market value at 12 January 2014 £
Principal private residence	480,000
10,000 shares in Sweeney plc	See note (1)
Shares in Dunstan Ltd	See note (2)
Cash and chattels	150,700
Outstanding liabilities (including income tax and capital gains tax)	12,650

Notes:

(1) The shares in Sweeney plc were quoted at 410 – 414p on 12 January 2014.

(2) Dunstan Ltd is an unquoted investment company. Todd inherited his shares, which represent a 15% holding, when his wife died in February 2013. There was no nil rate band left unused on his wife's death. Todd's shares in Dunstan Ltd were worth £24,900 in February 2013 and had a market value of £28,000 on 12 January 2014.

Todd made the following lifetime gifts:

- A cash gift of £390,000 to his son Toby on 4 May 2008.

- A gift of 8 acres of land to his daughter Lucy on 1 July 2012. Todd owned 8 acres of the site and his wife owned an additional 2 acres. The relevant values on 1 July 2012 were as follows:

	£
Value of 8 acres	120,000
Value of 2 acres	20,000
Value of the whole 10 acre site	190,000

Requirement

Calculate the inheritance tax payable as a result of Todd's death.   **(12 marks)**

12 Andrei Johnson (J10)

(a) Andrei Johnson decided to make the following disposals during 2013/14:

- 15 July 2013: A gift of a commercial property worth £454,700 to a discretionary trust. The trustees will pay any inheritance tax due. Andrei had purchased the property for £420,600 in May 1998.

- 17 October 2013: The sale of qualifying corporate bonds for £40,500. These were purchased for £31,270 in June 2001.

- 5 November 2013: The sale of a house previously occupied by Andrei as his principal private residence. The house was purchased on 5 November 2001 and was occupied by Andrei until 5 November 2008. On that date, he moved into a new flat and made an election for the new property to be his principal private residence. The original house was empty until it was sold. The capital gain arising on the disposal of the house was £210,000, before any reliefs.

- 3 February 2014: A gift of 6,500 shares in Wilkes Ltd, an unquoted investment company, to his son Jack. Andrei subscribed for his shares at par in May 1990. Wilkes Ltd has an issued share capital of 10,000 £1 ordinary shares which, just before the gifts were held as shown below.

	No. of shares
Andrei Johnson	7,500
Ruby Johnson (Andrei's wife)	2,000
Jack Johnson (Andrei's son)	500
	10,000

The values of the shareholdings in Wilkes Ltd are as follows:

	Price per share
Up to 25%	£10
26% - 50%	£12
51% - 74%	£25
75% - 100%	£30

Andrei is a higher rate taxpayer in 2013/14.

Requirement

Calculate the capital gains tax payable by Andrei for 2013/14, showing the tax treatment of all items. **(6 marks)**

(b) Andrei has been told that he may have only two years to live and is therefore keen to understand the inheritance tax payable as a result of the above transactions and on his death. In answering this part, use the information in part (a) and make the following assumptions:

- Andrei dies on 1 May 2016 with an estate worth £2.1 million, which will be left to his son Jack. Andrei made no lifetime gifts other than the ones shown in part (a) above.

- The commercial property gifted on 15 July 2013 is estimated to be worth only £356,000 on 1 May 2016. The values of all the other assets are expected to remain unchanged.

Requirement

Calculate the inheritance tax payable as a result of Andrei's expected death. **(10 marks)**

(16 marks)

13 Sam Ridge (M11)

(a) Sam Ridge, a retired author, lives in London. He has recently been diagnosed with a terminal illness and is making plans on the basis that he will die on 31 March 2015.

Sam owns the following assets, with estimated market values at 1 April 2014 unless stated otherwise:

(1) His home in London worth £969,000. Sam has lived there for over thirty years. There is an outstanding mortgage of £110,000 over this property.

(2) A flat in Wales worth £230,000. This was inherited from his aunt when she died in May 2010. The value of her chargeable estate on death was £442,000 and she left the entire estate to Sam. She had made one lifetime transfer of £38,000 in cash to her daughter in January 2006.

(3) A rental property in London worth £240,000, which has always been let on one-year leases. The property was purchased in January 1996 for £180,500.

(4) A painting worth £17,000 which he acquired for £2,100 in January 1998.

(5) Cash of £34,000, plus £14,000 in various ISA accounts.

(6) A grand piano worth £40,000 which was purchased for £5,000 in June 1987.

(7) 12,000 shares in Rime plc which were purchased for £29,900 in April 2009. The shares have recently decreased in value and yesterday they were quoted at 210 – 214p with marked bargains of 204p, 206p and 220p.

(8) A life assurance policy on Sam's life. The policy is written in trust for Sam's son, Cole. The market value of the policy is £159,000 and proceeds payable are £210,000.

Sam has made no lifetime gifts. In his will, he leaves the whole of his estate to Cole.

Requirement

Calculate the inheritance tax payable as a result of Sam's death, assuming that he dies on 31 March 2015. Use the values of assets provided above. **(14 marks)**

(b) Rather than wait until he dies, Sam has now decided to give the rental property and the piano to Cole in June 2014.

Sam has taxable income for 2014/15 of £24,410.

Requirement

Using the information in part (a), calculate the capital gains tax liability that will arise on these two gifts to Cole. You are not required to change your answer to part (a). **(5 marks)**

(19 marks)

14 Julio Mandel (J11)

Julio Mandel undertook the following transfers, which were his only lifetime gifts:

1 February 2014	Gift of Julio's principal private residence to his daughter. The property cost £202,700 on 1 February 1981 and had a market value of £910,000 on 1 February 2014. The market value of the property at 31 March 1982 was £210,700. Julio had sold other assets in October 2013 just sufficient to use his annual exempt amount for capital gains tax.

Julio occupied the property as shown below:

Period	Months	
01.02.81 – 31.01.91	120	Occupation by Julio
01.02.91 – 31.07.94	42	Julio worked elsewhere in the UK and the property was empty
01.08.94 – 31.01.02	90	Occupation by Julio
01.02.02 – 31.07.02	6	Julio worked elsewhere in the UK and the property was rented out
01.08.02 – 31.01.06	42	Julio took a break from work and lived in Africa for some time. The property continued to be rented out.
01.02.06 – 01.02.14	96	Occupation by Julio

2 March 2014	Gift of £240,000 in cash to a discretionary trust set up for the benefit of Julio's grandchildren. The trustees agreed to pay any inheritance tax due on the transfer.

Having made the gifts described above, Julio died suddenly on 1 June 2014 at the age of 52. He was survived by two children, but had never married. Julio left his entire estate, valued at £340,000, to his son. There was a bank loan of £2,900 outstanding on Julio's death and funeral expenses totalled £2,300.

Julio had started a small business consultancy as a sole trader on 6 April 2014 and made trading profits of £10,975 until the time of his death. Julio had notified HMRC of his new business, but at the time of his death he had paid neither income tax nor any national insurance contributions in respect of the venture. Julio was a basic rate taxpayer and his only other source of income from 6 April 2014 until his death was bank interest of £8,400 (net).

Requirements

(a) Calculate the capital gains tax payable by Julio for 2013/14 as a result of the disposal of his principal private residence. Show how any reliefs are calculated. **(6 marks)**

(b) Calculate the inheritance tax payable as a result of Julio's death. **(12 marks)**

(18 marks)

15 Alice and John (S11)

Alice and John have been together for a number of years and have five children together. Alice and John want to know the amount of inheritance tax that would be payable on Alice's death. Alice owns the following assets:

- A house worth £700,000 with a mortgage secured on it of £200,000.

- A life assurance policy on her own life written into trust for the benefit of the children. In the event of her death the children will receive £450,000 in total.

- 30,000 shares held in A plc. As at today, the shares are quoted at 210-215p with marked bargains of 210p, 214p and 216p.

- 2,000 shares in B Ltd, an unquoted investment company with 50,000 issued shares. John owns 3,000 shares in B Ltd. As at today, a holding of less than 5% of the shares is valued at £4.50 per share whereas a holding of 5-10% is valued at £5.10 per share.

Cash, chattels and other personal effects worth £945,000.

Alice's only previous lifetime transfer was the gift of £106,000 in cash to a discretionary trust set up in September 2010 for the benefit of the grandchildren.

Under the terms of Alice's will, John inherits £1 million with the balance of the estate left to the children.

Requirements

If Alice were to die today, calculate the inheritance tax that would be due as a result of her death assuming:

- Alice and John are married; and
- Alice and John are not married. **(12 marks)**

Notes: You should present your answer as an inheritance tax computation in two columns using the headings (i) Married; and (ii) Not married.

16 Bill (D11)

Bill has two children, Jason and Suki, and made the following lifetime gifts:

13 May 2004	A cash gift of £100,000 to his son Jason.
1 June 2010	A cash gift of £390,000 to the trustees of a discretionary trust for the benefit of his two children. The trustees agreed to pay any inheritance tax due on the transfer.
5 July 2012	Cash gifts of £150 to each of his five grandchildren.
18 August 2013	A gift of a painting to his son Jason on the occasion of Jason's marriage. The painting was purchased on 13 June 1993 for £2,100 and was valued at £20,000 in August 2013.
9 March 2014	A gift to his daughter Suki of 20,000 shares in Wolf plc, an investment company, quoted at 330 – 334p with marked bargains of 331p, 335p and 337p. Immediately prior to the gift, Bill owned 30,000 shares. Bill purchased his shareholding in May 2004 for £55,275.

Jason was planning to sell the painting, but it was valued at £18,000 in September 2014 and he therefore decided to keep it in the hope that it would increase in value.

Bill died suddenly on 15 September 2014 and left his estate, valued at £1.2 million, to his two children in equal shares. Bill had taxable income of £27,010 in 2013/14.

Requirements

(a) Calculate the capital gains tax payable by Bill for 2013/14. **(6 marks)**

(b) Calculate the inheritance tax payable as a result of Bill's death, indicating the amount of and reasons for the availability of any reliefs and/or exemptions. Make clear your treatment of the use of the nil rate band. **(16 marks)**

(22 marks)

17   Megan (M12)

Megan died on 1 January 2014. At the time of her death she owned the following assets:

- Land in Wales worth £245,000.
- Cash, chattels and other personal effects worth £415,000.

On 31 December 2000 Megan gave £248,000 in cash to a discretionary trust set up for the benefit of her children.

On 1 February 2007 Megan gave £185,000 in cash to her daughter.

Megan's husband died on 1 January 2009. He left £234,000 to his children and the rest of his estate to Megan. He had made no lifetime transfers.

Under the terms of Megan's will, £200,000 is gifted to a UK registered charity with the balance of the estate left to her children.

Megan's funeral cost £6,337.

Requirement

Calculate the inheritance tax due, if any, as a result of Megan's death.   **(12 marks)**

18   Tina Chang (J12)

(a)   Tina Chang died on 1 November 2013. Tina left £250,000 in cash to her husband Miguel, and the rest of her estate to her son Noah.

Tina's estate on death comprised the following, as valued at 1 November 2013:

- A house in London worth £790,000 on which there was a mortgage of £145,000 outstanding.

- 1,000 shares in WMK plc, which were quoted at 103p – 106p. On 1 November 2013 there were marked bargains of 100p, 102p and 106p.

- Tina's share of a piece of land owned jointly with Miguel in the proportions 30% by Tina, 70% by Miguel. The relevant values were:

	£
Value of a 30% interest	31,000
Value of a 70% interest	75,000
Value of the entire piece of land	149,000

- A life insurance policy on Tina's own life. The policy was not written into trust. It pays proceeds of £120,000 and had a market value at 31 October 2013 of £96,000.

- Cash of £250,000.

- Paintings worth £92,000.

On 15 May 2008 Tina made a gift of an apartment in Oxford worth £344,000 to a discretionary trust. The trustees agreed to pay the inheritance tax due. On 1 November 2013, the apartment was worth £302,000.

Requirement

Calculate the inheritance tax payable as a result of Tina's death indicating the availability and amount of any relief(s).   **(12 marks)**

(b) Noah has sold a painting he had inherited from his mother Tina. The probate value of the painting was £3,900 and Tina had purchased it in March 2000 for £4,200.

Noah sold the painting in February 2014 for £15,650 and paid selling costs of £480. He intends to use the money from the sale to purchase shares in Lynch Ltd at a cost of £9 per share. He has taxable income of £12,000 for 2013/14 and no further capital gains.

Requirement

Calculate the number of shares in Lynch Ltd that Noah may purchase using the after-tax proceeds from the sale of the painting. **(4 marks)**

(16 marks)

19 Felicity Sharp (M13)

Felicity Sharp has non-savings income for 2013/14 of £22,745. In addition, she has made the following disposals during the year:

- Sold 2,000 shares in Legato plc, an investment company, to her sister for £7 each when the market value was £10.50 each. Felicity had purchased 4,800 shares for £9,200 in June 2009. The shares were the subject of a one-for-four rights issue at £5.50 per share in March 2011. Felicity took up all of her rights.

- Sold a painting for £25,900 which originally cost £5,100 in March 2004.

- Sold 2,000 shares in Staccato Ltd for their market value of £55,000. The shares originally cost £39,000 in January 1980 and were worth £42,000 in March 1982.

Requirement

Calculate the capital gains tax payable by Felicity for 2013/14. **(8 marks)**

20 Delia Major (M13)

Delia Major is worried about her health and has asked for an assessment of her inheritance tax position, based on her dying in December 2014.

Delia is a partner in a business called Brightlights. Delia also owns a commercial building, Argyle Towers.

By December 2014 Delia estimates that the value of her share in the Brightlights partnership will be £300,000 and that the value of Argyle Towers will be £230,000. Delia estimates that the remainder of her estate on death will be worth £1.7 million.

Under the terms of her will, Delia will leave £1 million to charity and the rest of her estate to her son, Bernard.

Delia has made the following lifetime transfers:

1 April 2007:	Gift of £296,000 to a discretionary trust for the benefit of her two grandchildren.
1 March 2008:	Gift of £50,000 to Bernard.
18 June 2008:	Gifts of £250 each to her two grandchildren.

In addition, since 3 September 2009, Delia has paid £10,000 to Bernard for his children's school fees on 3 September each year. Delia has always used her salary from Brightlights to pay the fees and the payments have not affected Delia's standard of living.

Requirement

Calculate the inheritance tax that would be payable as a result of Delia's death if she were to die in December 2014. Show your treatment of all the transfers above and indicate the availability and amount of any exemptions. **(11 marks)**

Income tax – the unincorporated trader

21 Preparation question: capital allowances

Francis prepared accounts for the ten-month period to 31 March 2014.

The following capital expenditure was incurred in this trading period.

(i) 30 January 2014 New computer equipment costing £5,000.

(ii) 1 February 2014 New motor car for Francis costing £32,000 (CO_2 emissions 155 g/km), second-hand motor car for sales manager costing £10,000 (CO_2 emissions 127 g/km). Francis used his car for business purposes 90% of the time.

(iii) 2 March 2014 New plant costing £151,840, second-hand plant costing £79,844.

(iv) 10 March 2014 New refrigeration equipment costing £25,000. This equipment qualifies as energy efficient as listed on the UK Energy Technology list.

Prior to 1 June 2013, all equipment was leased so there were no tax written-down values brought forward on this date. The new plant purchased on 2 March 2014 is expected to be used in the business for the next 30 years.

Requirements

(a) Calculate the maximum capital allowances which can be claimed by Francis in this period of account.

(b) Outline the relief available to Francis in respect of expenditure on office accommodation.

Note: Ignore VAT.

Guidance notes

1 You should first read through the question, and note all the different types of asset involved.

2 You can then plan how your answer will look. It is best to set out a capital allowance computation using the standard pro forma.

3 Each type of asset should be tackled separately. By breaking a question down into small pieces in this way, it becomes much more manageable.

4 Note the length of the period of account. Will this affect WDAs?

22 Preparation question: adjustment of profits

Archer has been in business since 6 April 2004 as a gentlemen's outfitter. The accounts for the year ended 30 June 2014 showed a draft adjusted trading profit before capital allowances of £9,173.

The following matters also need consideration in connection with the above accounts, and have not been considered in calculating the draft adjusted trading profit.

(1) Capital allowances on fixtures and fittings, a van and a car have been agreed as £11,960.

(2) The draft adjusted trading profit includes a deduction of £24,000, being the lease premium paid by Archer when he took out a new ten year lease on his business premises on 1 October 2013.

(3) Stock on hand at 30 June 2014 was included in the financial accounts at £6,170, which comprised the following.

	£
Conventional clothing (cost £2,580; market value £3,680)	2,580
Trendy clothing (cost £3,590; market value £2,650)	3,590
	6,170

At 1 July 2013 the stock consisted entirely of conventional clothing and the value brought into the accounts was the cost price of £4,120; the market value at that date was £5,360.

(4) During the year clothing costing £100 with a retail market value of £95 was taken from stock by Archer for his private use. The £100 was recorded as drawings, with no impact on profit.

(5) Archer uses a room in his home for business purposes. He has calculated that he worked at home for 26 hours per month except for one month during the year when he worked at home for 55 hours. Archer claims the fixed rate deduction for use of his home for business purposes.

Requirement

Compute Archer's adjusted trading income for the year ended 30 June 2014.

23 Preparation question: change of accounting date

Sarah has been trading since 1 July 1986 as a retailer of children's clothing. She has unrelieved overlap profits of £11,500 (four months).

Her tax adjusted trading profits for the last couple of years have been:

	£
Year ended 30 November 2012	24,000
Year ended 30 November 2013	40,500

Sarah is contemplating changing her accounting date to 31 March. The estimated future adjusted trading profits of the business are:

	£
Year ended 30 November 2014	25,500
Period ended 31 March 2015	14,000

Requirement

Calculate the assessable profits for all relevant tax years, assuming that Sarah does change her accounting date.

24 Preparation question: cash basis of accounting for small businesses

Mr Hainey has a grocery shop and has been trading for several years. He and his wife live in the flat above the shop. Mr Hainey has elected to use cash basis of accounting for the year to 31 March 2014 and the accounts for this year are set out below.

	£	£
Total receipts from sale of goods		72,000
Payments for purchases of goods for resale		(48,300)
Gross profit (net receipt)		23,700
Other receipts: Proceeds from sale of equipment		3,000
Expenses paid:		
Light and heat	1,850	
Rent of shop and flat	2,250	
Postage and stationery	185	
Telephone	200	
Accountancy	500	
Legal and professional fees	650	
Motor vehicle expenses	2,525	
Wages	2,100	
Cleaning	500	
Sundry expenses	160	
Purchase of weighing scales	500	
		(11,420)
Net profit (receipts) for year		15,280

Notes:

(1) Purchases of goods includes goods for own consumption which cost £400

(2) One third of light and heat, rent and telephone expenses related to the flat above the shop. Mr Hainey has not elected to use the fixed rate monthly adjustment for private use of business premises.

(3) Legal and professional expenses were in respect of fees incurred on an unsuccessful bid to acquire premises next door.

(4) Motor vehicle expenses are in respect of a car and a van. The car has been leased since 6 April 2013. It would have cost £16,200 to buy and has CO_2 emissions of 165g/km. The car leasing expenses in the year were £600 and the cost of fuel for the car was £800.

The balance of £1,125 relates to payments for the servicing and fuel for the van. The van was acquired in the previous year and the cost was covered in full by the annual investment allowance.

Mr Hainey has summarised his mileage for both the car and the van as follows for the year ended 31 March 2014:

Car

Personal journeys	1,000
Travel to visit clients	5,000
Travel to visit potential clients	2,000
	8,000

Van

Personal journeys	1,000
Deliveries to clients	3,000
	4,000

Mr Hainey would like to claim the fixed rate mileage allowance where possible.

(5) The wages are paid to Mrs Hainey for secretarial duties. From 1 April 2013 she has been paid £175 per month.

(6) Sundry expenses include the following:

	£
Cash donations to national charities	5
Subscription to chamber of trade and commerce	25
Subscription to golf club	25
	55

(7) The tax written down values on the capital allowances pools at 1 April 2013 were nil.

(8) Mr Hainey's accountant has informed him that he has an 'adjustment expense' for tax purposes of £800 as a result of changing over to the cash basis of accounting. This has not been reflected in the above figures.

Requirement

Calculate the taxable trading profits for the year ended 31 March 2014. Explain your treatment of the proceeds from the sale of the equipment and the payment for the weighing scales.

25 Elinor (J09)

(a) On 1 January 2014, Elinor decided to set up her own unincorporated business as a photographer. Her business is standard rated for VAT purposes. Elinor's cumulative turnover for the new business to 31 May 2014 was £56,900.

On 1 June 2014, Elinor accepted a contract worth £14,300 to sell her photos to a customer who is VAT registered in France (an EU country). On 13 June 2014, Elinor accepted a second contract worth £8,000 to sell her photos to a French customer who is not VAT registered. Both customers paid for their photos at the time they placed their orders.

Requirement

Explain when Elinor is required to notify HMRC of the need to register for VAT, assuming she does not wish to register any earlier than necessary. Include a brief description of the potential VAT treatment of the two contracts accepted by Elinor in June 2014. **(4 marks)**

(b) Elinor's first VAT return showed a net payment to be made to HMRC. However, Elinor has received a repayment of £900 from HMRC directly into her bank account. Elinor realises that this is an error and she is not entitled to this repayment. However, she has told her chartered accountant that she intends to keep the money and say nothing to HMRC about it.

Requirement

Explain the action the chartered accountant should take in response to this issue. **(4 marks)**

(c) In order to raise additional finance for her expanding business, Elinor has prepared forecast accounts for the year ending 31 December 2014. She estimates her trading profit for the year ending 31 December 2014 to be £89,000 (after capital allowances of £18,500 on the tax written down value brought forward in the main pool). In preparing this estimate, Elinor has treated all of the issues described above correctly, but has not made any deductions in respect of the following:

- Elinor will purchase a van on 1 November 2014. The van will cost £13,000 (VAT inclusive) and will be used by her 80% for business purposes and the rest of the time will be used by her new assistant for private purposes.

- Elinor has employed an assistant from 1 April 2014. He is paid £1,280 per month and Elinor pays him £50 per month towards the cost of qualifying childcare.

Requirements

(i) Compute Elinor's revised trading profit for the year ending 31 December 2014. **(5 marks)**

(ii) Compute the trading income assessment for Elinor for all relevant tax years, identifying any overlap profits. **(3 marks)**

(16 marks)

26 Jose Cranem (S09)

Jose Cranem runs 'Dee Minor' a small unincorporated business he set up in 2002 to make hand-crafted wooden toys.

Information about Dee Minor

Dee Minor operates from a small factory, the freehold of which was purchased on 1 August 2012 for £140,000. Previously, Jose had operated his business from rented premises.

The recent tax adjusted trading profits (after deducting capital allowances) for the business are as follows:

	£
Year ended 30 June 2012	110,130
Year ended 30 June 2013	93,800

Jose accepted an offer to sell his business and prepared final accounts for Dee Minor for the six months ended 31 December 2013. The tax adjusted trading profit (before deducting capital allowances) for this period was £62,090. The tax written down values at 1 July 2013 were as follows:

	£
Main pool	17,190
Jose's car (used 40% for business purposes)	13,000

Sale of Dee Minor

On 31 December 2013, Jose sold the business of Dee Minor to Agricette Ltd, a leading toy manufacturer. Agricette Ltd prepares accounts to 31 December each year. The consideration for the sale was £252,100, allocated as follows:

	Consideration £
Goodwill	80,000
Factory	160,000
Plant and machinery	12,100
	252,100

Jose kept his car, which originally cost £32,000, and had a market value of £7,900 at 31 December 2013. The main pool of plant and machinery was transferred to Agricette Ltd for £12,100 on 31 December 2013. None of the items in the main pool were worth more than £6,000 and all had originally cost less than £6,000. Jose made no disposals in 2013/14 other than the sale of his business.

Jose has unrelieved overlap profits from commencement of £2,700.

Other income and payments

During 2013/14, Jose received UK bank interest of £1,200 and dividends of £8,900 from a UK company. On 14 April 2013, Jose made a £120 donation under Gift Aid to a local charity.

Requirements

(a) Calculate Jose's tax adjusted trading profit for the six months ended 31 December 2013. **(3 marks)**

(b) Calculate Jose's trading income assessment for 2013/14. **(2 marks)**

(c) Calculate Jose's income tax payable for 2013/14. **(8 marks)**

(d) Calculate the taxable gains arising as a result of the sale of the business on 31 December 2013. **(4 marks)**

Ignore VAT. **(17 marks)**

27 George (D10)

George, an unincorporated trader, commenced to trade on 1 January 2013. He prepared his first set of accounts for the 16 month period to 30 April 2014, and thereafter intends to prepare accounts annually. George registered for VAT on 1 January 2013 and makes wholly standard rated supplies.

George made a tax adjusted trading profit of £220,873 (before capital allowances) in the 16 month period to 30 April 2014. George was unsure of three items which he treated as follows when he adjusted the original accounting profit figure in order to calculate the tax adjusted profit:

- In May 2013 George purchased a new car with CO_2 emissions of 180g/km for £18,000 plus VAT at 20%. George deducted the full £3,600 VAT from the original profit figure in order to calculate the tax adjusted profit. The car is used for personal use by George 35% of the time.

- In November 2013 George took goods from the business which had cost £150 and had a sales value of £195 for his own use. George adjusted the original profit figure by deducting the £150 from cost of sales in order to calculate the tax adjusted profit.

- In December 2013 George sent a number of product samples to ten customers. On average each customer received one trade sample worth £100. George disallowed the expenditure by adding back £1,000 to the original profit figure in order to calculate the tax adjusted profit.

George purchased the following assets in the 16 months ended 30 April 2014.

		£
January 2013	Office equipment	21,500
May 2013	Office furniture	92,000
August 2013	Electrical system for part of factory	24,000

All figures are stated exclusive of VAT.

Requirements

(a) Calculate George's tax adjusted profit after capital allowances for the 16 month accounting period ended 30 April 2014. **(5 marks)**

(b) Calculate George's taxable trading income for all relevant tax years. State the dates of the basis periods applicable to each tax year and the amount of any overlap profit arising. **(4 marks)**

(9 marks)

28 Paula Petrova (D11)

(a) Paula Petrova has run her own unincorporated business "Pointy Shoes" for many years.

Her latest finalised accounts were prepared for the year ended 31 January 2013 and the tax adjusted trading profits were £62,900. Paula then changed her accounting date and prepared accounts for the 14 months ended 31 March 2014. Her draft results for the 14 months ended 31 March 2014 are as follows:

	Note	£	£
Gross trading profit			194,500
Add: interest receivable	1		1,400
Less:			
Depreciation		3,925	
Repairs and renewals	2	4,830	
Staff costs	3	76,200	
Paula's car expenses	4	4,700	
Other allowable expenses		25,330	
			(114,985)
Profit for the period			80,915

Notes:

(1) This is the amount of interest receivable on Paula's business bank account.

(2) Repairs and renewals comprise the following:

	£
New water heating system	3,300
Redecoration of business premises	815
Repair to the air conditioning unit following a water leak	275
Replacement ceiling tiles following the water leak	440
	4,830

(3) Staff costs include wages of £950 paid to Paula's part-time assistant. She is paid monthly and has been employed at the same wage since 1 February 2014. Neither employee nor employer Class 1 national insurance contributions have been accounted for in respect of this employment. The assistant is not contracted out of the State Second Pension. Staff costs do not include any payments to Paula.

(4) Paula's car expenses comprise the following:

	£
Expenses on her Fiat car (see below)	4,400
Expenses on her new Toyota car (see below)	300
	4,700

Capital allowances

At 1 February 2013, the tax written down values of Paula's assets were as follows:

	£
Fiat car	14,800
Main pool	3,180
Special rate pool	600

The Fiat car was purchased on 1 April 2008 and Paula used it 60% for business purposes.

Paula made the following acquisitions and disposals during the 14 months ended 31 March 2014:

Acquisitions:		£
15 April 2013	Office furniture	1,800
28 June 2013	Toyota car which is used 60% for business purposes by Paula. The car has CO_2 emissions of 150 g/km	18,000
Disposals:		
5 February 2014	Fiat car (proceeds)	10,100

Paula has overlap profits brought forward of £6,286 arising on commencement of her business which represents a two month overlap period.

Requirements

(i) Calculate the tax-adjusted trading profits (after capital allowances) for Pointy Shoes for the 14 months ended 31 March 2014. Ignore VAT. **(13 marks)**

(ii) Calculate Paula's trading income assessment for 2013/14, stating the assessment period. **(2 marks)**

(b) Paula's husband Noel started to work for Tap Shoes Ltd on 1 June 2013, having taken a career break for a year. He received the following from Tap Shoes Ltd:

- Salary of £45,000 pa paid monthly on the last working day of the month.

- A car for private use from 1 July 2013. Noel used the car 30% for business purposes. The car had CO_2 emissions of 90g/km and a list price of £21,000, although Noel made a capital contribution towards the cost of the car of £2,500. Noel was reimbursed for all diesel costs in connection with the car, totalling £8,800.

- General expense allowance of £90 per month totalling £900 for 2013/14, which was all spent on entertaining clients.

Noel has been employed on a part time basis by Ice Ltd from 1 January 2009. He earned a salary of £7,000 from Ice Ltd for 2013/14. HMRC has agreed to a deferment on the payment of national insurance contributions on this employment.

The total income tax paid under PAYE in respect of Noel's employments for 2013/14 was £9,300. Noel is not contracted out of the State Second Pension.

Noel made contributions to his personal pension scheme of £12,000 (net) during 2013/14.

Noel is an investor in a Real Estate Investment Trust and received amounts paid out of tax exempt property income of £2,400 on 10 April 2013. In addition, Noel received dividends from a UK company of £18,000 during 2013/14.

Requirement

Calculate Noel's income tax and Class 1 national insurance payable/repayable for 2013/14, making clear your treatment of all items. Ignore VAT. **(15 marks)**

(30 marks)

29 Kirsty (M12)

(a) Kirsty commenced to trade on 1 January 2013. Kirsty has forecast an accounting profit for the fifteen months ending 31 March 2014 of £36,000 after accounting for the following items in the profit and loss account:

	Note	£
Entertaining	(1)	2,450
Staff costs including Class 1 Secondary NICs	(2)	23,000
Depreciation		3,846
Property costs	(3)	28,000
Overdraft interest payable		2,400

Notes:

(1) Entertaining includes the following expenses:

	£
Client entertaining	842
Staff entertaining	600
Advertising in local restaurants	1,008
	2,450

(2) Staff costs include all relevant costs except for any Class 1A National Insurance Contributions due. Teresa, who commenced work on 6 April 2013, is Kirsty's only employee to receive benefits. For 2013/14 Teresa received the following benefits in addition to her salary of £10,000:

- Use of a leased diesel van with a list price of £10,450 and CO_2 emissions of 127g/km. Kirsty pays the monthly leased cost of £125 in addition to both business and private fuel. Teresa's private mileage is approximately 20,000 miles pa.

- Provision of a computer worth £750 with agreed business usage by Teresa of 55%.

- Vouchers redeemable for £100 worth of meals in local restaurants which cost Kirsty £85.

- Kirsty paid £25 per month for Teresa's mobile telephone. Approximately 25% of Teresa's usage was for private calls.

(3) Property costs

	£
Lease premium for five year lease granted on 1 January 2013	22,000
Annual rental of £3,000 payable yearly in advance	6,000
	28,000

Capital allowances

On 1 January 2013 Kirsty purchased computing equipment (including the computer provided to Teresa) at a total cost of £4,500 and fixtures and fittings at a cost of £12,000.

Requirements

(i) Calculate Kirsty's tax-adjusted trading profit after capital allowances for the fifteen months ending 31 March 2014. **(12 marks)**

(ii) Calculate Kirsty's taxable trading income for all relevant tax years. State the dates of each basis period. **(2 marks)**

Note: Ignore VAT

(b) Kirsty sold two assets during 2013/14:

	Chargeable Gain / (Allowable Loss) £
Painting	7,555
Necklace	21,350

Neither of the assets has been used in her business.

Requirement

Calculate Kirsty's capital gains tax liability for 2013/14 assuming for the purposes of this part only that she has total income for 2013/14 of £34,000. **(3 marks)**

(17 marks)

30 Preparation question: income tax

Sean, who was born on 10 May 1940, is married to Grainne, who was born on 25 July 1933. Sean has the following income and outgoings for the tax year 2013/14.

		£	
(a)	Share of partnership profits	14,000	
(b)	Interest on a deposit account with the Scotia Bank	2,240	(net)
(c)	Profits on the letting of an investment property. This figure does not include a £20,000 premium received in respect of a ten year lease signed on 6 June 2013	7,800	
(d)	Dividends received on UK shares	2,700	(amount received)

Grainne has net income for the year of £6,000.

Requirements

(a) Calculate the income tax payable by Sean for 2013/14.

(b) Explain how your calculation would have changed if Sean had made a Gift Aid donation of £8,000 (amount paid) during the tax year.

Guidance notes

1 The major part of this question requires you to calculate an individual's overall tax position. You should start by heading your answer and laying it out: non-savings, savings and dividend income. Next show net income and the personal allowance. It will then be more difficult to overlook anything.

2 Start with non-savings income and any deductions made specifically from it.

3 Insert the types of savings and dividend income, remembering that amounts are always included gross in the tax computation even if the amounts are actually received net.

4 Net income should be shown, as it is an important figure in some computations, particularly those involving individuals born before 6 April 1948.

5 After deducting the personal allowance to find the taxable income, you need to calculate tax payable. Remember to extend the basic rate band by the gross amount of the Gift Aid paid.

31 Preparation question: benefits

James Hodge is the sales director of Waterpipes plc, a UK company, with a salary of £40,000 a year. The company also provides him with the following.

(a) Company-owned computer equipment that had cost the company £6,600 on 6 October 2010. The private use of the computer by James is insignificant.

(b) On 1 November 2013, the company made him a loan of £50,000 at 1.5% a year, with interest payable monthly in arrears, to assist his purchase of a new home. Assume an official rate of interest of 4%.

(c) On 6 April 2011 the company paid £4,000 for a photocopier / fax machine to be installed at James' house. James has always had business and private use of the machine. On 6 October 2013 James purchased the machine from the company for £50, when its market value was £270.

During 2013/14 James travelled 12,000 miles on business. He does not have a company car, but is reimbursed 35p for each business mile.

He contributes 4% of his salary (excluding benefits) to a registered occupational pension scheme.

He has a pension of £1,500 a year from a company for which he had previously worked.

Requirement

Compute James's taxable income for 2013/14. Do not calculate tax payable.

Guidance notes

1 Deduct contributions to an occupational pension scheme from employment income.
2 The loan was made part way through the year, so pro rate the benefit.

32 Preparation question: pensions

Tom has self-employment income of £350,000 for the tax year 2013/14 and makes gross contributions of £275,000 to his personal pension during the year. He has made the same level of contributions for each of the last four tax years.

Adrienne, has earned a salary of £210,000 per annum for the previous three years. She has paid £2,500 per month into her personal pension since 2008/09. On 1 December 2013 she made an additional lump sum payment of £32,000 into her pension fund.

Requirements

(a) State the maximum amount of gross pension contributions for which Tom will be entitled to tax relief and the actual amount he will have paid into the pension during the year.

(b) Explain how tax relief is given for Tom's pension payments and calculate his income tax liability for the 2013/14 tax year.

(c) Explain to Adrienne the tax consequences of the pension contributions she made in 2013/14.

Guidance notes

1 Tax relief is available on contributions up to the amount of earnings for the relevant tax year. Where an individual does not have any earnings for a particular tax year, tax relief is available on gross contributions of up to £3,600.

2 Remember though that the annual contribution allowance is £50,000. Any tax-relieved contributions in excess of this are taxed at the individual's marginal rate, with the tax being paid under the self-assessment system. If an individual has not used the annual allowance in full the unused amounts can be carried forward for three tax years.

3 The personal allowance is tapered where adjusted net income exceeds £100,000 and reduces to nil when adjusted net income exceeds £118,880. Adjusted net income is total income less gross Gift Aid donations and gross personal pension contributions made by the individual. Employer contributions, if any, do not affect the adjusted net income working.

33 Preparation question – trust income tax

Trevor Rushing set up the Rushing Family Discretionary Trust many years ago with £200,000 of cash. The trustees have since invested the trust funds and received the following income from investments during the 2013/14 tax year:

	£
Bank interest received	12,000
Dividends received	27,000
Rental income	14,500

At 6 April 2013 the balance in the trust's tax pool, brought forward from previous years, was £1,500.

The trustees made an income payment of £20,000 to one of the beneficiaries on 12 February 2014.

Requirements

(a) Calculate the income tax payable by the trustees of the Rushing Family Discretionary Trust for 2013/14.

(b) Show the balance in the trust's tax pool at the end of the year.

(c) Show the amounts that would be entered on the Form R185 given to the beneficiary, in respect of the income distribution in February 2014.

Guidance notes

1 Do not forget the basic income tax rules that require all income to be entered gross in an income tax computation, even where they are received net.

2 Apply the appropriate basic rate of tax to the first £1,000 of the trust's income.

3 Apply the appropriate trust tax rates to the remainder of the income.

4 The tax pool is a running total of all the tax actually paid or suffered by the trustees that is available to cover the 45% tax credit required for distributions to beneficiaries.

5 The R185 form shows the amount that the beneficiary actually receives as well as the 45% tax credit that comes with the payment.

34 Preparation question – overseas aspects of income tax

Cassie, age 55, is resident and domiciled in the UK. She received the following income during the year ended 5 April 2014:

Employment income from UK employer	£25,000
Property income – overseas property (gross)	£42,000
Pension income from overseas former employer (gross)	£6,000
Savings income – UK interest (amount received)	£3,200

The tax deducted from Cassie's employment income via PAYE was £7,379.

Cassie also paid overseas tax of £7,200 in respect of the overseas property. No overseas tax was deducted in relation to the overseas pension.

Requirement

Calculate Cassie's total UK income tax payable for 2013/14.

Guidance notes

1 Do not forget the basic income tax rules that require all income to be entered gross in an income tax computation, even where they are received net.

2 Remember the special rule for taxing overseas pension income where the individual is UK resident and domiciled.

3 As tax has also been paid overseas, double taxation relief is available.

4 Include all income, both UK and overseas, in the computation first and calculate the income tax liability. Then you can compare this with the liability without the overseas income that has suffered some foreign tax.

35 Stefan Blitzburger

Stefan Blitzburger was sent to the UK by his employer in May 1995, since when he has continued to be UK resident. He still considers himself to be domiciled in Germany, where he was born.

During the 2013/14 tax year, Stefan received the following UK and overseas income:

Employment income	£250,000
Dividends from his portfolio of UK quoted companies (amount received)	£19,350
Savings income – UK interest (amount received)	£9,600
Property income – overseas property (gross)	£130,000
Dividend income from Eurohypo AG, a company quoted on the German stock exchange (amount received)	£9,150

Stefan did not remit any of the overseas property income, which had suffered tax of £45,500 in Germany, to the UK during the year ended 5 April 2014. However, he did remit his overseas dividends, which were paid net of 15% withholding tax.

His employer deducted income tax of £87,948 via PAYE.

Stefan made a remittance basis claim for the year.

Requirement

Calculate Stefan's income tax payable for 2013/14. **(15 marks)**

36 The Breville Trust

Barry Breville set up the Breville Trust on 1 May 2013 with cash, quoted shares and a rental property, all of which generated income for the trust during the year ended 5 April 2014. Barry has previously set up one other trust.

The Breville Trust is a discretionary trust for the benefit of Barry's nephews and nieces and during the 2013/14 year the trustees exercised their discretion and made an income payment of £5,000 each to two of the beneficiaries.

The trustees received the following income during the tax year:

	£
Bank interest received	3,000
Dividends received	9,000
Rental income	12,000

The trustees also had the following items of expenditure:

	£
Expenses relating to the let property	4,300
General trust administration expenses	1,575

Requirements

(a) Calculate the income tax payable by the trustees of the Breville Trust for 2013/14. **(11 marks)**

(b) Show the amounts that would be entered on the Form R185 given to each beneficiary in respect of the payments received from the trust. **(2 marks)**

(13 marks)

37 The Oyster Trust

(a) The Oyster Trust is a life interest trust, of which Marc Pearl is the life tenant.

During 2013/14 the trustees received the following income:

	£
Bank interest received	4,000
Dividends received	10,800
Rental income	16,200

The trustees also had the following items of expenditure:

	£
Expenses relating to the let property	6,800
General trust administration expenses	1,100

The trustees made an income payment of £1,000 to Marc during the year but did not pay out the balance of the income to him until after the end of the tax year.

Requirements

(i) Calculate the income tax payable by the trustees for 2013/14. **(6 marks)**

(ii) Show the entries on the Form R185 given to Marc for 2013/14. **(4 marks)**

(b) The Crayfish Trust is an unconnected discretionary trust. The trustees made the following disposals of trust property during the tax year:

- 15 October 2013: The sale of a house previously occupied by a beneficiary, Tom, as his principal private residence. The trustees had purchased the house for Tom's use on 16 May 2003 and Tom had lived there until 15 November 2009, when he moved into his own flat. He made an election for the new property to be his principal private residence. The house remained empty until it was sold. The capital gain arising on the disposal of the house was £350,000, before any reliefs.

- 12 February 2014: Sold 1,000 shares in Shellac plc for £15,000. The trustees had purchased 400 shares for £1,500 in June 2004 and a further 1,100 shares in October 2009 for £4,500.

- 1 March 2014: The sale of an antique necklace for £4,995. The original cost of the necklace was £3,250 in June 2001.

Requirement

Calculate the trustees' capital gains tax payable, assuming they claim all available reliefs. **(8 marks)**

(18 marks)

38 William Pembroke (J09)

(a) William Pembroke has been employed by Norfolk Ltd for many years. He earns an annual salary of £59,000. As a result of a recent promotion to Head of Corporate Solutions, William has been offered the choice of either a company car or additional salary.

The company car offered to William has a list price of £37,000 and CO_2 emissions of 177g/km. Additional accessories worth £1,000 will be supplied with the car. William will be required to pay £2,300 towards the cost of the car, but Norfolk Ltd will pay all running costs (including the provision of petrol for both private and business purposes). As an alternative to the provision of the car, William has been offered additional salary of £8,000 pa.

Requirement

Calculate William's additional income tax and national insurance contributions each year if he

(i) Accepts the company car arrangement, or

(ii) Takes the additional salary. **(5 marks)**

(b) William decided to take the additional salary rather than the company car. He was also provided with the following benefits by Norfolk Ltd during 2013/14:

- A loan of £7,000 on 6 June 2013 on which interest is payable by William at 3% pa.

- An award of £1,000 under a staff suggestion scheme.

- The use of a computer that cost £2,250 and had first been provided to William on 1 January 2010. William's private use of the computer was insignificant.

- Free advice in respect of William's home computer network from Norfolk Ltd's in-house IT experts. The advice would normally have been the subject of an internal recharge of £200.

In addition, William received building society interest of £220 on 5 May 2013 and dividends of £225 from Norfolk Ltd on 1 March 2014. He made a donation of £320 under Gift Aid on 13 February 2014. William pays £448 per month into his personal pension scheme.

On 1 May 2013, William purchased a property and immediately let it out unfurnished. The tenants paid a lease premium of £3,000 in return for the grant of a five-year lease over the property at an annual rent of £14,400.

Requirement

Using the information in parts (a) and (b) of this question, compute William's income tax liability for 2013/14, making clear your tax treatment of all items. **(13 marks)**

(18 marks)

Note: **Assume an official rate of interest of 4%.**

39 Lea Oswald (J10)

Lea Oswald was employed by Dallas Ltd until 31 January 2014. Lea had been employed by Dallas Ltd for 12 years. Her employment income during 2013/14 was as follows:

Salary and benefits from Dallas Ltd

- £48,000 pa salary from Dallas Ltd.

- Use of a petrol company car until 31 January 2014 which has a list price of £32,000 and CO_2 emissions of 164g/km. Lea was also provided with unlimited fuel for business and private purposes.

- Use of a company flat. Dallas Ltd rented the flat for £1,750 per month but terminated the lease when Lea moved out on 31 January 2014. The accommodation did not qualify as job-related.

- Use of a laptop computer which cost £2,900 when it was first provided on 30 April 2013. Lea used the laptop 80% for private purposes. Lea purchased her laptop computer from Dallas Ltd on 31 January 2014 for £300. The market value of the computer at that date was £800.

On 1 March 2014, Lea received dividends of £4,000 from Washington Ltd and made a £600 donation to charity under Gift Aid.

Requirement

Calculate Lea's income tax liability for 2013/14, showing your treatment of all items. **(9 marks)**

40 Violet (D10)

Violet works full-time for Red Ltd, a co-operative. Violet owns 1,000 shares in Red Ltd which she purchased for £32,000 two years ago financed by a bank loan taken out for the same amount at an annual interest rate of 4.25%.

Violet received the following remuneration package from Red Ltd during 2013/14:

- Basic salary of £62,050 pa.

- Company car, a Renault Clio, with CO_2 emissions of 93g/km with a list price of £16,450. The Clio was unavailable to Violet for the whole of October 2013 as it needed to be repaired. Red Ltd pays for all her petrol when she is driving the Clio.

- Holiday voucher with a face value of £2,000 which cost Red Ltd £1,800. Violet used the voucher as part payment for a family holiday to Africa.

- A contribution of £5,000 to Red Ltd's occupational pension scheme on Violet's behalf. Violet personally contributes a further £2,000 per year.

Whilst the Clio was being repaired, Violet drove her own car for the whole of October 2013 and claimed a mileage allowance from Red Ltd of 52p per mile. During October 2013 Violet drove 2,800 business miles.

In addition to her employment income Violet received interest of £1,500 from her National Savings and Investments (NS&I) Direct Saver account and £2,000 interest from her National Savings Certificates. She also received dividends from Red Ltd of £10,800. Violet also made a personal pension contribution of £800 during 2013/14.

Violet owns a 75% share and her husband owns a 25% share in a house which is rented out to tenants. However, no declaration regarding actual ownership has been made to HMRC. The total rental income for the year was £10,400. Agents' fees were payable of £1,040 plus VAT at 20%. Mortgage interest payable on the rental property for the year was £2,800.

Violet is not contracted out of the State Second Pension.

Requirements

(a) Calculate Violet's income tax liability for 2013/14. **(14 marks)**

(b) Calculate the employee's and employer's national insurance contributions payable for 2013/14 by Violet and Red Ltd respectively. Clearly show the amounts payable for each Class of national insurance contributions payable. **(5 marks)**

(19 marks)

41 Mary Queen (M11)

(a) Mary Queen was employed by Mariner Ltd, a company that designs and builds yachts, until she resigned on 31 August 2013 to set up her own business. Mary's employment income for 2013/14 is as follows:

Employment arrangements

- A salary of £74,200 pa from Mariner Ltd. Mary normally received a contractual bonus of 5% of her salary each year. When she resigned, Mariner Ltd refused to pay the full amount and Mary settled for a bonus of £1,000.
- Use of a petrol company car with a list price of £24,000 and CO_2 emissions of 120g/km. Mary returned the car to Mariner Ltd on 31 July 2013.
- For the month of August, Mary was paid a mileage allowance of 35p per mile for 500 business miles that she drove in her own car.
- A £340 entertaining allowance of which £270 was spent on client entertaining.
- An interest-free loan of £3,500, which was written off by Mariner Ltd on 31 August 2013.
- Gifts of sailing equipment from two different customers. The first gift was worth £120 and the second gift was worth £150.

Mary's new business

Mary set up her own yacht-design business. She started trading on 1 September 2013 and will draw up her first accounts for the eight months to 30 April 2014. Her projected results for the eight months to April 2014 include the following:

- Estimated revenue of £48,000.
- A new car purchased on 1 August 2013 for £20,200. The car has CO_2 emissions of 115g/km. The petrol and running expenses total £3,175. Mary estimates that she will use the car 60% for business purposes.
- Computer equipment purchased for £6,100 on 3 September 2013.
- A three-year lease over office space. Mary entered into this lease on 1 September 2013, paying a premium of £2,400 for the grant of the lease and rent of £1,100 per month.
- Other allowable costs of £2,900.

Other information

During 2013/14 Mary received ISA interest of £1,000 and dividends of £1,600 from a UK company. She paid £15,000 (net) into her personal pension scheme.

Requirements

(i) Calculate Mary's taxable employment income for 2013/14, making clear your treatment of each item. **(7 marks)**

(ii) Calculate Mary's tax-adjusted trading profit for the eight months ending 30 April 2014, making clear your treatment of each item. **(8 marks)**

(iii) Calculate Mary's income tax liability for 2013/14. **(6 marks)**

(iv) Explain the different types of income on which Mary pays national insurance contributions for 2013/14. Calculations are not required. **(3 marks)**

Note: **Ignore VAT**

(b) Mary's husband, Albert Ross, is a self-employed chartered accountant working from home. Albert acts for Mariner Ltd, preparing the company's financial statements and providing tax advice. Albert has now agreed to act for his wife's new business. Both Mariner Ltd and Mary are tendering for work from the same company and both would like Albert's tax advice on the tender.

Requirement

Explain Albert's position with regard to the potential conflict of interest and any action that he should take. **(5 marks)**

(29 marks)

42 Henry Brocard (J11)

(a) Henry Brocard, born on 10 November 1955, was employed as the marketing director of Scalene Ltd, an unquoted UK trading company, throughout 2013/14. Henry's employment package for 2013/14 was as follows:

- Annual salary of £110,000.

- Provision of a petrol-fuelled company car with a list price of £45,000 and CO_2 emissions of 115g/km. Fuel was provided, and insurance and repairs to the car cost Scalene Ltd £4,900.

- Private medical insurance which cost Scalene Ltd £780 pa. Henry was injured in a car accident in January 2014 and his treatment cost £2,900, which was paid for by the insurance company.

In addition, Henry incurred the following expenses during 2013/14, none of which was reimbursed by Scalene Ltd:

- Subscription of £560 pa to a fine dining club. Henry eats there once every two weeks and sometimes invites professional contacts to join him.

- Personal pension contributions of £1,000 per month. This is the amount of contribution paid by Henry to his personal pension scheme each month.

- £1,230 on commuting from home to a temporary work place for a six-week secondment in January and February 2014.

Henry also received UK dividends of £10,800 and UK bank interest of £960 during 2013/14.

Requirement

Calculate Henry's income tax liability for 2013/14, making clear your treatment of each item.

(13 marks)

(b) Meg Brocard is Henry's wife and was 68 years old on 1 June 2013. On that date she decided to vest her pension benefits. Meg had a money-purchase scheme which was valued at £1,850,000 on 1 June 2013. Meg took up the maximum tax-free lump sum. The balance of the lifetime allowance was vested to provide pension-income benefits. The excess of the fund over the lifetime allowance was then taken as a lump sum.

Requirement

Explain the tax consequences of Meg's decisions. Include in your answer a computation of the lifetime allowance charge and the amount that the scheme administrator pays to Meg. **(5 marks)**

(18 marks)

43 Paola (S11)

Paola is employed by Delta Ltd. Details of Paola's remuneration package for 2013/14 are as follows:

A salary of £86,500 pa.

- Use of a diesel company car with a list price of £26,900 and CO_2 emissions of 127g/km. Paola pays for all her own fuel. Paola originally contributed £6,000 to the capital cost of the car. During 2013/14 Paola had a new accessory added to the car at a cost to Delta Ltd of £200.

- An interest free loan of £75,150 was written off by Delta Ltd on 6 April 2013.

- On 6 October 2013 Delta Ltd gifted a laptop computer to Paola which was worth £1,800. Paola had been using the computer wholly for private purposes since 6 April 2012. It had been purchased by Delta Ltd for £3,400 on 6 April 2012.

- Delta Ltd and Paola each contribute 5% of Paola's salary to an occupational pension scheme.

Paola donated £100 per month to charity via Delta Ltd's approved payroll giving scheme. Paola also contributed £8,000 in cash to her personal pension scheme in October 2013.

During 2013/14 Paola received dividends from Echo Ltd of £11,970 and interest on her bank deposit account of £2,500. In addition, in May 2013, Paola received interest of £250 on a holding of Treasury Stock. Paola made a cash donation via Gift Aid of £500 in July 2013. Paola is not contracted out of the State Second Pension.

Requirement

Calculate Paola's income tax liability and her primary Class 1 national insurance contributions liability for 2013/14. **(19 marks)**

44 Kristina Grey (J12)

(a) Kristina Grey used to run her own unincorporated business, 'Grey's Parties', as a sole trader. Grey's Parties was successful, but in 2013 Kristina accepted an offer of employment. She therefore ceased trading on 30 June 2013, preparing a final two-month set of accounts to that date.

Recent tax-adjusted trading profits were as follows:

	£
Year ended 30 April 2012	46,910
Year ended 30 April 2013	67,030

Kristina had overlap profit from commencement of £8,170.

The trading profit for the two months ended 30 June 2013 was £22,770. This figure has been adjusted for tax purposes except that Kristina has not made any deduction in her accounts for costs on cessation or deducted capital allowances for the period ended 30 June 2013.

Costs on cessation

Derek Grey is Kristina's husband and was employed full time by Grey's Parties until he was made redundant on 31 May 2013. Derek received £2,200 as statutory redundancy pay and a non-contractual payment as compensation for loss of office of £4,800.

Capital allowances

The tax written down values at 1 May 2013 were as follows:

	£
Main pool	5,800
Kristina's car	4,250

Kristina's car had been purchased in November 2012 and was used 60% by her for business purposes. The car has CO_2 emissions of 190 g/km. On cessation on 30 June 2013, Kristina kept the car, which had a market value of £5,100 at that date.

Derek was also provided with a Skoda car by Grey's Parties, which he used 45% for business purposes. The Skoda car was purchased for £18,600 in September 2010 and had CO_2 emissions of 105 g/km. A 100% first year allowance was claimed on this car in the year ended 30 April 2011. On 14 June 2013, the car was sold for £3,900.

The remaining plant and machinery (excluding cars) was sold for £1,000 on 27 June 2013. No item was sold for more than cost. Maximum capital allowances had always been claimed by Kristina on all qualifying items.

Requirements

(i) Calculate the tax-adjusted trading profit for Kristina's business for the two months ended 30 June 2013, making clear your treatment of each item. **(7 marks)**

(ii) Calculate the trading income assessments for Kristina for 2012/13 and 2013/14, stating the dates of each basis period. **(3 marks)**

Note: Ignore VAT and national insurance

(b) Kristina's new job is with On-Call Ltd, a close company. On-Call Ltd employed Kristina with effect from 1 August 2013. She is employed on the following terms:

- A salary of £95,000 pa.

- Use of a company car from 1 September 2013. The car has a list price of £25,000 and CO_2 emissions of 169g/km. On-Call Ltd pays for all diesel for the car, which costs the company £350 per month. Only 20% of the diesel is used for business travel by Kristina and she contributes £100 per month towards the cost of her private fuel.

- A contractual bonus of 5% of her annual salary paid in June each year.

Kristina has also purchased 5% of the ordinary shares in On-Call Ltd from one of the existing shareholders. In order to finance this, she took out a bank loan of £22,000 on 1 November 2013, just before the share purchase. Interest on the bank loan is payable at 7% pa.

Kristina receives £39,000 in dividends each December from Grace plc, an unconnected company in which Kristina invested on the advice of a friend.

Kristina makes personal pension contributions to a money-purchase scheme which she joined in 1994. Since 2005, Kristina has made personal pension contributions of £15,000 (gross) per tax year. She intends to increase these contributions to £57,000 (gross) in 2014/15 and 2015/16, and then £155,000 (gross) in 2016/17.

Requirements

(i) Calculate Kristina's income tax liability for 2013/14, based on the above information and your answer to part (a). Make clear your treatment of each item. **(10 marks)**

(ii) Calculate the employer's national insurance contributions in respect of Kristina's employment during 2013/14 payable by On-Call Ltd. **(2 marks)**

(iii) Calculate the amount of pension contributions on which Kristina will be entitled to tax relief for 2014/15 to 2016/17. Show the use of the annual allowance for each year. **(4 marks)**

(26 marks)

45 Cagney and Lacey

Cagney is employed by Angels Ltd and receives an annual salary of £63,000.

Cagney travelled 15,000 business miles during 2013/14 and claimed a mileage allowance of 50p per business mile from Angels Ltd.

Lacey commenced employment with Angels Ltd on 1 July 2013. She receives an annual salary of £42,000. She received a bonus of £6,000 in December 2013.

Cagney and Lacey are not contracted out of the State Second Pension (S2P).

Requirement

Calculate the employee's and employer's national insurance contributions payable in respect of Cagney's and Lacey's employment for 2013/14.   **(9 marks)**

46 Diana

Diana Artemis, who had previously been employed by Troy Ltd, resigned on 31 March 2014 and received no further remuneration from Troy Ltd.

On 31 March 2014, Diana bought her company car from Troy Ltd for £12,000, the agreed market value of the car at that date. On the same day, Diana also returned her company owned laptop that was worth £2,000 when it was first provided to her in February 2010. Diana used the laptop exclusively for business purposes.

Diana had used the fully expensed company car (including petrol) since it was first provided to her in August 2010. The car had an original list price of £50,000, CO_2 emissions of 212g/km and 65% of Diana's mileage in the car each year was for private purposes. Diana had been provided with the car and the laptop in addition to her salary of £33,800 pa and private medical insurance that cost Troy Ltd £240 per year. During September 2013, Diana made a claim for medical treatment that cost the insurance company £1,300. Troy Ltd also paid Diana £80 per week in childcare vouchers for 48 weeks during 2013/14, as part of a childcare scheme which was available to all employees. Diana had been in the childcare scheme since 2010.

Requirement

State, with supporting calculations, the types and amounts of national insurance contributions to be paid in respect of Diana's employment for 2013/14. Identify any items upon which no national insurance contributions are payable. Diana is not contracted out for national insurance purposes.

(8 marks)

47   Jim

Jim works for Bell Ltd. He received a gross salary of £54,000 and dividends of £10,000 from the company in the year ended 31 March 2014. Jim is contracted out for national insurance purposes.

Bell Ltd makes annual contributions of £6,000 to a registered company occupational pension scheme for Jim's benefit. Jim is not required to make any contributions to the scheme. In January 2014 Bell Ltd bought a new petrol company car for Jim's use at the list price of £35,000. The petrol car has CO_2 emissions of 158g/km and is used by Jim 60% for business motoring. Jim pays for all of his private petrol himself.

Bell Ltd prepares accounts to 31 March each year.

Requirement

Compute Jim's national insurance contributions for the year 2013/14 and Bell Ltd's employer's national insurance contributions in respect of the year ended 31 March 2014. State when these liabilities would fall due for payment.   **(10 marks)**

48   Alexander

Alexander was born on 10 January 1965. He runs a sole trader business and has the following results.

	Tax adjusted trading profits £	Accounting profit £
Year ended 31 December 2013	47,000	38,000
Year ended 31 December 2014	51,000	43,000

Alexander's son Gareth started his sole trader business on 1 January 2013 and has the following results.

	Tax adjusted trading profits £	Accounting profit £
Period ended 31 October 2013	5,000	3,000
Year ended 31 October 2014	19,500	6,300

Alexander's father Harry was born on 10 January 1944. His tax adjusted trading profit for his sole trader business for the year ended 5 April 2014 was £39,000.

Requirement

Calculate, with supporting explanations, the national insurance contributions payable by Alexander, Gareth and Harry in respect of their sole trader businesses for 2013/14.   **(10 marks)**

49 Preparation question: short accounting period

Armit Ltd started trading on 1 July 2013 and made up its first accounts to 31 March 2014. Armit Ltd is a small company for research and development purposes.

The sole shareholder and director of Armit Ltd is Jasmine Armit.

In the period between 1 July 2013 and 31 March 2014, the following income was received and expenses incurred.

	£
Trading profits (before capital allowances)	374,000
Bank interest receivable	1,950
Research and development expenditure (amount deducted to calculate trading profits)	20,000
Qualifying charitable donation made	11,000
Dividend paid to Jasmine	15,000
Capital additions:	
Van	8,800
Computer	3,200
Car (CO_2 emissions 85 g/km) (20% private use by Jasmine)	14,500
Car (CO_2 emissions 130 g/km) (15% private use by salesman)	9,667

Requirement

Compute the corporation tax payable by Armit Ltd for the period ending 31 March 2014.

Note: **Ignore VAT.**

Guidance notes

1 A good place to start would be to calculate the capital allowances computation.
2 Then you can calculate the taxable total profits.
3 What is the effect of a short accounting period on the limits for marginal relief?

50 Preparation question: marginal relief

Squad Ltd, a UK trading company, produced the following results for the year ended 31 December 2013.

	£
Income	
Adjusted trading profit	220,000
Rental income	103,000
Bank deposit interest accrued (non-trading investment)	6,000
Capital gains: 29 July 2013	32,500
25 October 2013	5,500
Capital losses brought forward at 1 January 2013	24,000
Qualifying charitable donations paid	4,000

Requirement

Compute the corporation tax payable by Squad Ltd for the year ended 31 December 2013.

Guidance notes

1 In calculating a company's taxable total profits, we must bring together all taxable profits, including gains. You must therefore start by preparing a proforma tax computation, and then select from the question all relevant profit figures.

2 Once you have found the taxable total profits, you can consider the rate of tax. You should find that marginal relief applies. If you do not, look carefully to see whether you have missed anything.

51 Preparation question: long period of account

Jasmine Ltd has always made up accounts to 31 March, but intends to draw up its next set of accounts for the 15 months to 30 June 2014. The estimated results of the company for the period are as follows:

	£
Adjusted trading profit before capital allowances	325,000
Plant and machinery tax written down value at 1 April 2013	40,000
Chargeable gain on disposal of an investment property on 10 June 2013	265,000
Qualifying charitable donation made in April each year	4,000
Dividend received from a 5% investment in a UK resident company on 10 August 2013	10,800

Jasmine Ltd purchased a computer on 4 December 2013 for £8,000. Jasmine Ltd has no associated companies.

Requirement

Calculate the corporation tax payable by Jasmine Ltd in respect of the 15 months ended 30 June 2014.

Note: **Ignore VAT.**

52 Preparation question: capital gains

Update Ltd makes up its accounts annually to 31 March, and has no associated companies.

During its accounting year ended 31 March 2014 Update Ltd disposed of the following assets.

(a) In June 2013, an office building was sold for £400,000. It had been purchased in July 1987 for £130,000.

(b) In July 2013, 8,000 shares in Shoot plc were sold for £48,000. The shares in Shoot plc had been acquired as follows.

May 1984	4,000 shares for £8,000
March 1988	4,000 shares for £10,000

There were no capital losses brought forward.

Update Ltd's taxable total profits for the year ended 31 March 2014, excluding capital gains, were £3,500,000.

Requirement

Calculate the amount of corporation tax payable as a result of the above transactions.

Note: **Assume RPI in June 2013 is 250.6 and in July 2013 is 251.7.**

Guidance notes

1   The building requires a basic capital gains computation.

2   The shares are in the s.104 pool. The s.104 pool includes indexation within it, first up to its starting point April 1985 and then up to each purchase or sale.

53 Atlantis Ltd (J04)

Atlantis Ltd is a trading company that sells plastic cutlery to the catering industry and is a 100% subsidiary of Kennedy Ltd.

The accounts for Atlantis Ltd for the year ended 30 November 2013 are as follows.

	£	£
Gross trading profit		660,972
Bank interest receivable (Note 1)	22,108	
Rent receivable (Note 2)	24,200	
Profit on sale of investment property (Note 3)	202,900	
Dividends received (Note 4)	8,900	
		258,108
Less:		
Staff costs (Note 5)	68,700	
Allowable administrative costs	139,158	
Depreciation	10,060	
Interest payable (Note 6)	16,856	
Qualifying charitable donations	2,000	
Research and development expenditure (Note 7)	46,740	
		(283,514)
Net profit for the period		635,566

Notes:

(1) The actual amount of interest received during the year ended 30 November 2013 was £22,500.

(2) Rent receivable relates to an overseas investment property. The accounts figure is the rental income received by Atlantis Ltd. This was received net of 18% withholding tax.

(3) The profit relates to the sale of a UK property, Apollo Place, which was sold for £814,300 on 16 September 2013. This property was purchased in May 2000 for £420,085 and extended during June 2001 at a cost of £34,100, excluding legal and professional fees in connection with the extension work of £2,980. Apollo Place has always been rented out to a succession of commercial tenants until 31 October 2012.

(4) The dividends were received from Gemini Ltd, a UK trading company in which Atlantis Ltd owns 15% of the ordinary share capital. Gemini Ltd performs research and development into new plastics.

(5) Staff costs include £15,250 paid by Atlantis Ltd to the group registered occupational pension scheme and £23,810 of directors' remuneration, both paid during the year.

(6) Interest payable

	£
Bank overdraft interest	488
Debenture interest payable to Kennedy Ltd	12,900
Costs in connection with the issue of the above debentures	3,200
Interest on overdue corporation tax	268
	16,856

The debentures were issued by Atlantis Ltd to raise funds for the purchase of 15% of the shares in Gemini Ltd.

(7) Research and development expenditure

	£
Payments to Gemini Ltd (a connected company for R&D purposes) for the cost of technical research on behalf of Atlantis Ltd	26,600
Staff costs	8,640
Research equipment	11,500
	46,740

Atlantis Ltd qualifies as a small company for research and development purposes.

(8)   The tax written down value on the main pool at 1 December 2012 is £9,800. The only additional items of plant and machinery purchased in the year to 30 November 2013 are a car (CO_2 emissions of 137g/km) for the new sales director costing £26,750 (purchased on 5 June 2013), which is used 60% for private purposes by the director, and a new lift installed in the offices at a cost of £277,600 (purchased on 23 August 2013). The new lift is expected to have a working life of 30 years, and replaces the old lift which had to be scrapped. There have been no other disposals of plant and machinery during the year.

Requirements

(a)   Calculate the corporation tax payable by Atlantis Ltd for the year ended 30 November 2013.

(23 marks)

(b)   Give a brief explanation of your treatment of the payments referred to in Note (5) above in relation to staff costs and in Note (7) above in relation to research and development expenditure. **(3 marks)**

Note: **Assume that the RPI in September 2013 is 253.1**

(26 marks)

54   Argus Ltd group (S09)

(a)   The Argus Ltd group comprises of three trading companies, all of which are incorporated in the UK and prepare financial statements to 31 March 2014. Argus Ltd owns 75% of Colossus Ltd, which in turn owns 70% of Unicorn Ltd.

Argus Ltd purchased Colossus Ltd on 1 January 2013 and as a result Colossus Ltd changed its accounting date and prepared financial statements for the 15 months ended 31 March 2014.

Tax adjusted profits

Colossus Ltd has trading profits before capital allowances for the 15 month period ended 31 March 2014 of £350,000. However, this was before any available deduction in respect of the following items:

	£
Interest payable on a loan taken out on 1 January 2014 in order to purchase a further 20% of the shares in Unicorn Ltd. Colossus Ltd had held 50% of the shares in Unicorn Ltd until 1 January 2014.	380
Patent royalties payable on 31 December 2013 in respect of Colossus Ltd's trade.	3,600
Interest payable on a loan taken out to purchase office premises (see below).	2,900
Qualifying charitable donation on 31 March 2013	700

Capital allowances

The tax written down value of the main pool at 1 January 2013 was £29,055 and Colossus Ltd claimed maximum capital allowances. Colossus Ltd sold office equipment on 13 March 2013 for £2,100 (which was less than the original cost) and purchased computer hardware on 1 February 2014 for £11,663.

Interest receivable

Colossus Ltd received loan interest of £2,400 for the 15 month period ended 31 March 2014. The interest accrued evenly over the 15 month period.

Office building

In addition, Colossus Ltd sold an office building on 14 March 2014 for £150,830 which had originally cost £55,000 in April 2008. Colossus Ltd had taken out a loan to partially fund this acquisition, the interest on which is shown above. Interest on the loan accrues evenly.

Colossus Ltd had capital losses brought forward at 1 January 2013 of £2,700.

Requirement

Calculate the corporation tax payable by Colossus Ltd for the fifteen months ended 31 March 2014.

(17 marks)

Note: **Assume the indexation factor between April 2008 and March 2014 is 0.226**

(b)   Unicorn Ltd is looking to raise new finance in November 2014 in order to expand its business. The following options are being considered:

- Take out a bank loan at an interest rate of 6.5% pa.

- Issue new shares to the existing shareholders.

- Sell a 13% shareholding in Ark Ltd, an unquoted UK trading company. This represents its entire shareholding in the company. The shares in Ark Ltd were purchased in January 2012.

Requirement

Briefly describe the corporation tax consequences for Unicorn Ltd of each of the above options.

(4 marks)

(21 marks)

55   Zita Ltd (D10)

(a)   Zita Ltd, an unquoted trading company, recorded an accounting profit for the year ended 31 December 2013 of £3,288,558 after accounting for the following items:

	Note	£
Patent royalties payable (trade related)		420,455
Research and development expenditure incurred	(1)	450,000
Loss on disposal of 5% loan stock	(2)	27,500
Rental income	(3)	108,000
Interest receivable	(4)	55,483
Interest payable	(5)	215,445
Staff costs	(6)	489,235
Receipts arising from investments in Zuppa Ltd	(7)	2,000,000

Notes:

(1)   The research and development expenditure charged to the profit and loss account for the year is £450,000.

A laboratory was built in August 2013 at a cost of £125,000. New computer hardware was installed in the new laboratory at a cost of £25,000. Both the cost of the new laboratory and the computer hardware were capitalised in the financial accounts and are items of qualifying research and development capital expenditure.

Zita Ltd qualifies as a large company for research and development purposes.

(2)   In March 2013 Zita Ltd sold loan stock for £372,500 which had originally cost £400,000 in January 2006. The loan stock was held for investment purposes.

(3)   Zita Ltd has rented out the top floor of its London office block since 2000. The building has 10 floors. The cost of security and utilities for the whole building is paid by Zita Ltd. These costs amounted to £1.2 million for the year ended 31 December 2013, and are included in calculating the accounting profit above. The rent receivable for 2013 was £144,000. The tenant paid the rent due for the last three months of 2013 in July 2014.

		£
(4) Bank interest receivable		52,150
Interest receivable on loan stock		3,333
		55,483

		£
(5) Overdraft interest payable		15,445
Interest payable on loan to purchase London office		200,000
		215,445

(6)   Included in staff costs are pension costs of £128,000 of which £28,000 had been accrued but not paid by 31 December 2013.

(7) In July 2013 Zita Ltd received dividends of £1,440,000 from its 15% holding in Zuppa Ltd, an unquoted trading company. In October 2013 Zita Ltd sold its shareholding in Zuppa Ltd realising a profit on disposal of £560,000. The shares were originally acquired in January 2005 for £4,440,000.

Capital allowances

The accountant has calculated the capital allowances due for the year ended 31 December 2013 to be £205,831. This does not include any adjustment required in relation to the items mentioned in notes (1) to (7) above.

Requirement

Calculate Zita Ltd's corporation tax liability for the year ended 31 December 2013.   **(14 marks)**

Notes: Ignore VAT

Assume the RPI for October 2013 was 254.2.

(b) Zita Ltd is a partially exempt VAT registered trader.

In the three months ended 31 December 2013 Zita Ltd's VAT records show the following:

	£
Input VAT relating to standard rated supplies	355,242
Input VAT relating to exempt supplies	31,733
Non-attributable input VAT	189,390
Standard rated supplies (VAT exclusive)	6,455,879
Exempt supplies	301,548

In addition to the above:

- Zita Ltd purchased private fuel for an employee at a total cost of £2,400 (VAT inclusive) for the three months ended 31 December 2013. The fuel was used in a company car with CO_2 emissions of 206g/km. The car is used for both the taxable and exempt parts of the business.

- Zita Ltd purchased a new delivery van for use in the taxable part of the business. The van cost £7,596 (VAT inclusive).

Requirement

Calculate the net VAT payable / repayable for the three months ended 31 December 2013.

(7 marks)

(21 marks)

56   Sylon Ltd (M11)

(a) Sylon Ltd is a UK company which manufactures plastic containers and prepares accounts to 31 December each year. For the year ended 31 December 2013 it generated a trading profit (before deduction of interest payable and capital allowances) of £1,603,300. The following information is available in order to complete the corporation tax computation for the year:

Interest payable/receivable

Sylon Ltd incurred the following amounts of interest payable:

	£
Interest on a loan taken out to purchase new machinery	4,160
Interest on a loan taken out to purchase Sylon Ltd's headquarters (Biers House)	12,800
Interest on a loan taken out to purchase loan stock in Pegasus plc, an unconnected UK company	2,900
	19,860

Sylon Ltd received interest of £6,800 on the loan stock in Pegasus plc for the year ended 31 December 2013.

Capital allowances

The tax written down value of the main pool of plant and machinery at 1 January 2013 was £70,670 and the tax written down value of the special rate pool at 1 January 2013 was £18,900.

Sylon Ltd undertook the following transactions during the year:

Acquisitions:		£
12 January 2013	Machinery	91,000
3 March 2013	Rewiring of the office building	162,900
Disposal:		
1 August 2013	A lorry purchased for £16,000 in August 2008	9,400

Other property transactions

Sylon Ltd undertook the following transactions during the year ended 31 December 2013:

1. On 1 August 2013, Sylon Ltd sold an investment property (Brook Avenue) for £150,600 which it had purchased in May 2008 for £80,000.

2. On 1 November 2013, in order to expand its business, Sylon Ltd purchased new retail premises (Buck Mews) for £145,000. However, 10% of the retail space was rented out to an unconnected party from 1 November 2013 for £3,000 per month.

3. Sylon Ltd's headquarters (Biers House) was purchased in April 2002 and since that time 20% of the floor space has been rented out as surplus office space to an unconnected company at an annual rental of £20,400.

Share transactions

In addition to the loan stock held in Pegasus plc, Sylon Ltd also owns ordinary shares in Pegasus plc. The shares were acquired as follows:

1 January 2007	Purchase of 1,000 shares @ £22.50 per share
15 May 2009	Rights issue of 1 for 5 @ £18 per share

Sylon Ltd took up all of its rights on 15 May 2009, but then sold 900 of its shares in Pegasus plc for £29,089 in January 2013.

Sylon Ltd has a number of associated companies and therefore pays corporation tax at the main rate.

Requirement

Calculate the corporation tax payable by Sylon Ltd for the year ended 31 December 2013.

(15 marks)

Note: **The August 2013 RPI is 252.6. Ignore VAT.**

(b) The new finance director of Sylon Ltd has asked all department heads to submit spending budgets for the year ended 31 December 2014 and the head of sales and marketing has submitted the following:

Expenses:	£
Client entertaining	32,000
Staff entertaining (annual party for all 200 staff members)	55,000
Gifts of food hampers to clients (cost £55 each)	1,650
General expense allowance for head of sales and marketing	20,000

Capital costs:

New laptop to be used by the head of sales and marketing. It is proposed that the laptop will be sold in December 2014 for estimated proceeds of £2,000, and a short-life asset election will be made.	5,000

Sylon Ltd will pay corporation tax at the main rate of 23% for the year ending 31 December 2014.

Requirement

Calculate the total after tax cost of the above items of expenditure for the year ended 31 December 2014.

(7 marks)

(22 marks)

Note: **Ignore VAT and national insurance**

57 Bryde Ltd (J11)

(a) Bryde Ltd is an unquoted UK trading company which prepares accounts to 31 December each year. Leon Carter is the managing director and he owns 100% of the ordinary share capital. The draft results for the year ended 31 December 2013 show the following:

	Notes	£	£
Trading profit			401,900
Profit on the sale of an investment property	(1)		4,970
Rental income receivable	(2)		14,000
UK dividends received	(3)		34,000
Bank interest receivable			3,500
			458,370
Depreciation		13,100	
Interest payable	(4)	4,910	
Legal and professional fees	(5)	5,800	
Entertaining	(6)	730	
Staff costs		108,000	
Other allowable expenses		77,600	
			(210,140)
Profit for the year			248,230

Notes:

(1) The sale of the investment property gave rise to a chargeable gain of £2,380.

(2) Rental income receivable comprised the following:

	£
Rent receivable from Leon on an unfurnished flat owned and provided by Bryde Ltd while he is working in London	1,500
Rent receivable on the investment property	12,500
	14,000

(3) Dividends received from 30% holding in Garfield Ltd, a UK company.

(4) Interest payable comprised the following:

	£
Bank overdraft interest	1,310
Interest payable on a loan taken out to fund expansion of the business	1,600
Interest payable on a loan taken out to fund the purchase of a 10% shareholding in Euclid plc in November 2013	2,000
	4,910

(5) Legal and professional fees comprised the following:

	£
Legal fees in connection with the loan to purchase shares in Euclid plc	1,100
Accountancy and audit fees	4,490
Legal fees incurred in respect of new staff contracts	210
	5,800

(6) Entertaining comprised the following:

	£
General expense allowance for Leon (£450 was spent entertaining clients)	500
Staff entertaining	230
	730

The written down value of the main pool at 1 January 2013 was £12,890. In February 2013 a Toyota car was purchased for £15,000 (VAT inclusive) which had CO_2 emissions of 90 g/km. The car was used 60% for private purposes by Leon. In May 2013 computer equipment was purchased for £4,000 (VAT inclusive). Bryde Ltd is registered for VAT.

Bryde Ltd has no associated companies.

Requirement

Calculate the corporation tax payable by Bryde Ltd for the year ended 31 December 2013.

(13 marks)

(b) Bryde Ltd is contemplating purchasing 45% of the ordinary shares in Loomis Ltd on 1 July 2014.

Bryde Ltd estimates that its own results for the year ending 31 December 2014 will be as follows:

	£
Trading profit	320,000
Interest income	3,000
Other taxable income	4,000

In order to fund the acquisition of shares in Loomis Ltd, Leon is considering the following transactions:

- Bryde Ltd will take out a bank loan of £85,000 on 1 July 2014 at an interest rate of 6% pa.

- Bryde Ltd will sell a 9% shareholding in Garfield Ltd (an unquoted trading company) for estimated proceeds of £51,000. Bryde Ltd acquired a 30% shareholding in Garfield Ltd on 1 August 2013 for £15,300. Leon wants to proceed with the sale on 1 July 2014 but the buyer would like to delay the sale until September 2014.

The estimated results for Bryde Ltd for the year ending 31 December 2014 do not take account of the tax effect of these transactions.

Requirements

(i) Explain the corporation tax consequences of taking out the bank loan in order to fund the purchase of the shares in Loomis Ltd. **(2 marks)**

(ii) Calculate Bryde Ltd's capital gain if the sale of the shares in Garfield Ltd was made in July 2014 and also if it were instead delayed until September 2014. **(3 marks)**

(18 marks)

Note: **Assume the following retail price indices:**

August 2013	252.6
July 2014	260.4
September 2014	261.8

58 HEP Ltd group (D11)

(a) HEP Ltd owns 100% of the shares in Lock Ltd and Ardna Ltd. In turn, Lock Ltd owns 51% of the shares in Shannon Ltd.

The shares in Ardna Ltd were acquired on 1 September 2013.

HEP Ltd is an unquoted trading company and Roberto Kane, the group financial controller, has done some preliminary work on the preparation of the corporation tax computation for the year ended 30 June 2014. He has calculated the draft adjusted trading profit for the year to be £478,900. However, this is before any deduction for interest payable or research and development costs as Roberto is unsure of the availability and amount of any allowable deductions for these items. He has performed all other relevant adjustments to profit. The following information has been provided:

Interest payable

	£
Interest on overdue corporation tax	450
Interest on a bank loan taken out to fund the purchase of debentures in Power plc	2,800
Bank overdraft interest	240
Interest on a loan to purchase a rental property	1,630
	5,120

Research and development

HEP Ltd incurred the following costs in undertaking a qualifying research and development (R&D) project. HEP Ltd is a small or medium-sized enterprise for R&D purposes. No deduction for any of these amounts has been made in arriving at the draft adjusted trading profit of £478,900.

	£
Cost of staff directly engaged in R&D	23,000
Laboratory equipment	15,500
Consumable materials	4,910
Computer software	12,740
	56,150

HEP Ltd undertook the following transactions during the year ended 30 June 2014:

Crusha Ltd: A 16% shareholding in Crusha Ltd, an unquoted trading company, was purchased on 1 April 2011 for £35,200. Half of this shareholding was sold on 1 August 2013 for £9,400.

River Plaza: HEP Ltd purchased the freehold of this property on 13 January 2002 for £260,100 and sold it on 4 March 2014 for £408,089.

Other income

HEP Ltd received bank interest of £12,800 and debenture interest of £4,000 during the year ended 30 June 2014. In addition, it received rent of £40,400 for the year. No dividends were received during the year.

Requirement

Calculate the corporation tax payable by HEP Ltd for the year ended 30 June 2014. **(12 marks)**

Note: **Assume the RPI in August 2013 was 252.6 and in March 2014 was 258.1**

Note: **Ignore VAT**

(b) Roberto, the group financial controller of HEP Ltd, who is a chartered accountant, has received the following email from his manager, the HEP Ltd group finance director:

"Dear Rob,

There are some other things that I want to make you aware of:

- I want to avoid paying any corporation tax instalment payments so please can you draft an email to all departments of the HEP Ltd group to bring forward any capital expenditure plans for the second half of 2015 to the year ending 30 June 2015, so that we claim capital allowances as soon as possible.

- The projected results do not include directors' bonuses, which have yet to be determined, but are anticipated to be £120,000. Please make sure these are deducted for tax purposes. If HMRC ask, tell them that the bonuses will be paid in January 2016, although they will actually be paid in May 2016. If you do that for me I will make sure your expense claims are put through as soon as possible with no questions asked.

Thanks"

Requirement

Explain the corporation tax and ethical issues that Roberto should consider before replying to this email. **(8 marks)**

(20 marks)

Note: **Ignore VAT**

59   Red Ltd (M12)

Red Ltd's finance director has asked you to recalculate Red Ltd's entitlement to capital allowances for the year ending 31 March 2014. He has provided you with the following information regarding transactions during the year ending 31 March 2014:

- The tax written down values brought forward at 1 April 2013 are £888,150 for the main pool and £431,500 for the special rate pool.

- Red Ltd purchased new IT equipment for £43,000 which has a useful life of six years after which it will be scrapped.

- Red Ltd purchased new air conditioning units for its head office at a cost of £82,000.

- Red Ltd purchased various items of main pool plant and machinery with a total cost of £175,000.

Requirement

Calculate Red Ltd's maximum entitlement to capital allowances for the year ending 31 March 2014. Explain your treatment of the IT equipment and your use of the annual investment allowance. **(5 marks)**

Note: **Ignore VAT**

60   Alpha Ltd (M12)

(a)   In January 2014 Alpha Ltd, a trading company with no associated companies, made the following capital disposals:

- On 1 January 2014 Alpha Ltd agreed to sell its shareholding in X Ltd to Y plc in two parts. It sold 700 shares (a 7% holding) on 1 January 2014 for £2.5 million. In addition, Alpha Ltd provisionally agreed to sell its remaining 600 shares (a 6% holding) on either 31 December 2014 or 31 March 2015. The two companies have yet to negotiate a price for the second disposal.

   Alpha Ltd originally purchased 1,300 shares (representing a 13% holding) in X Ltd, a trading company, on 1 January 2010 for £1.3 million.

- On 5 January 2014 Alpha Ltd sold a property for £150,000 which it had purchased on 10 February 2006 for £195,000.

Requirements

(i)   Calculate the chargeable gain, if any, arising on the disposal of the shares in X Ltd on 1 January 2014, and any allowable loss on the disposal of the property on 5 January 2014.
(2 marks)

(ii)   Explain to Alpha Ltd the tax consequences of disposing of its remaining 6% holding of shares in X Ltd on 31 December 2014 or alternatively on 31 March 2015.   **(4 marks)**

Note: **Assume an RPI for January 2014 of 256.0**

(b) On 7 February 2014 Alpha Ltd sold 4,000 of its shares in E Ltd for £260,000. E Ltd has 100,000 issued shares. Alpha Ltd purchased the shares as follows:

Date	Number	Total Cost £	
1 January 1980	1,000	2,000	Market value on 31.3.82 was £3,000
1 January 1990	2,000	10,000	

E Ltd made a 1 for 2 bonus issue on 1 January 1985. E Ltd made a 1 for 5 rights issue at £6 per share on 1 January 1995. Alpha Ltd took up all of its rights.

Requirement

Calculate the chargeable gains arising on disposal of the shares in E Ltd on 7 February 2014. In answering this part, you should:

(i)   First calculate the number of shares held immediately prior to the disposal;
(ii) Then match the shares being sold to the shares held; and
(iii) Finally calculate any gains arising.   **(10 marks)**

Note: Assume an RPI for February 2014 of 257.0

(c) As at 1 April 2013 Alpha Ltd had a capital loss brought forward of £18,400.

Alpha Ltd has forecast its tax adjusted trading profit for the year ending 31 March 2014 as £78,200. The profit includes a deduction for qualifying research and development (R&D) revenue expenditure of £22,000, which is the amount actually spent. Alpha Ltd is a medium sized enterprise for R&D purposes.

For the year ending 31 March 2014 Alpha Ltd has interest income of £42,000, rental income of £5,800 and a qualifying charitable donation of £2,100 paid on 1 January 2014.

Requirement

Using the information above and your answers to parts (a) and (b), calculate Alpha Ltd's corporation tax liability for its year ending 31 March 2014.   **(5 marks)**

(21 marks)

61   Coe Ltd group (J12)

(a) Ovett Ltd is a UK resident, wholly owned trading subsidiary of Coe Ltd, which also owns 75% of Cram Ltd.

Ovett Ltd's adjusted trading profit before deduction of capital allowances for the year ended 31 March 2014 is £179,674. However, due to an error with the computer accounting system, the four items below were ignored in the preparation of the financial statements. Therefore any tax-allowable element of the following four items will need to be deducted, along with capital allowances, in arriving at the final tax-adjusted trading profit.

- Operating lease costs of £8,100 for a car used by the sales director. The car has a list price of £23,000 and CO_2 emissions of 85 g/km. The car is used 75% of the time for business purposes. The lease was taken out on 1 May 2013.

- 20 free samples given to Ovett Ltd's biggest customer. The samples have a retail value of £12 each and cost £6 per item to manufacture.

- A trade-related patent royalty of £20,000. The royalty was paid to another UK company without any deduction of tax.

- On 1 May 2012 Ovett Ltd paid a premium of £5,000 on the grant of a six-year lease on a factory used in its trade.

Ovett Ltd's capital allowances for the year ended 31 March 2014 comprise an annual investment allowance of £15,000 and writing-down allowances of £92,400 in respect of plant and machinery.

On 1 May 2013, Ovett Ltd sold a warehouse for £525,900 which it had purchased for trade purposes on 1 May 1998 for £307,000. Since purchase, the property had been rented out to an unconnected company for an annual rent of £78,000, payable quarterly in advance.

At 1 April 2013, Ovett Ltd had a capital loss brought forward of £12,900.

Requirement

Calculate the corporation tax payable by Ovett Ltd for the year ended 31 March 2014. **(11 marks)**

Note: Assume an RPI of 250.0 for May 2013

Ignore VAT and national insurance

(b) Jackie is the new financial controller of Coe Ltd. She has prepared a draft corporation tax computation for Coe Ltd for the year ended 31 March 2014.

Jackie is unsure of the treatment of some items. Her draft computation is as follows:

	Notes	£	£
Draft adjusted trading profits			400,190
Less:			
Add:			
Interest on a loan to purchase a new lorry	(1)	930	
Interest on a loan to purchase a 2% shareholding in an unconnected company		790	
			1,720
Less:			
Bank interest receivable	(2)		(2,845)
Capital allowances:			
Annual investment allowance on new lorry	(1)		(20,000)
WDA on main pool	(3)		(3,000)
Research and development	(4)		(70,000)
Tax-adjusted trading profit			306,065
Add: Dividend received from Cram Ltd			10,000
Taxable total profits			316,065
Corporation tax liability:			
£316,065 × 23%			£72,695

Notes:

(1) The lorry cost £20,000 on 1 March 2014. Jackie made no deduction for the lorry in arriving at the draft adjusted trading profits of £400,190.

(2) The figure of £400,190 includes the bank interest receivable of £2,845.

(3) The tax written down value on the main pool at 1 April 2013 was £17,000.

(4) £40,000 was spent in the year on qualifying research and development. Coe Ltd is classed as a small or medium sized enterprise for research and development purposes. No deduction for this cost has been made in arriving at the figure of £400,190.

Requirement

Using the information above, redraft the corporation tax computation for Coe Ltd for the year ended 31 March 2014, correcting any errors you identify. **(11 marks)**

Note: Ignore VAT

(c) Cram Ltd has used Steiner & Co as its tax advisers for the last six years. The chartered accountant at Steiner & Co who is in charge of the Cram Ltd engagement received the following email from Blake Goldberg, the former finance director of Cram Ltd.

"I know you have provided Cram Ltd with tax advice over the last six years and I trust your judgement. As you know several months ago I became the finance director of the parent company, Coe Ltd. I realise you don't advise me personally, but I should be grateful if you could help my wife with her latest tax return. She is a writer and isn't sure where on the return she should show a payment she has received for her first novel.

"If you can help with this, I'm sure I'll be able to offer you some work for Coe Ltd in future."

Requirement

Explain the ethical issues that the chartered accountant at Steiner & Co should consider before replying to this email. **(5 marks)**

(27 marks)

62 Reaper Ltd (D12)

Reaper Ltd, a VAT registered trading company, prepares accounts to 31 March each year and its draft results for the year ended 31 March 2014 are shown below:

	Notes	£	£
Gross profit			926,775
Less:			
Depreciation		3,600	
Trade related patent royalties payable (gross)		26,470	
Amortisation of goodwill	(1)	2,500	
Loss on the disposal of plant and machinery	(2)	5,900	
Administrative expenses (all allowable)		72,100	
Staff costs	(3)	117,350	
Legal fees	(4)	1,385	
Abortive costs of trying to raise loan finance	(5)	600	
Other allowable costs		88,600	
			(318,505)
UK bank interest receivable			15,700
UK dividends received	(6)		30,600
Interest payable	(7)		(14,500)
Profit for the year			640,070

Notes:

(1) The goodwill has been correctly accounted for in the draft results for the year ended 31 March 2014.

(2) All of the assets disposed of qualified for capital allowances.

(3) Staff costs include an annual salary of £19,000 for the production manager. On 1 October 2013 Reaper Ltd leased a van which it provided to the production manager. He uses it for his own private purposes most weekends. No payment has yet been made for the annual operating lease cost of the van of £8,000, and so no deduction has been made in the draft results above. The van has CO_2 emissions of 165 g/km and Reaper Ltd paid for all of the fuel for the van. National insurance contributions have not yet been accounted for in relation to the van.

(4) Legal fees comprised the following:

	£
Legal costs for the acquisition of a five year lease over a storage facility	380
Debt collection fees	185
Fees in connection with defending a faulty goods claim	820
	1,385

(5) Reaper Ltd incurred the abortive loan finance fees in an unsuccessful attempt to purchase 5% of the shares in a supplier company.

(6) Dividends were received from the following companies:

	£
Dividends from a 1% shareholding in Fox plc	1,100
Dividends from an 80% shareholding in Butcher Ltd	29,500
	30,600

Reaper Ltd has no other shareholdings.

(7) Interest payable comprised the following:

	£
On a loan to purchase plant and machinery	3,400
On a loan to purchase the shares in Butcher Ltd	4,900
Bank overdraft interest	6,200
	14,500

Reaper Ltd made the following acquisitions and disposals during the year:

Acquisitions:

		£
1 August 2013	Plant and machinery	60,000
21 October 2013	Car (CO_2 emissions 147 g/km)	28,500
3 March 2014	Thermal insulation	23,100

Disposal:

		£
5 March 2014	Computer equipment	5,000

The figures for acquisitions and disposals are inclusive of VAT at the standard rate, except for the thermal insulation which is inclusive of VAT at the reduced rate.

The tax written down values at 1 April 2013 were as follows:

	£
Main pool	73,100
Special rate pool	13,970

Requirement

Calculate the corporation tax payable by Reaper Ltd for the year ended 31 March 2014. **(22 marks)**

63   Rex Wood (J12)

(a)   Rex Wood operates an unincorporated business selling standard-rated goods. In June 1996, Rex bought a building which he opted to tax. The building cost Rex £161,000, and was used in Rex's trade.

Rex decided to sell the building to Esther Green at market value of £394,000 on 1 March 2014.

These figures are stated exclusive of any VAT. No VAT was accounted for on the sale of the building and no mention of VAT was made in the sale and purchase agreement.

Rex is an additional rate taxpayer and has already used his annual exempt amount for 2013/14.

Requirements

(i)   Calculate the capital gains tax payable on the sale of Rex's building.   **(2 marks)**

     Note: **Ignore VAT for the purposes of this part only**

(ii)   Explain the VAT treatment of the sale.   **(3 marks)**

(b)   Esther Green sells standard-rated goods in the UK and also the same goods in other EU countries. Esther has provided you with the following information for the quarter ended 31 May 2014 in order to prepare her VAT return:

Sales:	£
All sales are stated exclusive of VAT where relevant.	
Sales to UK customers	25,900
Sales to VAT-registered businesses in other EU countries	15,220
Sales to non-VAT registered individuals in other EU countries	3,670
Sale of machinery in the UK	2,000

UK purchases and expenses:	
All purchases and expenses are stated inclusive of any VAT.	
Expenses incurred related to the UK business	870
Expenses incurred related to the business in other EU countries	2,900
Purchase of a car for use 65% for private purposes by Esther	15,000
Purchase of a computer for use 30% for private purposes by Esther	890
Purchase of plant	3,910

Requirement

Calculate the VAT payable to HMRC for the quarter ended 31 May 2014, stating your treatment of the sales to other EU countries.   **(9 marks)**

(c)   Tom, one of Esther's friends who operates a similar business, has given her a list of particular suppliers he uses, saying:

"These suppliers often offer discounts. If you ask, though, they will also give you an invoice without any numbers on it. You can fill in whatever figures you like and deduct the full amounts in your income tax return, even though you actually paid less. This sort of thing happens all the time. All you are doing is avoiding tax."

Requirement

Explain whether this is a legal way of avoiding tax and the consequences for Esther of doing as Tom suggests.   **(6 marks)**

                                             (20 marks)

64 Apollo Ltd (M11)

Apollo Ltd is registered for VAT and sells goods to customers in the UK and elsewhere in the EU via its website. Supplies for the three months ended 31 March 2014 were as follows:

Sales:	£
To UK customers	48,300
To VAT-registered customers elsewhere in the EU	3,700
To non VAT-registered customers elsewhere in the EU	8,400

All of the above figures are inclusive of VAT where appropriate.

Apollo Ltd incurred standard-rated costs of £13,700 (VAT exclusive) for the three months ended 31 March 2014.

On 1 March 2014, Apollo Ltd granted a four-year lease over one of its properties, Thrace House, to Tigh Ltd. Under the terms of the lease, the monthly rent was £1,800 and Apollo Ltd charged a lease premium of £6,000. The option to tax has been exercised in respect of this building. The above figures relating to the lease premium and the rent are exclusive of VAT.

Requirement

Calculate the VAT payable by/repayable to Apollo Ltd for the three months ended 31 March 2014, making clear your treatment of each item. **(6 marks)**

65 Artifex Ltd

(a) Artifex Ltd bought a building on 15 January 2011 for £420,000 (inclusive of VAT). Artifex Ltd used the building 60% for taxable purposes in the year to 31 March 2011. Taxable use increased to 75% in the year to 31 March 2012 but then fell to 40% in the year to 31 March 2013. Artifex Ltd sold the building on 5 October 2013 for £360,000 (inclusive of VAT). Taxable use in the period from 1 April 2013 to 5 October 2013 remained at 40%.

Requirement

Calculate the initial input recovery and subsequent adjustments required for all other years, under the capital goods scheme, in respect of the building. **(8 marks)**

(b) The bookkeeper has received an invoice for a total cost of £2,800 for airline travel for Artifex Ltd's managing director. The invoice includes an amount for the flight and an amount for the in-flight meals however VAT at zero rate has been applied to the total cost.

Requirement

Explain why the zero rate of VAT has been applied to the total invoice value despite its being made up of differing supplies. **(4 marks)**

(12 marks)

66   Crescent Ltd

(a)   Crescent Ltd is a UK incorporated company that manufactures and supplies goods and services to a variety of customers in the UK and the rest of the EU.

The following summarises the VAT position for Crescent Ltd for the quarter ended 30 November 2014, but the VAT return has not yet been filed.

	£
Standard rated supplies – UK customers	31,500
Exempt supplies – UK customers	3,960
Sales to Brooke SA – Brooke SA is VAT registered in France	6,769
Standard rated sales via mail order to non-VAT registered customers in France	3,555
Input tax relating to standard rated supplies	1,832
Input tax relating to exempt supplies in the UK	930
Input tax relating to sales to Brooke SA	680
Input tax relating to mail order standard rated sales to non-VAT registered customers in France	676
Input tax relating to the UK head office which provides administrative support in respect of all sales activities	1,060

All of the above figures are exclusive of VAT, where relevant.

Requirement

Calculate, with supporting explanations, the amount of input tax that Crescent Ltd can deduct for the quarter ended 30 November 2014. Include an explanation of the UK VAT treatment of the French sales.   **(9 marks)**

(b)   In a move to expand its activities, Crescent Ltd secured a bank loan of £366,000 on 1 December 2013 with interest payable at 6% pa. The funds have been applied as follows:

(1)   £201,000 to fund the purchase of a new factory on 1 December 2013 for use in its trade.

(2)   £55,000 to fund the purchase of shares and debentures in Cryer Ltd on 1 December 2013. Debenture interest received by Crescent Ltd up until 31 August 2014 was £10,200. The additional debenture interest accrued to 30 November 2014 is £3,400.

(3)   £110,000 which was used to purchase a 99 year lease over a new property, Lyttelton Place, on 1 December 2013. Lyttelton Place was let out to a temporary tenant until 1 November 2014 at a monthly rent of £4,200. From 1 November 2014, the property was occupied as the administrative headquarters of Crescent Ltd. Crescent Ltd spent £3,300 on repairs and maintenance of the property during the year ended 30 November 2014.

Crescent Ltd has adjusted trading profits of £563,590 for the year ended 30 November 2014, before making any adjustments for the above items. In addition, no deductions have been made for interest payable as a result of the above transactions.

Additionally, Crescent Ltd sold an investment property, Dingly House, on 1 March 2014 for £156,000. Dingly House had been purchased by Crescent Ltd in April 2003 for £73,250, but had been empty since October 2013.

Requirements

(i)   Calculate the taxable total profits for Crescent Ltd for the year ended 30 November 2014.
                                                                                                          (11 marks)

(ii)   Briefly explain the stamp duty and stamp duty land tax implications of the purchases.
                                                                                                          (4 marks)

Note: **The RPI at March 2014 is 258.1.**

                                                                                                          (24 marks)

67 Crista (D12)

Crista set up her own business on 1 November 2013. Her VAT-exclusive supplies for each month from that date were as follows:

	Standard rated supplies £	Exempt supplies £
November 2013	2,900	
December 2013	1,800	
January 2014	4,100	
February 2014	4,900	
March 2014	9,700	
April 2014	10,400	
May 2014	14,700	
June 2014	17,500	6,200
July 2014	13,400	8,900
August 2014	2,100	3,000
September 2014	10,400	Nil
October 2014	42,000	3,000

As Crista knew that her supplies were going to increase dramatically in October 2014, she notified HMRC of the need to register for VAT on 1 October 2014 and started charging 20% VAT on her taxable supplies from that date.

In addition, Crista sold plant and machinery used in her business on 4 September 2014 for proceeds of £3,700 and no VAT was charged.

Crista is concerned that she may have registered late for VAT and has sent the following email to her tax adviser:

"Can you explain to me when I should have contacted HMRC and when I should have started charging VAT? I don't understand which supplies are relevant. If I have not charged enough VAT on any of my sales, can you tell me the correct amount to pay and whether I will suffer this cost? I am aware that there may be some penalties for not contacting HMRC at the right time, even if this is simply an oversight on my part. Please could you let me know how much these may amount to?"

Requirement

Answer Crista's questions with supporting calculations where appropriate. **(8 marks)**

68 Bactrian Ltd (M13)

Bactrian Ltd is registered for VAT and produces only standard-rated goods. In order to expand its business, the company has begun to sell its goods outside of the UK.

Figures for the quarter ended 28 February 2014 are as follows:

	£
Sales	
Supplies in the UK	39,500
Supplies to non-trading customers in other EU countries	12,900
Purchases	
Materials purchased in the UK	8,100
Computer advice from a non-EU supplier	190
Car purchased in the UK and used 80% for business purposes	6,280
Motor expenses including fuel costing £600 for employee Mary Drode	1,750

All the above figures exclude any VAT.

Half of Mary Drode's mileage was for work-related travel. The relevant VAT-inclusive fuel scale rate for the quarter is £450.

Requirement

Calculate the VAT payable by Bactrian Ltd for the quarter ended 28 February 2014, clearly showing your treatment of each of the above figures. **(5 marks)**

69 Dave Eaton

Dave Eaton has been living in the UK since he began working for Spud Ltd in the UK 15 years ago, but he is domiciled in Whereatania. He married his wife, Karen, who is UK resident and domiciled, on 1 June 2012 and the couple currently has no children.

On 1 September 2013, Dave's employer, Spud Ltd, sent him on a three month secondment to the Whereatanian office. Karen stayed in London for the duration of the secondment, apart from occasional trips to visit Dave in Whereatania.

Income

Dave's income and benefits from employment during 2013/14 were as follows:

- A monthly salary of £6,250 for his UK duties. This increased to £7,750 for the three months that he was on secondment. This was paid by the UK company.

- Accommodation in a one bedroom apartment in Whereatania for the duration of the secondment. The apartment cost Spud Ltd the equivalent of £1,250 per month.

- A return flight for the start and end of the secondment, plus a further flight to the UK to visit his wife costing £195 each.

- Spud Ltd also paid for three return flights for Dave's wife to visit him during the secondment. Again, each flight cost £195.

- Spud Ltd paid an amount equal to 1% of Dave's salary into his personal pension.

Dave also received the following income during 2013/14:

- UK bank interest of £3,000.
- UK dividends of £1,080.

He had no overseas sources of income during 2013/14.

Capital transactions

During 2013/14 Dave made the following disposals:

- He sold his flat in east London for £382,000 on 28 February 2014.

  Dave had paid £225,000, including stamp duty land tax and legal costs of £2,500, for the flat on 1 July 2001 and moved in two months later on 1 September 2001, once the flat had been fully redecorated. From 1 September 2002 the house was let to tenants while Dave moved in with his then girlfriend. He moved back in on 1 May 2007 when the relationship ended and lived there until he married Karen, at which time they both moved into their shared marital home. Dave made an election to continue to treat the flat as his principal private residence.

- He sold a rifle for £25,000 on 12 May 2013. He incurred selling fees of £75.

  Dave had purchased the rifle for £10,000 in July 2006 at an auction and had incurred a 5% auctioneer's fee.

- He sold 5,000 shares in Killian plc for £16.50 per share on 15 October 2013.

  Dave had purchased 6,000 shares on 12 November 2004 when they were worth £3 per share. There had been a rights issue in September 2009 offering two shares for every share held at a cost of £7.50 per share, which Dave had taken up.

- He sold five acres of land for £625,000 on 31 March 2014.

  He had purchased a 12 acre plot of land in Whereatania in 2000 for an equivalent value of £207,800, including fees. The remaining seven acres were valued at £1,050,000 in March 2014. He transferred £200,000 received in respect of the gain to his UK bank account. He received no interest from the bank account containing the rest of the proceeds during the 2013/14 tax year. There is no system of capital gains tax in Whereatania.

Dave makes a claim to use the remittance basis in 2013/14.

Requirements

(a) Explain why Dave was UK resident in 2013/14.   **(3 marks)**

(b) Calculate Dave's total income tax and capital gains tax liabilities for 2013/14, showing your treatment of each item.   **(21 marks)**

                                                                                           (24 marks)

70 Amanda (S09)

(a) Amanda has been employed as an accountant by Carpet Ltd since 6 April 2013. Carpet Ltd provides professional training services. Amanda is paid an annual salary of £68,000 and was provided with the following during 2013/14:

   (1) The use of a laptop computer which cost £2,000 when it was first provided to Amanda on 1 November 2013. Amanda's private use of the laptop is insignificant.

   (2) Medical insurance which cost Carpet Ltd £420 for 2013/14. During December 2013, Amanda received medical treatment which cost the insurance company £1,800.

   (3) Childcare payments of £80 per week paid directly by Carpet Ltd to a registered child carer.

   (4) Amanda cycles from home to work each day and is provided with £200 per year by Carpet Ltd in order to encourage her to do that. However, she is also provided with a petrol company car which she uses to visit clients and for private purposes. The car was first provided to Amanda on 6 April 2013 and has a list price of £15,000 and CO_2 emissions of 147g/km. Amanda made a contribution of £500 on 6 April 2013 towards the cost of the car.

   (5) Carpet Ltd pays 5% of Amanda's gross salary into an occupational pension scheme. Amanda has decided to match that contribution each tax year.

   (6) When Amanda joined Carpet Ltd, she made it clear that she wished to undertake educational courses over the next year in order to further her career. Carpet Ltd offered Amanda the following three options for 2013/14:

   Option One: attend training courses run by Carpet Ltd during 2013/14, the value of which is £7,000 (based on the price of these courses charged by Carpet Ltd to the general public). There were plenty of spaces available on the courses as a number of clients had cancelled due to the economic downturn; or

   Option Two: undertake a course of study with another tuition provider, the cost of which would be £5,500. Carpet Ltd agreed to make an interest free loan of £5,500 to Amanda (repayable in one year's time) should she wish to pursue this course; or

   Option Three: accept a one off cash payment of £3,000 to pursue a training course of her choice with an independent supplier. Amanda would use the money to train as a legal assistant.

   Amanda assessed these options and decided to pursue Option One.

Requirements

   (i) State, with calculations, the income tax and NIC payable by Amanda in respect of the three options detailed in note (6) above.   **(4 marks)**

   (ii) Calculate Amanda's employment income for 2013/14 assuming that, in respect of note (6) above, she chose Option One.   **(8 marks)**

   Note: **Assume that the official rate of interest throughout 2013/14 was 4%.**

(b)   Amanda purchased 17 Appian Road, a commercial property, on 1 January 1994. The property had been rented out unfurnished since 1 May 2012 for a monthly rental of £1,200. The tenants moved out on 1 November 2013 and the property was empty during November while Amanda extended the property at a cost of £6,900 and undertook some repairs costing £200. Amanda's son, Kenneth, runs KW Ltd and Amanda rented out the property to KW Ltd from 1 December 2013. When KW Ltd moved into the property on 1 December 2013 it paid a lease premium of £2,100 on the grant of a five year lease over the property at an annual rental of £10,000.

Amanda has property losses brought forward at 6 April 2013 of £1,100.

Requirement

Calculate Amanda's property income for 2013/14.

(4 marks)

(c)   Amanda is a chartered accountant and she also reviews the tax returns of her son, Kenneth, for free. It has come to her attention that Kenneth has been overstating the travel expenses that he claims from KW Ltd. These expenses are shown as deductible in his latest draft income tax return and, in addition, Kenneth has been reimbursed amounts that he did not actually spend.

When Amanda asked Kenneth about these discrepancies, he replied that "HMRC has it in for me. I put in a few extra expense claims from time to time for money I have not spent, but it all balances out in the end."

Requirement

State the ethical threats to which Amanda is exposed and explain the action she should take.

(6 marks)

(d)   Amanda's estate comprised the following at 31 July 2014:

	Estimated market value at 31 July 2014 £
Principal private residence	644,070
17 Appian Road – a rental property	280,500
Shares in Windsor Ltd (unquoted investment company)	33,930
Chattels and cash	40,710
Liabilities	11,100

Amanda is currently reviewing her tax situation, including the amount of inheritance tax that would be payable were she to die in the near future. She intends to leave her entire estate to her son, Kenneth.

Amanda's civil partner, Cyd, died on 1 July 2007 and Amanda inherited the whole of her estate, worth £1.75 million. Cyd had made no previous lifetime gifts.

Amanda has made no lifetime gifts.

Requirement

Calculate the inheritance tax payable in the event of Amanda's death, indicating the amount and availability of any exemptions and assume that:

- Amanda dies on 31 December 2017; and
- Amanda's estate at death has the same market value as at 31 July 2014.

(5 marks)

(27 marks)

71   Wentworth Ltd (M10)

(a)   Russell Ltd is a trading company. It is owned 75% by Musgrove Ltd. Musgrove Ltd is the 95% subsidiary of Wentworth Ltd, which also owns 65% of Elliot Ltd.

Russell Ltd's draft trading profit for the year ended 31 December 2013 is £346,700. This figure has already been adjusted for corporation tax purposes for everything except capital allowances and research and development expenditure.

The following information is also available:

	Notes	£
Loss on sale of fixed interest debentures	(1)	5,570
Interest receivable on the fixed interest debentures		8,000
Interest payable	(2)	5,920
UK dividends received from a 12% ordinary shareholding in Benwick Ltd		4,860
Qualifying charitable donation to a national charity		13,570

Notes:

(1) In December 2013 Russell Ltd sold fixed interest debentures in Croft plc. The above loss is computed correctly according to tax rules.

(2) Interest payable comprises:

	£
Bank overdraft interest	2,970
Interest on a loan taken out to acquire the debentures in Croft plc	1,200
Interest on a loan to purchase new machinery	1,750
	5,920

Capital allowances

The tax written down value of the main pool at 1 January 2013 was £26,900 and the tax written down value of the managing director's car was £23,000 (purchased in February 2009 and used 60% for private purposes). During the year ended 31 December 2013, Russell Ltd undertook the following acquisitions and disposals:

Acquisitions:		£
12 March 2013	Office furniture	35,900
3 May 2013	Computer equipment	8,100
17 June 2013	Car (CO_2 emissions 150 g/km) – no private use	13,000
Disposals:		
1 October 2013	Plant and machinery	2,000
23 November 2013	Car (originally cost £8,700 in June 2007) – no private use	2,910

Capital transactions

17 Harville Road: This property was purchased in June 2003 for £390,000. Russell Ltd sold the property in May 2013 for £612,880.

Lyme Court: This property was purchased for £327,868 in February 2013.

Benwick Ltd: Shares in Benwick Ltd, an unquoted trading company, were purchased for £12,800 in June 2006 and sold in May 2013 for £17,400.

Russell Ltd has capital losses brought forward at 1 January 2013 of £22,100.

Research and development

Some of the funds generated by the above disposals were used to undertake a qualifying research and development project. The following costs of the research were deducted in full in arriving at the draft trading profit:

	£
Research staff	31,000
Computer hardware	5,800
Computer software	1,900
	38,700

Russell Ltd is a small company for research and development purposes.

Requirements

(i) Calculate the corporation tax payable by Russell Ltd for the year ended 31 December 2013, assuming all beneficial claims and elections are made. Briefly explain the tax treatment of the sale of shares in Benwick Ltd. **(23 marks)**

   Notes: **Ignore VAT. The RPI for May 2013 is 250.0.**

(ii) State the stamp taxes consequences of the capital transactions made by Russell Ltd during the year ended 31 December 2013. Ignore VAT. **(5 marks)**

(b) The company accountant has raised some queries regarding VAT.

He advises you that Musgrove Ltd, a VAT registered company, wants to expand and sell goods to customers in the EU (who may or may not be VAT registered). The goods would be standard rated if sold in the UK.

He needs to complete the VAT return started by the bookkeeper. He has a list of purchases at their VAT inclusive values and he needs to know how some of the items should be treated for VAT purposes. These are as follows:

- Newspapers
- Stamps
- Wages
- Annual insurance premium
- Office stationery
- Books for the in-house library

Requirements

(i) Explain to the company accountant the VAT consequences of the plans to expand to other parts of the EU.

(2 marks)

(ii) For each item listed explain to the company accountant what type of supply it is for VAT purposes.

(3 marks)

(33 marks)

72 Alec Ealing (M10)

(a) Alec Ealing is the managing director and majority shareholder of Lavender Ltd, an unquoted trading company. Lavender Ltd prepares accounts to 31 March each year.

In the past, Alec has received no salary from Lavender Ltd but Alec decided to implement the following from 1 January 2014.

- A salary of £450 per month (gross)

- A company car (petrol) from 1 January 2014, the details of which are as follows:

List price: £19,200
CO_2 emissions: 159g/km
Operating lease payments per month payable by Lavender Ltd: £635
The lease was taken out on 1 January 2014.

Lavender Ltd has a draft trading profit after capital allowances for the year ending 31 March 2014 of £117,000. However, this figure does not reflect any costs deductible in respect of the above plans.

Requirement

Compute the tax adjusted trading profit for Lavender Ltd for the year ending 31 March 2014.

(4 marks)

Note: **For the purposes of this part, ignore VAT.**

(b) In January 2012, Alec was granted a 25-year lease over Guinness House, a property in London. Alec paid a premium of £216,000 for the grant of the lease and pays rent of £1,200 each year. Alec rents out Guinness House as a furnished property for short periods, never exceeding three weeks, to individuals who wish to stay in a luxury property. During 2013/14 Guinness House was available for the whole year and was occupied for over half that time. The following information is relevant in respect of the property for 2013/14:

	£
Rental income	27,000
Allowable costs	3,490
Cost of new furniture	3,100

Requirement

Calculate Alec's assessable property income in respect of Guinness House for 2013/14. **(5 marks)**

Note: **For the purposes of this part, ignore VAT.**

(c) In addition to the income described in parts (a) and (b) above, Alec received bank interest of £240 and dividends from Mob Ltd of £36,000 during 2013/14. Instead of contributing to a pension fund, Alec pays £1,000 per month into a savings account. He also makes a donation of £50 per month under Gift Aid.

Requirement

Calculate Alec's income tax liability for 2013/14. **(6 marks)**

(d) Lavender Ltd is registered for VAT. All of its existing supplies to its regular UK customers are standard rated and these totalled £62,000 for the three months to 31 March 2014. In addition, on 1 January 2014, Lavender Ltd accepted two contracts to supply its products to new customers in March 2014 as follows:

Contract One

Goods were sold to Hill Ltd for £26,000. The supply of these goods is exempt for VAT purposes.

Contract Two

Goods were sold to MB Ltd for £15,000. The supply of these goods is zero-rated for VAT purposes.

Lavender Ltd incurred the following standard rated costs during the three months ending 31 March 2014:

	£
Relating to existing UK customers	33,920
Relating to Contract One	11,700
Relating to Contract Two	7,920
Costs relating to the whole business	12,700

All of the above figures are exclusive of VAT, where appropriate.

Requirement

Calculate the VAT payable by/repayable to Lavender Ltd for the three months ending 31 March 2014. **(5 marks)**

(e) Lavender Ltd's business continues to expand and Alec has accepted a one-year contract to make standard rated supplies to a new client, commencing on 1 April 2014. To meet this extra demand, Alec is considering the following options:

Option One: Subcontract the extra work at a fee of £20,000 (VAT inclusive).

Option Two: Employ an extra member of staff for a year at a salary of £13,000. Under this option, additional plant and machinery would be purchased at a cost of £3,900 (VAT inclusive) which would be sold for £1,000 (VAT inclusive) at the end of the one-year contract.

Lavender Ltd expects to pay corporation tax at the small profits rate for the year ending 31 March 2015.

Requirement

Calculate the net cost of each of the two options. **(6 marks)**

(26 marks)

73 Rosa Gergiev (M10)

(a) Rosa Gergiev started up her own unincorporated business 'Light Touch' on 1 June 2012 designing and selling light fittings. Her recent tax adjusted trading profits are as follows:

	£
9 months ended 28 February 2013	28,800
12 months ended 28 February 2014	69,140

In order to fund the expansion of her business Rosa made the following disposals:

30 June 2013: Sale of antique jewellery for £15,000. Rosa had inherited the jewellery from her mother in May 1991 when it had a probate value of £3,000.

12 July 2013: Sale of 10,000 shares in Adage Ltd, an unquoted investment company, for £87,800. The shares had been given to Rosa by her father in May 2010 when they had a market value of £46,000.

Requirements

(i) Calculate the trading income assessments for the first two tax years of Rosa's business and any overlap profits arising. **(3 marks)**

(ii) Calculate the capital gains tax payable by Rosa for 2013/14. **(5 marks)**

(b) Rosa's cousin Valerie, a chartered accountant, prepares Rosa's self-assessment tax return every year. Valerie derives most of her professional income from her work for Rosa and other members of the Gergiev family. Rosa has told Valerie that on her tax return for 2013/14 she does not wish to declare income from a flat she rents out.

Requirement

Identify the ethical threats to which Valerie is exposed in this situation and explain which of the fundamental principles applicable to chartered accountants she would breach by knowingly preparing an incorrect return for Rosa. **(5 marks)**

(13 marks)

74 Charlie Schott (J10)

(a) Charlie Schott owns 95% of the ordinary shares in Lincoln Ltd (an unquoted trading company). Charlie is the managing director of Lincoln Ltd. The draft results for Lincoln Ltd for the year ended 31 March 2014 are as follows:

	Notes	£	£
Gross trading profit			302,990
Add:			
Bank interest receivable		3,100	
Rental income	(1)	17,900	
UK dividends received from a 15% shareholding in Moss Ltd		11,700	
			32,700
Less:			
Depreciation		7,910	
Loss on the sale of Penn House	(2)	70,800	
Lease premium amortisation	(3)	2,400	
Staff costs	(4)	370,596	
Interest payable	(5)	18,110	
Other allowable costs		172,340	
			(642,156)
Loss for the year			(306,466)

Notes:

(1) The rental income shown above is in respect of Penn House. Lincoln Ltd purchased the freehold of Penn House for £600,400 in January 2008 and has rented out 20% of the space since 31 March 2010. The rest of the property is used for trading purposes.

(2) Penn House was sold for £590,000 on 31 December 2013. Lincoln Ltd has capital losses brought forward of £12,900.

(3) On 1 April 2013, Lincoln Ltd was granted a five-year lease over a warehouse and paid a lease premium of £12,000 on that date. The rent payable on the warehouse was £36,000 pa and is included in other allowable costs of £172,340 above.

(4) Included within staff costs is a bonus of £18,000 for Charlie Schott for the year ended 31 March 2014. The amount was determined on 23 April 2014 and paid on 1 June 2014.

(5) Interest payable comprised the following:

	£
Bank overdraft interest	3,910
Hire-purchase interest on the purchase of machinery (see below)	1,200
Interest on a loan taken out to purchase Penn House	13,000
	18,110

The tax written down values brought forward at 1 April 2013 were as follows:

	£
Main pool	46,900
Special rate pool	1,980

Lincoln Ltd made the following acquisitions during the year:

		£
7 May 2013	Car – CO_2 emissions of 170g/km	14,300
3 June 2013	Machinery bought on hire-purchase	52,890
1 November 2013	New electrical systems in factory	4,710
8 February 2014	Low emission car	13,000

On 2 March 2014, machinery was sold for £1,800 (which was less than its original cost).

Lincoln Ltd has a subsidiary, Kennedy Ltd, in which it owns 95% of the ordinary shares.

Requirements

(i) Calculate the trading loss and the corporation tax liability for Lincoln Ltd for the year ended 31 March 2014. **(18 marks)**

(ii) Explain the stamp duty land tax implications for Lincoln Ltd of the purchase of the leased warehouse. **(3 marks)**

(b) Abe House is the only asset of significant value owned by Kennedy Ltd, which does not undertake any trading activities. Abe House was purchased in April 1999 for £197,500. The shares in Kennedy Ltd were acquired on 1 August 2003 for £8,000.

Lincoln Ltd has been contacted by a purchaser that would like to acquire Abe House on 1 June 2014 by one of two methods. The purchaser has made two proposals and is prepared to pay £350,000 to acquire either:

- Abe House only, or

- Lincoln Ltd's 95% shareholding in Kennedy Ltd.

Requirement

Using the information provided in parts (a) and (b), explain, with supporting calculations, the corporation tax consequences for Lincoln Ltd and Kennedy Ltd of the two proposals for the disposal. You are not required to calculate corporation tax liabilities. **(4 marks)**

Note: **Assume the RPI for June 2014 is 260.0.**

(c) Yesterday, Charlie Schott sent the following email to the chartered accountant who handles his tax affairs:

"I want to change the bonus arrangements for next year. As you are aware, my bonus is normally paid on 1 June following the year end, but for the year ending 31 March 2015, I should like to delay this payment until 1 February 2016. I know you have said we can only claim a deduction in the accounts for the year ended 31 March 2015 if payment is made within nine months. However, I'm sure we can stretch that limit just this once."

Requirement

Explain the action that the chartered accountant should take.

(6 marks)

(31 marks)

Note: **Ignore VAT.**

75 Martina McQueen (J10)

(a) On 1 January 2014, Martina McQueen set up her own unincorporated business as a designer and manufacturer of glassware. Martina has been invited to tender for a substantial new contract providing glassware to a local shop. She is also already selling her products in other EU countries to both VAT-registered and non-VAT registered customers. As Martina's business expands, she is becoming increasingly concerned about the need to account for VAT. Martina's supplies are classified as standard-rated for VAT purposes and she understands that once she is VAT registered, she can recover her input tax.

Requirement

Explain to Martina the circumstances in which she will be required to register for VAT. Make clear your treatment of her sales outside the UK. **(4 marks)**

(b) Martina has decided to register for VAT voluntarily with effect from 1 January 2014. She has prepared the following information for the year ending 31 December 2014:

	£
Revenue:	
Sales of glassware (VAT exclusive)	86,060
Costs:	
Tax-deductible expenses	12,200
Client entertaining	460
Purchase of computer for use in the business	3,900
Purchase of a new car on 1 June 2014 for Martina, which she uses 70% for private purposes. CO_2 emissions of 115g/km	11,500

All of the above costs should be assumed to be inclusive of VAT at 20%.

Requirements

(i) Calculate the tax-adjusted trading profit for Martina for the year ending 31 December 2014. **(4 marks)**

(ii) Compute the trading income assessments for Martina for her first two tax years of assessment and identify any overlap profits arising. **(3 marks)**

(c) Martina has decided to employ a part-time assistant from 1 January 2015 as she anticipates that her trading profit will rise substantially over the next year and she will become an additional rate taxpayer. The assistant will receive a salary of £12,900 pa and will have the use of a van, which will be leased by Martina. Martina will incur leasing and business fuel costs of £7,200 pa . The assistant will be allowed unlimited private use of the van, but will be required to pay for his own private fuel.

Martina's husband does not approve of the plan to employ an assistant as he thinks it is a waste of money and not tax efficient. He has offered to find time to do the same job for a salary of £7,000 pa plus childcare vouchers from Martina's business of £160 per week. He would not need the use of a van, but would use his own car to meet all delivery needs. He estimates that he would drive 5,000 business miles pa and would require a mileage allowance of 50p per mile. Martina's husband is a basic rate taxpayer.

Requirement

Calculate the cost to the business of each of the suggested options. **(9 marks)**

(20 marks)

76   Yelena, Katya and Alina (S10)

(a)   Yelena, Katya and Alina have been in partnership since 1 January 2001, preparing accounts to 30 June each year. Yelena receives a salary of £37,000 pa and Katya a salary of £41,500 pa. Alina does not receive a salary. The remaining profits/losses are allocated equally between the partners.

The partnership's adjusted trading profit before capital allowances for the year ended 30 June 2014 is £72,900.

At 1 July 2013 the tax written down values of the partnership assets were as follows:

	£
Main pool	15,870
BMW car used by Yelena (60% private use)	14,600

The partnership undertook the following transactions during the year ended 30 June 2014:

Acquisitions:		£
13 August 2013	Computer equipment	3,965
1 May 2014	Toyota car for use by Yelena (60% private use) with CO_2 emissions of 90 g/km	See below

Disposals:	
1 May 2014	BMW car (purchased in February 2013) used by Yelena was traded in for the Toyota car. The part exchange value on the BMW was £8,000 and a further £7,000 was paid in cash.

All of the above figures are inclusive of VAT at 20% where appropriate and the partnership is registered for VAT and makes wholly standard rated supplies.

Requirements

(i)   Calculate the tax adjusted trading profits for the partnership for the year ended 30 June 2014.

(5 marks)

(ii)   Show the allocation of the partnership profit for the year ended 30 June 2014.   **(3 marks)**

(b)   The partners have decided to incorporate their business on 31 December 2014. The budgeted tax adjusted trading profit (after capital allowances) for the six months ending 31 December 2014 has been prepared and Yelena's share is estimated to be £33,417.

Yelena has unrelieved overlap profits from commencement of the partnership of £2,900.

Requirement

Using the information given in (a) and (b) above, calculate the trading income assessment for Yelena for 2014/15.   **(2 marks)**

(c)   Yelena has employed a chartered accountant, who is a sole trader, to advise her on her personal tax affairs. The accountant has accepted the engagement but has recently discovered that, for the tax year 2012/13, Yelena deliberately understated her trading income and overstated her pension contributions on her tax return and, as a result, paid £15,000 less tax than she should have. Yelena has indicated to her chartered accountant that she sees no reason to pay the extra £15,000 of tax to HMRC.

Requirement

Explain why Yelena's actions constitute money laundering and explain the actions that her chartered accountant should take.   **(6 marks)**

(16 marks)

77 Quark Ltd (S10)

(a) Spin Ltd is the 75% subsidiary of Quark Ltd which also owns 100% of the shares in Charm Ltd. Due to poor results, it has been decided that Spin Ltd's operations will be closed down. Spin Ltd's draft accounts for the final four months ended 31 July 2014 show the following:

	Notes	£	£
Trading loss			(98,310)
Profit on the sale of Hadron House	(1)	137,200	
Rent receivable	(2)	8,400	
UK bank interest receivable		1,430	
			147,030
			48,720
Depreciation		13,200	
Interest payable	(3)	12,340	
Legal and professional fees	(4)	2,390	
Closure costs	(5)	57,790	
Other allowable costs		23,940	
			(109,660)
			(60,940)

Notes:

(1) Hadron House was sold on 13 July 2014 for £210,000. It had been purchased in April 2005 for £104,000. From 13 July 2014 onwards, any remaining staff of Spin Ltd were relocated to the headquarters building of Quark Ltd, which had been purchased for £200,000 in May 2014.

(2) Since April 2005, 20% of Hadron House had been rented out to an unconnected tenant. The tenant's lease terminated on 12 July 2014.

(3) Interest payable comprised the following:

	£
Interest on a loan to purchase Hadron House	2,900
Bank overdraft interest	8,100
Interest payable on a loan from Quark Ltd to help meet payroll costs in July 2014	1,340
	12,340

(4) Legal and professional fees comprised the following:

	£
Debt collection fees	1,890
Costs incurred defending an alleged motoring offence by an employee while on company business	500
	2,390

(5) Closure costs include £43,000 of statutory redundancy payments.

The tax written down values at 1 April 2014 were as follows:

	£
Main pool	24,800
Special rate pool	900

On 1 July 2014, Spin Ltd sold plant and machinery (which had originally been added to the main pool) for proceeds of £12,800. No items were sold for more than original cost. On cessation, all other items which had previously attracted capital allowances were scrapped.

Requirements

(i) Calculate the tax adjusted trading loss for Spin Ltd for the four months ended 31 July 2014.

(7 marks)

(ii) Calculate Spin Ltd's corporation tax liability for the four months ended 31 July 2014.

(7 marks)

(iii) Calculate the stamp duty land tax payable on the purchase of Quark Ltd's new headquarters.

(1 mark)

Notes: **Assume an indexed rise of 10% between April 2005 and July 2014. Ignore VAT.**

(b) Michelle Green was employed by Spin Ltd and following the closure of Spin Ltd will be relocated to the Quark Ltd group headquarters. She will continue to be paid a salary of £60,000 pa. However, as Michelle will have to re-locate from Cardiff to London, Quark Ltd is assessing the following two options to compensate her:

Option One: Michelle will live rent free in a house in London owned by Quark Ltd. The house cost £235,000 in April 2011 and has an annual value of £17,000 pa. Local property agents have stated that the house has a rental value of £2,000 per month although the property has been empty for the last year.

Option Two: Michelle will receive an expense allowance of £1,000 per month to cover the cost of travelling from Cardiff to London each week.

Assume Quark Ltd pays tax at the small profits rate.

Requirement

Calculate the annual after tax cost to Quark Ltd of both option one and option two.   **(7 marks)**

Note: **Assume the official rate of interest is 4% pa.**

(c) Michelle needs to raise extra funds and is therefore considering **one** of the following:

1   Reducing her personal pension contributions, starting on 1 October 2014, from £1,400 (gross) per month to £600 (gross) per month. She would resume her previous level of contributions on 1 October 2015.

2   Selling a painting which she purchased in May 1999 at a cost of £5,900. A buyer has offered to pay £8,200 for the painting on 1 December 2014.

3   Selling a vintage car which she inherited from her father in March 1997 when it was worth £5,950. A dealer has offered to purchase the car in September 2014 for £7,600.

Michelle also makes regular disposals of shares each year, sufficient to utilise her capital gains tax annual exempt amount, and is a higher rate taxpayer.

Requirement

Calculate the amount of after tax funds generated by undertaking each of the above options.

(6 marks)

(28 marks)

78   Murray and Carla Gellman (S10)

Murray Gellman died suddenly on 1 February 2014. He had been born on 14 July 1944. His wife Carla had died in June 2012. The details of Murray's tax affairs at the time of his death are as follows:

Income tax:

Murray was a self-employed lecturer and prepared accounts to 5 April each year. He has no overlap profits and his trading income for the period 6 April 2013 to 31 January 2014 is estimated to be £18,560.

Murray also owned a property which he rented out for £19,500 pa. The last tenants moved out when their lease terminated on 31 December 2013. Murray had incurred £1,200 of repair expenditure in January 2014 in anticipation of the property being advertised for rent from 1 February 2014.

In addition, on 1 May 2013 Murray received dividends of £2,070 from Baryon Ltd (see below) and also received bank interest of £6,200 during 2013/14.

Inheritance tax:

Murray's estate at death comprised the following:

	Market value at 1 February 2014 £
Principal private residence	670,000
Rental property	300,000
5% holding in Lepton plc	See below
Cash and chattels	320,000
Outstanding liabilities (excluding tax)	28,900

The shares in Lepton plc were quoted at 416-419p on 1 February 2014. The marked bargains on that day were 412p, 418p and 420p.

Murray previously owned shares in Baryon Ltd, an unquoted investment company. The shares cost £32,000 in May 2001 and Murray gave the shares to his son, George, on 12 June 2013, when they were worth £41,000. The only other lifetime gift made by Murray was a gift to a discretionary trust in August 2006. The gross chargeable value of the gift was £635,000.

On her death in June 2012, Murray's wife left her entire estate to her husband. She had made no lifetime gifts. Murray left his entire estate to his son George.

On 7 July 2011, Murray's father, Stephen, died and left the whole of his chargeable estate of £360,000 to Murray. Stephen had made no lifetime gifts.

Murray had settled his income tax liability for 2012/13, but had not yet paid any income tax or capital gains tax in respect of 2013/14.

Requirements

(a) Calculate Murray's income tax payable for 2013/14.   **(6 marks)**

(b) Calculate the inheritance tax payable as a result of Murray's death.   **(15 marks)**

                                                                             (21 marks)

Note: Ignore national insurance.

79 Trevor Knott (J11)

(a) Trevor Knott is a sole trader who started trading on 1 January 2013 and prepared his first set of accounts for the 14 months ended 28 February 2014. Trevor makes wholly standard rated supplies, but has not yet registered for VAT. His draft accounts for the 14 months ended 28 February 2014 show the following:

	£
Sales	77,500
Expenses:	
Allowable expenses	32,075
Client entertaining	2,590
Repairs relating to Trevor's car	1,900

Trevor purchased his car on 1 December 2013 for £21,000 and it has been used 30% for business purposes since that date. The car has CO_2 emissions of 165g/km. Trevor also purchased a computer in July 2013 for £1,800 for use only in the business.

All of the above figures are inclusive of VAT, where appropriate.

Requirements

(i) Calculate the tax-adjusted trading profit for Trevor for the 14 months ended 28 February 2014, making clear your treatment of all items. **(5 marks)**

(ii) Calculate Trevor's taxable trading income for all relevant tax years and any overlap profit arising. **(3 marks)**

(b) On 1 March 2014 Trevor accepted a contract from a new client worth £73,000. The work will be performed in March 2014 and paid for in May 2014. The supplies to the new client are exempt from VAT, whereas all of Trevor's other supplies are standard rated. Standard rated sales (excluding VAT) are as follows:

	£
January 2013 - December 2013	5,200 per month
January 2014	8,500
February 2014	9,000
March 2014 - May 2014	10,000 per month

Requirement

Explain when Trevor will be required to submit his application for VAT registration to HMRC. **(4 marks)**

(c) Trevor decided to register for VAT voluntarily, and has been registered since 1 March 2014. He has prepared his first VAT return for the quarter ended 31 May 2014 using the standard *de minimis* test for partial exemption purposes. However, he has recently heard that there are simplified partial exemption tests and is wondering whether either Test One or Test Two may apply to his business.

Trevor's input tax for the quarter to 31 May 2014 was as follows:

Total input tax (no blocked tax)	£1,500
Input tax directly attributable to exempt supplies	£1,200
Input tax directly attributable to taxable supplies	£230

Requirement

Explain whether Trevor's business passes either of the two simplified partial exemption tests. **(6 marks)**

(18 marks)

80 Bute Traders (M12)

You work as a tax assistant for a firm of chartered accountants. You have been given the following information in relation to three unconnected clients:

Gerald

Gerald is a new client and has written a letter to the firm which includes the following comment:

'I have read the engagement letter but I don't understand the bit where it refers to agents and principals. I really don't see the difference; you're my accountant aren't you? You're meant to do everything for me regarding tax. I thought that was what I'm paying for?'

Bute Traders

Bute Traders is an unincorporated VAT registered business. Bute Traders is partially exempt. During the year ended 31 December 2013 Bute Traders' own bookkeeper completed the partial exemption calculations when filing the quarterly VAT returns. However, the annual partial exemption adjustment is always prepared by your firm.

Your manager has told you that Bute Traders failed both Test One and Test Two when applied to the year as a whole and that therefore you need to complete the annual partial exemption adjustment. You have been given the following figures for the year ended 31 December 2013 regarding outputs:

	£
Standard rated taxable supplies (excluding VAT)	341,300
Exempt supplies	55,000
	396,300

Bute Traders' input tax for the year ended 31 December 2013 is:

	£
Wholly attributable to standard rated supplies	50,045
Wholly attributable to exempt supplies	5,850
Non-attributable	12,000
	67,895

The input VAT recovered during the year ended 31 December 2013 amounted to £64,570. In addition the bookkeeper has stated that no input tax was recovered on plant and machinery purchased in July 2013. This plant and machinery was purchased for use in all parts of the business for £15,000 excluding VAT.

Splott plc

Splott plc is a VAT registered business which disposed of two properties in December 2013.

The first property was an office building for which Splott plc received £1 million on sale. It had been purchased as a newly constructed office building in January 2012.

The second property was an investment property which Splott plc had owned for many years and rented out. Splott plc had exercised an option to tax on this property. The property was sold for proceeds of £2.5 million.

Requirements

(a) Explain to Gerald, illustrating your answer with an example for each, the difference between a chartered accountant acting as an agent and as a principal when providing tax services. **(4 marks)**

(b) Calculate the annual adjustment required, if any, to the input VAT recovered by Bute Traders for its year ended 31 December 2013. **(7 marks)**

(c) Explain, with supporting calculations, the amount of VAT, if any, that Splott plc should have charged on the disposal of each property. Calculate the stamp duty land tax payable on each purchase. **(5 marks)**

(16 marks)

81 Michael Lyon (M13)

(a) Michael Lyon was employed as the personnel manager of Lecker plc, a cookery training company, for several years until he left the company on 30 September 2013. Michael's annual salary was £52,000. Michael's other remuneration from 6 April 2013 to 30 September 2013 was as follows:

- Furnished accommodation which cost £134,000 in January 2010. By the time the accommodation was first provided to Michael on 1 April 2011 it had increased in value to £155,000. The accommodation has an annual value of £12,000. The furniture cost £2,900 when first provided to Michael on 1 April 2011. Michael paid rent of £768 per month until he moved out on 30 September 2013.

- A mileage allowance of 42p per mile. Michael drove 4,000 business miles between 6 April and 30 September 2013.

- A free parking space near Lecker plc's premises. This cost Lecker plc £80 per month.

- Reimbursement of £340 spent by Michael entertaining Lecker plc's clients.

- Michael attended a cookery course provided by Lecker plc in May 2013. The normal fee for that course was £550. However, as there were spaces available Michael attended free of charge. In addition, Lecker plc purchased additional ingredients costing £75 for Michael's use on the course.

Requirement

Calculate Michael's assessable employment income for 2013/14, making clear your treatment of each item. **(7 marks)**

Note: **The official rate of interest is 4% pa.**

(b) Michael started an unincorporated business on 1 October 2013 and registered for VAT immediately. The provisional accounts for the seven months to 30 April 2014 show a net profit of £40,202 after deducting the following expenses:

	Notes	£
Staff costs		12,420
Depreciation		2,870
Saffron House expenditure	(1)	29,400
Michael's car expenses	(2)	2,580
Light and heat		1,200
Repairs and renewals	(3)	1,425
Bank interest on business start-up loan		720
Legal and professional fees	(4)	440
Sundry expenses	(5)	1,543

Notes:

(1) Michael paid a premium of £5,400 on 1 October 2013 to secure a seven-year lease over his business premises, Saffron House. Rent of £24,000 is payable annually in advance.

(2) Michael uses the car 60% of the time for business purposes. Car expenses consist of a parking fine of £60 incurred by Michael on a business trip, and £2,520 in total spent on fuel for his car in the period.

(3) Repairs and renewals comprise the following:

	£
Redecoration of Saffron House reception area	520
Technologically efficient hand dryer	630
Replacement of carpet tiles in the reception area	275
	1,425

(4) Legal and professional fees comprise the following:

	£
Overdraft arrangement fee	74
Accountancy fees	366
	440

(5) Sundry expenses comprise the following:

	£
Catering costs at a party for local clients	870
Gifts to 20 clients of a spoon showing Michael's business logo	90
Various allowable expenses	583
	1,543

Capital items

In addition to the above, Michael purchased the following for use in his business:

		£
23 October 2013	Michael's car with CO_2 emissions of 93g/km (Note 2)	13,500
4 March 2014	Paintings for display in reception area	1,600

Other outgoings and income

Michael paid £180 in March 2013 for VAT registration advice for the business, but has not included any amount for this in his provisional accounts for the seven months to 30 April 2014.

During 2013/14, Michael received UK dividends of £2,250. He also received £4,160 from a real estate investment trust, paid out of tax-exempt property income. Michael made a personal pension contribution of £4,000 on 2 April 2014.

Requirements

(i) Calculate Michael's tax-adjusted trading profit for the seven months ending 30 April 2014, assuming that he claims the maximum possible capital allowances. Briefly explain your treatment of the £180 paid for VAT advice. **(12 marks)**

(ii) Using the information above and your answer to part (a), calculate Michael's income tax liability for 2013/14. **(6 marks)**

Note: All figures are stated exclusive of VAT. **(25 marks)**

82 Harry and Zinnia Wormwood (J13)

(a) Harry Wormwood was married to Zinnia and they had two children, Michael and Matilda. When Harry died in January 2007, he left the whole of his estate to Zinnia. Harry's only lifetime transfer was a gift of £55,000 to Michael in January 2005 on the occasion of Michael's marriage.

Zinnia died on 1 April 2014, leaving all her assets to Michael and Matilda. Zinnia's second husband Bruce inherited nothing on Zinnia's death. Zinnia had made no lifetime transfers.

At the time of her death, Zinnia owned the following assets:

- A property in London worth £1.5 million on 1 April 2014. There was a mortgage of £300,000 outstanding on the property.

- A holding of 2,000 shares in Trunchbull plc. On 1 April 2014 the shares were quoted at 630p to 646p and the marked bargains were 632p, 636p and 643p.

- Trust assets valued at £225,000 on 1 April 2014. Zinnia was the only life tenant of an interest in possession trust created on 1 January 1995.

- Two paintings. These form part of a set of three paintings, and the values on 1 April 2014 were:

	£
Two paintings owned by Zinnia (value given is total for the two)	150,000
Third painting owned by Bruce	90,000
Total value of the three paintings valued as a set	400,000

Michael and Matilda do not have sufficient savings to settle the inheritance tax liability. They are concerned that they will be unable to pay the inheritance tax liability on the estate on time, as most of Zinnia's assets are not readily convertible into cash.

Requirements

(i) Calculate the inheritance tax payable as a result of Zinnia's death. **(10 marks)**

(ii) State the date by which Michael and Matilda should pay the inheritance tax due in order to avoid paying any interest. **(1 mark)**

(iii) Assuming Michael and Matilda wish to pay the inheritance tax as late as they legitimately can, explain when the liability could be paid and whether the amount(s) would be subject to interest. **(4 marks)**

(b) You work as a trainee for a firm of chartered accountants. Your line manager, Roald, has recently taken over responsibility for the tax affairs of Zinnia's interest in possession trust. You have reviewed the files for the trust and have realised that the previous manager Patricia, who is married to Roald, had not organised the trust's affairs in the most tax efficient way. The trust would have paid at least £10,000 less tax per year over the last fifteen years if Patricia had acted competently. You are unsure what to do with this information.

Requirement

With reference to the conflict resolution process set out in the ICAEW's code of ethics, explain the relevant factors for consideration when deciding the best course of action in this situation.

(5 marks)

(20 marks)

Answer Bank

1 Preparation question: chargeable gains

(i) The painting

	£
Proceeds	31,800
Less MV 31.3.82	(16,800)
Gain	15,000

(ii) The land

	£
Proceeds	108,000
Less incidental costs of sale	(1,970)
Net sale proceeds	106,030

Less: Cost $\dfrac{A}{A+B} \times £200,000$

$\dfrac{108,000}{108,000 + 612,000} \times £200,000$ (30,000)

	£
Gain	76,030

(iii) The Book plc shares

s.104 pool

	No. of shares	Cost £
Acquisitions		
1 May 1986	20,000	18,000
1 March 1989	4,000	4,000
1 May 2002	4,000	10,628
	28,000	32,628
Disposal		
1 July 2013	(24,000)	(27,967)
c/f	4,000	4,661

	£
Proceeds	84,000
Cost	(27,967)
Gain	56,033

(iv) The property

	£
Proceeds	120,000
Less cost	(50,000)
Gain (Note)	70,000

Capital gains tax position

	£
Gain on painting	15,000
Gain on land	76,030
Gain on shares	56,033
Gain on property	70,000
	217,063
Less annual exempt amount	(10,900)
Taxable gains	206,163

	£
Capital gains tax	
(£32,010 − £27,010) = £5,000 × 18%	900
(£206,163 − £5,000) × 28%	56,326
	57,226

2 Preparation question: chargeable gains

John Major

Capital gains tax – 2013/14

	£
Cricket bat (W1)	7,833
Treasury stock – exempt	–
Land (W2)	8,295
	16,128
Annual exempt amount	(10,900)
Taxable gains	5,228
Capital gains tax £5,228 × 28%	1,464

WORKINGS

(1) Cricket bat

	£
Sale proceeds	10,700
Less: Cost	(1,300)
Gain	9,400
	7,833

Gain cannot exceed $\frac{5}{3} \times (£10{,}700 - £6{,}000)$

(2) Land

	£
Market value (note)	13,500
Less: Cost £16,000 × $\dfrac{£13{,}500}{£13{,}500 + £28{,}000}$	(5,205)
Gain	8,295

Note: The sale is to a connected person; therefore market value is substituted for sale proceeds, regardless of the actual sale proceeds received.

Norma Major

Capital gains tax – 2013/14

	Chargeable gains £
Statue (W1)	31,700
Nero plc shares (W2)	20,617
Livia plc shares (W3)	12,231
Augustus plc shares (W4)	637
	65,185
Annual exempt amount	(10,900)
Taxable amount	54,285
Capital gains tax £54,285 × 28%	15,200

Due date for payment under self assessment is 31 January 2015.

WORKINGS

(1) Henry Moore statue

	£
Market value (Note)	48,000
Less: Value when inherited	(16,300)
Gain	31,700

Note: Norma sold the statue for less than it was worth to her sister, a connected person. The actual sale proceeds received are irrelevant; the full market value of the statue must be used to compute the gain.

(2) **Nero plc shares**

	£
Proceeds (March 2014)	23,350
Less: Cost (see below)	(2,733)
Gain	20,617

Working (Nero plc)	No. of shares	Cost £
December 1987 – purchase	4,500	4,599
August 1998 – rights issue	2,250	3,600
	6,750	8,199
March 2014 – disposal	(2,250)	(2,733)
Pool c/f	4,500	5,466

(3) **Livia plc shares**

	£
Proceeds (June 2013)	18,430
Less: cost (see below)	(6,199)
Gain	12,231

Working (Livia plc)

	Number	Cost/MV 31.3.82 £
January 1980 – purchase	1,500	3,750
April 1987 – purchase	2,400	5,793
	3,900	9,543
May 1992 – bonus issues 1:2	1,950	–
	5,850	9,543
June 2013 disposal	(3,800)	(6,199)
Pool c/f	2,050	3,344

(4) **Augustus plc shares**

Gift of shares – March 2014

	£
Market value at date of gift (12,000 × £1.60)	19,200
Less: Deemed cost (below)	(18,563)
Gain	637

Working: Augustus plc shares

	No. of shares	Cost £
January 1998 – purchase	40,000	61,875
Disposal – March 2014	(12,000)	(18,563)
Balance c/f	28,000	43,312

3 Preparation question: PPR relief

(a) **Sebastian**

Capital gains tax computation – 2013/14

	£
Principal private residence (W1)	13,600
Less: Annual exempt amount	(10,900)
Taxable gains	2,700
Capital gains tax (£2,700 @ 28%)	756

WORKINGS

(1) **Principal private residence (PPR)**

	£
Sale proceeds	200,000
Cost	(46,000)
Extension	(18,000)
Gain before relief	136,000
Less: PPR relief (W3) (£136,000 × $^9/_{10}$)	(122,400)
Gain after PPR	13,600

(2) **PPR relief**

Period of ownership   10 years
Period of occupation   9 years

The exempt gain is made up of six years actual occupation together with the three years permitted period of absence for no specific reason, thus leaving one year not covered by the PPR exemption.

Note that 'use of the house rent free' by Sebastian's cousin does not constitute 'letting' for the purposes of obtaining letting relief.

(b) **Amy**

	£
Sale proceeds (July 2014)	350,000
Cost (June 2003)	(500,000)
New kitchen (July 2004)	(12,000)
Loss	(162,000)
Allowable loss (W1) = £162,000 × 19/134	(22,970)

WORKINGS

(1) **Principal private residence relief**

		Notes	No. of months	Exempt	Chargeable
1.6.03 – 31.5.07	Owner-occupation		48	48	
1.6.07 – 31.1.09	Working overseas	(i)	20	20	
1.2.09 – 31.12.09	Owner-occupation		11	11	
1.1.10 – 31.7.14	Empty	(ii)	55	36	19
			134	115	19

Notes:

(i) Periods of working overseas are deemed occupation if *at some time* they are preceded by and followed by periods of actual occupation.

(ii) The last 36 months of ownership are exempted if the property has *at some time* been the individual's principal private residence.

The period from 1 January 2010 to 31 July 2011 will not qualify for PPR and therefore the loss relating to this period will form an allowable loss which can be set against future capital gains.

4 Preparation question: inheritance tax

Inheritance tax payable as a result of Birket's death

Lifetime gifts made within seven years before death

Date of death   December 2014
Seven years before   December 2007

Gift to Rudolf on 26 June 2001 is more than seven years before death and therefore no tax is payable. As a PET which never becomes chargeable, it is not accumulated.

	CLT 10 Jan 2008 £	PET 1 Apr 2010 £	CLT 15 Aug 2011 £
Value transferred		43,000	
Marriage exemption		(1,000)	
Annual exemption Current year		(3,000)	
Previous year b/f		(3,000)	
Gross chargeable amount	140,500	36,000	202,625
Lifetime tax (W1)	Nil	N/A	3,625
IHT payable on death (W2)	Nil	Nil	13,695
Payable by			Trustees
Due date			30 June 2015

IHT on estate (on assumed death in December 2014)

	£	£
Value of business		524,000
Quoted shares in Kariba plc (450,000 × £2.30)		1,035,000
Other assets		886,350
		2,445,350
Less: Debts and funeral expenses (£37,300 + £2,450)		(39,750)
		2,405,600
Less: Exempt bequests: Charitable		(285,000)
Chargeable estate		2,120,600

	£
Nil rate band at death (December 2014)	325,000
Gross chargeable transfers (December 2007– December 2014)	
(£140,500 + £36,000 + £202,625)	(379,125)
Nil rate band available	Nil
IHT due on estate (£2,120,600 × 36%)	763,416

Payable by   Executors
Due date   30 June 2015

Note: The exempt gifts to charity of £285,000 exceed 10% of the baseline figure for the estate of £2,405,600 (net value of estate less available nil rate band but before charitable gift), therefore the IHT due on the estate will be calculated at 36% instead of 40%. This is automatic (no election is required).

WORKINGS

(1) IHT during lifetime – 15 August 2011 CLT

	£
Valuation	205,000
Less: Annual exemption	
2011/12	(3,000)
b/f 2010/11	(3,000)
	199,000
Nil rate band at gift – August 2011	325,000
Less: Transfers in previous seven years	(140,500)
Remaining nil rate band	184,500
Tax $\frac{20}{80}$ (199,000 – 184,500)	3,625
Gross chargeable transfer (199,000 + 3,625)	202,625

Lifetime tax is payable by Birket unless otherwise agreed.

(2) IHT on death – lifetime gifts

	CLT 10 January 2008		PET 1 April 2010		CLT 15 August 2011	
	£	£	£	£	£	£
Gross chargeable transfer (GCT)		140,500		36,000		202,625
Nil rate band at death (December 2014)	325,000		325,000		325,000	
GCT in previous 7 years						
(10.01.01 – 10.01.08) (Note)	Nil					
(01.04.03 – 01.04.10)			(140,500)			
(15.08.04 – 15.08.11) (£140,500 + £36,000)					(176,500)	
Nil rate band available		(325,000)		(184,500)		(148,500)
Taxable amount		Nil		Nil		54,125
IHT on death @ 40%		Nil		Nil		21,650
Taper relief (15 August 2011 – December 2014)						3 – 4 years
Chargeable % after taper relief						80%
IHT chargeable on death						17,320
Less: IHT payable in lifetime (W1)						(3,625)
IHT payable on death						13,695

Note: The gift on 26 June 2001 is not accumulated as it is a PET which never becomes chargeable.

5 Dahlia Simmons

(a) IHT liability

Dahlia has a French domicile. Since she has only been resident in the UK for 15 out of the last 20 years she does not have a deemed UK domicile. Thus, IHT will only apply to her UK assets.

Lifetime transfer 1 October 2011 – Death tax on chargeable lifetime transfer

		£
Transfer		1,000,000
AE	2011/12	(3,000)
	2010/11	(3,000)
		994,000
NRB		(325,000)
Taxable		669,000
Tax @ 40%		267,600
Less: lifetime tax paid (no taper relief as <3 years) (W1)		(133,800)
Tax payable		133,800

Death estate

	£	£
House in London	600,000	
Less: spouse exemption	(600,000)	
		Nil
Flat in Paris (excluded property – where situated)		Exempt
French branch of Barclays Bank (excluded property – overseas branch)		Exempt
UK branch of Barclays Bank		25,000
UK unquoted shares		20,000
Canadian quoted shares (excluded property – registered overseas)		exempt
		45,000
Less: Charitable exemption		(10,000)
Chargeable estate		35,000
Less: nil rate band (fully utilised by transfer on 1 October 2011)		(Nil)
Taxable at 36% (Note)		35,000
IHT due		12,600

Note: The net chargeable estate (ie before the charity exemption and after the available nil rate band, which, here, is £Nil) is £45,000, so a charitable legacy of at least £4,500 (10% × £45,000) results in a death tax rate of 36% rather than the usual 40%.

WORKING

(1) **Lifetime tax – October 2011**

	£
Gift	1,000,000
Less: AE 2011/12 and 2010/11 b/f	(6,000)
	994,000
Less: nil rate band	(325,000)
Available nil rate band	669,000
IHT @ 20%	133,800

(b) Payment

The IHT on the lifetime gift is payable by trustees.

The IHT on the death estate is payable by the executors.

Both are due for payment by 31 May 2014, ie by the end of the month six months following death.

Marks

(a) IHT liability
Non-UK domiciled & not deemed domiciled | 1
Lifetime transfer
AEs × 2 | ½
Nil rate band | ½
Tax @ 40% | ½
No taper relief | ½
Deduct lifetime tax | ½
Calculation of lifetime tax (W1) | 1
Death estate
London property – spouse exemption | 1
Paris property – excluded property | 1
French branch bank account – excluded property | 1
London branch bank account | ½
UK shares | ½
Canadian company shares – excluded property | 1
Charity exemption | 1
No nil rate band remaining | ½
Death tax rate
Net chargeable estate | 1
Donation exceeds 10% | 1
Tax at 36% | 1

14

(b) Payment
Lifetime gift
Payable by the trustees | ½
Due date for death tax on lifetime gift | 1
Death estate
Executors pay the tax | ½
Due date | 1

3
17

6   Nicola Jones

(a)   UK resident and domiciled

	£
Vase (W1)	8,131
Shares (W2)	24,135
Chargeable gain	32,266
Annual exempt amount	(10,900)
Taxable gains	21,366
Capital gains tax liability @ 28%	5,982

(b)   UK resident but not UK domiciled

	£
Vase (W1)	8,131
Shares – not taxable as gain not brought into the UK (remittance basis)	Nil
Taxable gain	8,131
Tax @ 28%	2,277
Add: Remittance basis charge (as resident for at least 7 out of last 9 tax years)	30,000
CGT liability	32,277

Note: As Nicola claims to use the remittance basis she is not entitled to the annual exempt amount.

WORKINGS

(1) **Vase**

	£
Proceeds	16,000
Less: part disposal cost	
$\dfrac{16,000}{16,000+45,000} \times £30,000$	(7,869)
Gain	8,131

(2) **Shares**

	£
Proceeds: €34,450 ÷ €1.25	27,560
Less: cost: €5,000 ÷ €1.46	(3,425)
Gain	24,135

Marking guide

		Marks
(a)	**UK R & D**		
	Gain on vase – part disposal	1½	
	Shares – conversion to sterling amounts	1½	
	AEA	1	
	CGT @ 28%	1	
			5
(b)	**UK R & ND**		
	Gain on vase taxable	½	
	Gain on shares not taxable as gain not remitted	1	
	No AEA	1	
	CGT @ 28%	½	
	Add remittance basis charge	1	
			4
			9

7 Nicolette Paulson

(a) **IHT on Nicolette's death estate**

	£	£
Free estate		
House in Sussex	625,000	
Less: spouse exemption	(625,000)	
		Nil
Shares in Matthews plc (W1) £3.84 × 20,000		76,800
Shares in Paulson Investments Ltd (W2) £350 × 8,000		2,800,000
Cash and chattels		225,220
Less: liabilities		(23,655)
Less: charity exemption		(500,000)
Total free estate		2,578,365
Settled property		
Life interest		250,000
Total chargeable estate		2,828,365
Less: nil rate band (W3)		(231,000)
Excess over nil rate band		2,597,365
IHT payable @ 36% (W4)		935,051
Less: QSR (W5)		(4,496)
Total IHT payable		930,555

WORKINGS

(1) **Shares in Matthews plc**

Valued at the lower of :
¼ up rule = 380 + ¼ (396 − 380) = 384p
Mid-bargain = (382 + 396)/2 = 389p

(2) **Shares in Paulson Investments Ltd**

As both Nicolette and Ray hold shares in Paulson Investments Ltd they are related property, so must use the value relating to their combined ownership, ie the value of a 100% holding.

(3) **Available nil rate band**

	£	£
2013/14 nil rate band		325,000
Less: Gift to daughter	105,000	
Less: Marriage exemption	(5,000)	
Less: AE × 2	(6,000)	
		(94,000)
Available nil rate band		231,000

Note: There is no IHT on this gift at death as it falls below the nil rate band.

(4) **Death tax rate**

The death rate of IHT is 36%, rather than 40%, where at least 10% of the net chargeable estate (ie the estate ignoring the charitable gift, but after deducting the available nil rate band) is left to charity. The test must be satisfied by both the free estate and the settled property unless the gift from one part of the estate satisfies the test for the entire estate.

	£
Estate including charitable legacy:	
£2,597,365 + £500,000	3,097,365
10% thereof	309,737

The 10% test is satisfied for both elements of the estate by the £500,000 charitable legacy.

(5) **IHT on grandmother's death (September 2010)**

	£
Net transfer	50,000
Gross transfer (£50,000 + £14,500)	64,500
QSR (3 – 4 years between the two deaths) is:	
£14,500 × $\frac{50,000}{64,500}$ × 40%	£4,496

(b) **Payment of IHT**

The IHT due must be split between the free estate and settled property elements. The executors pay the former and the trustees of the Paulson Trust the latter:

	£
Payable by the executors:	
$\frac{2,578,365}{2,828,365}$ × £930,555	848,303
Payable by the trustees:	
$\frac{250,000}{2,828,365}$ × £930,555	82,252

The IHT is due 6 months after the end of the month of death, ie by 30 September 2014.

(a) IHT payable

	Marks
House less spouse exemption	1
Shares in Matthews plc	1½
Shares in Paulson Investments Ltd – related property	1½
Cash and chattels	½
Deduct liabilities	½
Charity exemption	1
Settled property	1
Available nil rate band	1
Value of estate less nil rate band	1½
36% death tax rate	2
QSR	2
IHT	½
	14

(b) IHT payment

	Marks
Executors pay tax for free estate	1
Amount	1
Trustees pay tax for trust	1
Amount	1
Due date	1
	5
	19

8 The O'Donnell Trust

(a) Capital gains tax liability

	£
Painting (W1)	18,750
Treasury stock – exempt	–
PPR (W2)	10,787
	29,537
Annual exempt amount	(5,450)
Taxable gains	24,087
Capital gains tax liability @ 28%	6,744

WORKINGS

(1) Painting

	£
Proceeds	25,000
Less: costs of sale 5% × £25,000	(1,250)
Net sales proceeds	23,750
Less: cost	(5,000)
	18,750

Not more than 5/3 (£25,000 – 6,000) = £31,667

(2) Property

	£
Proceeds	425,000
Less: cost	(250,000)
	175,000
Less: PPR relief (W3) £175,000 × 131/146	(157,021)
Gains	17,979

CGT & IHT   89

Less: letting relief, lower of
- PPR relief: £157,021
- £40,000   (7,192)
- Gain attributable to letting: £7,192 (£175,000 × 6/146)

Chargeable gain   10,787

Note: The trustees can claim PPR relief and lettings relief as a beneficiary occupies the property as their main residence.

(3) **PPR periods**

	Total	Exempt	Chargeable
1.9.01 – 31.10.05 5 – actual occupation	50	50	
1.11.05 – 30.4.07 – up to 3 years absence any reason	18	18	
1.5.07 – 31.10.07 – actual occupation	6	6	
1.11.07 – 31.7.09 – up to 3 years absence any reason	21	18	3
1.8.09 – 31.10.09 – actual occupation	3	3	
1.11.09 – 31.07.10 – work overseas but did not resume occupation	9		9
1.08.10 – 31.10.10 – let	3		3
1.11.10 – 31.10.13 – last 36 months	36	36	
	146	131	15

(b) **Self assessment deadlines**

- The trustees' self assessment tax return is due on 31 January 2015 if filed online, or 31 October 2014 if they submit a paper return.
- The trustees' CGT payment is due on 31 January 2015.

Note: CGT is never payable by payments on account.

Marking guide

		Marks
(a)	CGT liability	
	Gain on painting	1
	Costs of sale	½
	Chattel restriction	1½
	Treasury stock – exempt	1
	PPR	
	Gain	1
	PPR relief	1
	Occupation periods (½ per line in working)	4
	Letting relief	1½
	AEA	1
	CGT liability	½
		13
(b)	Self assessment deadlines	
	Return – online deadline	1
	Return – paper deadline	1
	Payment	1
		3
		16

ICAEW

9 Joanne Cohen (J09)

(a) Capital gains tax

	£
Proceeds	980,500
Less: 31 March 1982 MV	(150,000)
	830,500
Less: PPR (W1)	(423,043)
£830,500 × 190/373	
	407,457
Less: letting relief as the lower of:	
PPR: £423,043	
Gain due to letting: £830,500 × 141/373 = £313,942	
£40,000	(40,000)
	367,457
Less: annual exempt amount	(10,900)
Capital gain	356,557
Capital gains tax liability:	
£356,557 × 28%	£99,836

W1

	Chargeable	Exempt	Total
1.4.82 – 31.1.91 actual occupation			
(ignore pre 31 March 82)		106	106
1.2.91 – 31.7.94 absent and no re-occupation	42		42
1.8.94 – 31.7.98 working elsewhere in the UK		48	48
1.8.98 – 30.4.10 let to tenants	141		141
1.5.10 – 30.4.13 last 36 months		36	36
	183	190	373

(b) Lifetime tax on CLT: 1 February 2013

	£
Gift	345,000
Less: annual exemption – 2012/13	(3,000)
– 2011/12	(3,000)
	339,000
Less: nil rate band available (no chargeable transfers in the previous 7 years)	(325,000)
	14,000
IHT @ 20/80 × £14,000	3,500
Gross chargeable transfer (£339,000 + 3,500)	342,500

IHT as a result of death on the CLT

	£
Gross chargeable transfer	342,500
Less: nil rate band (£325,000 + £325,000 – 100% unused NRB on Neil's death)	(650,000)
Taxable	Nil
IHT payable	Nil

IHT on death estate

	£
Shares in KD plc (W1) = 100,000 × £3.19	319,000
Land	430,000
Cash and chattels	412,000
	1,161,000
Less: liabilities	
Income tax	(12,910)
Capital gains tax (part (a))	(99,836)
Chargeable estate	1,048,254
Less: nil rate band remaining	
£(650,000 – 342,500)	(307,500)
Taxable	740,754
IHT payable: £740,754 × 40%	£296,302

The tax on the land may be paid in ten equal instalments. The first payment will be due on 31.12.14, although the remaining instalments will bear interest from this date.

The remaining tax on the death estate must be paid by 31.12.14 to avoid interest.

W1
¼ up rule: 318p + ¼ × (322−318) = 319p
Mid-marked bargain: (317 + 327)/2 = 322p
Therefore shares valued at the lower price of 319p

Marking guide

			Marks
(a)	Gain	1	
	PPR	4	
	Letting relief	1½	
	AEA	1	
	CGT liability	½	
			8
(b)	CLT Feb 2013		
	Lifetime tax		
	– AE	1	
	– NRB	½	
	– Tax	1	
	– GCT	1	
	Tax on death		
	– NRB (increased by 100%)	2	
	– IHT	½	
	Death estate		
	– Shares in KD plc (W1)	1½	
	– Land	½	
	– Cash and chattels	½	
	– Liabilities	1	
	– NRB	1	
	– IHT	½	
	Payment of IHT	2	
			13
			21

10 Pearl (D09)

(a)

	£
Gain on Table Ltd shares	
Proceeds (market value) (£2.45 × 100,000)	245,000
Less cost (£0.15 × 100,000)	(15,000)
Gain	230,000
Gain on Sofa plc shares	
Proceeds (W1) (£3.32 × 50,000)	166,000
Less cost – Mar 82 value (£0.80 × 50,000)	(40,000)
Gain	126,000
Total gains (£230,000 + £126,000)	356,000
Less AEA	(10,900)
Taxable gains	345,100
Capital gains tax @ 28%	£96,628

	£
(W1) Value of Sofa plc shares	
Value at lower of:	
¼ up = £3.30 + ¼ (£3.38 − £3.30)	3.320
Average marked bargains = £3.31 + £3.38 / 2	3.345

(b)

CLT – June 2007
The gross chargeable transfer of £302,500 (W1) is covered by the nil rate band at the date of death and so there is no additional IHT payable at death. There is no refund of lifetime tax paid.

PET – gift of cash to daughter 15 May 2013

	£	£
Gift		100,000
Less ME		(5,000)
Less AE 2013/14		(3,000)
Less AE b/f 2012/13		(3,000)
Gross chargeable transfer		89,000
Nil rate band remaining	£	
Nil rate band at death	325,000	
Less gross cumulative chargeable transfers since 16.05.06(W1)	(302,500)	
Taxed at 0%		(22,500)
Taxed at 40%		66,500
Death tax (no taper relief as < 3 years, no lifetime tax paid)		£26,600

Gift of painting to charity
Gifts to charity are exempt IHT

Sale of Table Ltd shares 15 August 2013
No transfer of value (so not a PET) as Ben paid market value for the shares.

PET – sale of Sofa plc shares 1 October 2013

	£	£
Gift (part a) £166,000 − £119,000		47,000
Nil rate band remaining:	£	
Nil rate band at death	325,000	
Less GCT since 01.10.06 (£302,500 + £89,000)	(391,500)	
Taxed at 0%		(Nil)
Taxed at 40%		47,000
Death tax (no taper relief as < 3 years, no lifetime tax paid)		£18,800

No AEs as allocated to first PET

Death estate
Fully exempt as bequeathed to charity

WORKING

(1) CLT June 2007 gross chargeable transfer

	£	£
Gift		308,000
Less AE 2007/08 and 2006/07 b/f		(6,000)
Chargeable transfer		302,000
Nil rate band remaining:	£	
Nil rate band at transfer – 2007/08	300,000	
Less cumulative chargeable transfers since 1 June 2000	(0)	
Taxed at 0%		(300,000)
Taxed at 20/80 (paid by donor)		2,000
Lifetime tax paid		500
Gross chargeable transfer = £302,000 + £500		£302,500

Marks

(a)   Gain on Table Ltd shares
       Proceeds   ½
       Cost   ½

       Gain on Sofa plc shares
       Proceeds   2
       Cost   1
       AEA   1
       CGT liability   _1_
                                                                               6

(b)   PET 15 May 2013
       ME   1
       AE   1
       NRB   1
       Tax   ½
       Gift of painting   ½
       Sale 15 August 2013
         Not a transfer of value   1

       PET 1 October 2013
         Value   1
         NRB   1
         IHT   ½
       Death estate   ½
       CLT June 2007(W1)
       AE   ½
       NRB   ½
       Tax   1
       GCT   _1_
                                                                            __11__
                                                                            __17__

11   Todd Lovett (M10)

Inheritance tax on PETs chargeable as a result of Todd's death
4 May 2008 – Cash gift

	£	£
Cash		390,000
Less: Annual exemptions – 2008/09		(3,000)
– 2007/08		(3,000)
Transfer of value		384,000
Nil band at death	325,000	
Less: gross chargeable transfers since May 2001	–	
Nil rate band remaining		(325,000)
Excess over nil band		59,000
IHT @ 40%		23,600
Taper relief: (5 to 6 years)		
£23,600 × 40%		£9,440

1 July 2012 – Gift of land

	£
Value transferred £190,000 × $\dfrac{120,000}{120,000+20,000}$	162,857
Less: Annual exemptions – 2012/13	(3,000)
– 2011/12	(3,000)
	156,857

	£	£
Nil band at death	325,000	
Less: gross chargeable transfers since July 2005	(384,000)	
Nil rate band remaining		Nil
Excess over nil band		156,857
IHT @ 40% (no taper relief)		£62,743

Inheritance tax on the death estate	£	£
Principal private residence		480,000
Shares in Sweeney plc		
$10,000 \times [410p + \dfrac{(414-410)p}{4}]$		41,100
Shares in Dunstan Ltd		28,000
Cash and chattels		150,700
		699,800
Less: liabilities		(12,650)
Chargeable estate		687,150
Nil band at death	325,000	
Less: GCTs in the previous 7 years £(384,000 + 156,857)	(540,857)	
Nil rate band remaining		Nil
Excess over the nil rate band		687,150
IHT @ 40% (no QSR as no tax payable on transfer to spouse)		£274,860

Marking guide

	Marks
PET on 4 May 2008	
– Gift	½
– AE	1
– Nil band	1
– Tax	½
– Taper	1
PET on 1 July 2012	
– Value	1½
– AE	½
– Nil band	1
– IHT	½
Death Estate	
– Residence	½
– Shares in Sweeney plc	1½
– Shares in Dunstan Ltd	½
– Cash and chattels	½
– Liabilities	½
– Nil band	½
– IHT	½
	12

12 Andrei Johnson (J10)

(a) Capital gains tax liability

	£
Commercial property (W1)	34,100
QCBs – exempt	–
PPR (W2)	35,000
Shares in Wilkes Ltd (W3)	156,000
Gains	225,100
Less: annual exempt amount	(10,900)
Capital gain	214,200
Capital gains tax liability @ 28%	59,976

WORKINGS

(1) Commercial property

	£
Proceeds (MV)	454,700
Less: cost	(420,600)
Capital gain	34,100

(2) PPR

	£
Gain before PPR relief	210,000
Less: PPR 10/12 × 210,000 (7 years actual occupation + last 3 years)	(175,000)
	35,000

(3) Shares in Wilkes Ltd

	£
Proceeds (£25 × 6,500) (Note: based on actual shareholding disposed of)	162,500
Less: cost	(6,500)
	156,000

(b) IHT on transfers chargeable as a result of Andrei's death

15 July 2013 – Gift of commercial property

		£
Gross chargeable transfer (W1)		448,700
Less fall in value relief (£454,700 – £356,000)		(98,700)
		350,000
Nil rate band in May 2016	325,000	
Less: gross chargeable transfers since 15.7.06	–	
Nil rate band remaining		(325,000)
Excess over the nil rate band		25,000
Inheritance tax @ 40% (no taper relief)		10,000
Less: lifetime tax paid (W1)		(24,740)
IHT payable		Nil

3 February 2014 – Gift of shares in Wilkes Ltd

		£
Value (W2) (No AEs as allocated to July 2013 CLT)		213,000
Nil rate band in May 2016	325,000	
Less: gross chargeable transfers since 3.2.07 (W1)	(448,700)	
Nil rate band remaining		–
Excess over nil rate band		213,000
Inheritance tax @ 40% (no taper relief)		£85,200

Inheritance tax on the death estate

	£	£
Value of estate		2,100,000
Nil rate band in May 2016	325,000	
Less: gross chargeable transfers in the 7 years prior to death (£213,000 + £448,700)	(661,700)	
Nil rate band remaining		–
Excess over the nil rate band		2,100,000
Inheritance tax @ 40%		£840,000

WORKINGS

(1) **15 July 2013 – Gift of commercial property**

	£	£
Value		454,700
Less: annual exemptions – 2013/14		(3,000)
– 2012/13		(3,000)
Transfer of value		448,700
Nil rate band in July 2013	325,000	
Less: gross chargeable transfers since 15.7.06	–	
Nil rate band remaining		(325,000)
Excess over nil band		123,700
Lifetime tax @ 20% (trustees paying tax)		£24,740

(2) **Diminution in value**

	Before transfer	After transfer
Andrei Johnson	7,500	1,000
Related property – Ruby Johnson	2,000	2,000
	9,500	3,000
Total %	95%	30%
Valuation per share	£30	£12

	£
Value of Andrei's gift:	
Before: 7,500 shares @ £30	225,000
After: 1,000 shares @ £12	(12,000)
Diminution in value	213,000

Marks

(a) Commercial property (W1)   1
     QCBs   ½
     PPR (W2)   1
     Shares in Wilkes Ltd (W3)   2
     AEA   1
     CGT @28%   ½
                                                          ___
                                                              6

(b) Lifetime tax (W1)
         Commercial property   ½
         AEs   1
         NRB   ½
         IHT @ 20%   ½
     IHT as a result of death
     Commercial property
         Fall in value   1
         AEs   ½
         NRB   ½
         IHT (and no taper)   ½
         Lifetime tax paid (no repayment)   ½
     Shares in Wilkes Ltd
         Diminution in value (W2)   2
         NRB   ½
         IHT   ½
     Death estate
         NRB   ½
         IHT   1
                                                          ___
                                                           10
                                                          ___
                                                           16

13   Sam Ridge (M11)

(a) **IHT on Sam's death estate**

	£
House in London	969,000
Less: mortgage	(110,000)
	859,000
Flat in Wales	230,000
Rental property in London	240,000
Painting	17,000
Cash	34,000
ISAs	14,000
Piano	40,000
Shares in Rime plc (W1) 211p × 12,000	25,320
Life assurance policy (in trust for Cole)	Nil
Chargeable estate	1,459,320
Less: nil rate band	(325,000)
Excess over nil rate band	1,134,320
IHT payable @ 40%	453,728
Less: QSR (W2)	(10,313)
	443,415

WORKINGS

(1) **Shares in Rime plc**

Valued at the lower of :
¼ up rule = 210 + ¼ (214 – 210) = 211p
Mid-bargain = (204 + 220)/2 = 212p

(2) **IHT on aunt's death (May 2010)**

	£
Chargeable estate	442,000
Less: nil rate band in 2010/11 (£325,000 – 32,000) (W3)	(293,000)
Chargeable estate	149,000
IHT on £149,000 × 40%	59,600
Net transfer is (£442,000 – 59,600)	382,400

QSR if Sam dies on 31 March 2015 is therefore:

$£59,600 \times \dfrac{382,400}{442,000} \times 20\%$

	£10,313

(3) **Aunt's lifetime gifts (Jan 2006)**

	£
Gift	38,000
Less: annual exemption 2005/06	(3,000)
2004/05 b/f	(3,000)
Chargeable value	32,000

(b)

Capital gains tax consequences of Sam's gifts:

	£
Gift of rental property	
Proceeds (MV)	240,000
Less: cost	(180,500)
Gain	59,500
Gift of piano	
Proceeds (MV)	40,000
Less: cost	(5,000)
	35,000

Not more than 5/3 (£40,000 – 6,000) = £56,667

Total gains

	£
Rental property	59,500
Piano	35,000
	94,500
Less: Annual exempt amount	(10,900)
Taxable amount	83,600
Capital gains tax:	
(£32,010 – £24,410) £7,600 × 18%	1,368
(£83,600 – £7,600) £76,000 × 28%	21,280
	22,648

Note: Were the rental property and the piano to be left to Cole on death, no CGT would be payable.

Marks

(a) IHT on death estate

House	½
Less mortgage	½
Flat	½
Rental property	½
Painting and cash	½
ISAs	½
Piano	½
Life assurance policy	1
NRB	½
IHT	½
QSR deduction	½
Shares in Rime plc (W1)	
Lower of	½
Quarter up	1
Mid-bargain	1
IHT on aunt's death (W2)	
Chargeable estate	½
NRB	1
IHT	½
Net transfer	½
QSR	1½
Value of lifetime gift (W3)	1½
	14

(b) CGT consequences

Gain on rental property	1
Gain on piano	1
Chattel restriction	½
AEA	1
CGT	1½
	5
	19

14 Julio Mandel (J11)

(a) **Capital gains tax liability**

	£
Proceeds	910,000
Less: MV at 31.3.82	(210,700)
	699,300
Less: PPR (W1) £699,300 × 376/382	(688,316)
Gains	10,984
Less: letting relief, lower of	
PPR: £688,316	
£40,000	
Gain attributable to letting: £10,984	(10,984)
Capital gain	Nil
Capital gains tax liability	Nil

WORKINGS

(1)

	Total	Exempt	Chargeable
1.4.82 – 31.1.91 – ignore pre 31.3.82	106	106	
1.2.91 – 31.7.94 – up to 4 years working in the UK	42	42	
1.8.94 – 31.1.02 – actual occupation	90	90	
1.2.02 – 31.7.02 – 6 months exempt working in the UK	6	6	
1.8.02 – 31.1.06 – up to 3 years absence any reason	42	36	6
1.2.06 – 31.1.11 – actual occupation	60	60	
1.2.11 – 31.1.14 – last 36 months	36	36	
	382	376	6

(b) **IHT on transfers chargeable as a result of Julio's death**

1 February 2014 – Gift of PPR £

		£
Value		910,000
Less: annual exemptions – 2013/14		(3,000)
– 2012/13		(3,000)
Transfer of value		904,000
Nil rate band in June 2014	325,000	
Less: gross chargeable transfers since 1.2.07	–	
Nil rate band remaining		(325,000)
Excess over nil rate band		579,000
Inheritance tax @ 40% (no taper relief)		£231,600

2 March 2014 – Gift to discretionary trust £

		£
Value		240,000
Less: annual exemptions		–
Transfer of value		240,000
Nil rate band in June 2014	325,000	
Less: gross chargeable transfers since 2.3.07	(904,000)	
Nil rate band remaining		–
Excess over nil rate band		240,000
Inheritance tax @ 40% (no taper relief)		£96,000
Less: Lifetime tax paid (W1)		–
IHT payable		£96,000

Inheritance tax on the death estate £

		£
Value of estate		340,000
Less: outstanding liabilities		(2,900)
Funeral expenses		(2,300)
Income tax liability [(£10,975 + £10,500 – £9,440) × 20%] – £2,100		(307)
Class 2 NI liability (£2.70 × 52 × 2/12)		(23)
Class 4 NI liability (£10,975 – £7,755) × 9%		(290)
Nil rate band in June 2014	325,000	
Less: gross chargeable transfers in the 7 years prior to death		
£904,000 + 240,000	(1,144,000)	
Nil rate band remaining		–
Excess over the nil rate band		334,180
Inheritance tax @ 40%		£133,672

WORKING

2 March 2014 – Gift to discretionary trust £ £

	£	£
Value		240,000
Less: annual exemptions		–
Transfer of value		240,000
Nil rate band in March 2014	325,000	
Less: gross chargeable transfers since 2.3.07	–	
Nil rate band remaining		(325,000)
Excess over nil band		Nil
Inheritance tax		£Nil

			Marks
(a)	Proceeds less MV82	½	
	Deduction of PPR as fraction	1	
	Letting relief	1	
	CGT payable	½	
	PPR (W1) (½ for each line of the table)	3½	
		6½	
	Max		6
(b)	*Lifetime tax (W1)*		
	Value	½	
	NRB (no IHT)	1	
	IHT as a result of death		
	Gift of PPR		
	Value	½	
	AEs	½	
	NRB	½	
	IHT	½	
	Gift to discretionary trust		
	Value less AE's	½	
	NRB	½	
	IHT	½	
	Lifetime tax paid	½	
	Death estate		
	Value	½	
	Less liabilities	½	
	Funeral expenses	½	
	IT liability	2	
	Class 2 NI	1	
	Class 4 NI	1	
	NRB	½	
	IHT	½	
			12
			18

15 Alice and John (S11)

Inheritance tax on the death estate

	£	Married £	Not married £
House less mortgage (£700,000 – £200,000)		500,000	500,000
Life assurance – written into trust		–	–
Shares in A plc (W1)		63,375	63,375
Shares in B Ltd			
Related property rules apply if married			
Value of 10% holding = £5.10 × 2,000		10,200	
Normal valuation rules apply if not married			
Value of 4% holding = £4.50 × 2,000			9,000
Cash and chattels		945,000	945,000
Chargeable estate		1,518,575	1,517,375
Less: exempt transfer to spouse if married		(1,000,000)	–
		518,575	1,517,375
Nil rate band	325,000		
Less: gross chargeable transfer (W2)	(100,000)		
Nil rate band remaining		(225,000)	(225,000)
Excess over nil rate band		293,575	1,292,375
Inheritance tax @ 40%		117,430	516,950

WORKINGS

(1) Shares in A plc

¼ value = £2.10 + ¼ (£2.15 – £2.10) = £2.1125
Mid-marked bargain = (£2.10 + £2.16)/2 = £2.13
Therefore value at the lower: £2.1125 × 30,000 =
£63,375

(2) Lifetime Transfer September 2010

	£
Gift of cash to discretionary trust	106,000
Less: annual exemptions – 2010/11	(3,000)
– 2009/10	(3,000)
Chargeable transfer	100,000

As this is less than the nil rate band in September 2010, no lifetime tax would have been paid.

	£
Gross chargeable transfer	£100,000

Marking guide

	Marks
House	1
Life assurance	1
A plc shares – value	2
B Ltd shares – related property	1½
B Ltd shares – normal valuation	1
Cash	1
Exempt transfer to spouse (married column only)	1½
Remaining NRB	1
IHT	1
CLT Sept 2010 (W2)	1
	12

16 Bill (D11)

(a) Capital gains tax liability

	£
Painting (W1)	17,900
Shares (W2)	29,350
Gains	47,250
Less: annual exempt amount	(10,900)
Capital gain	36,350
Capital gains tax liability:	
(£32,010 – £27,010) = £5,000 × 18%	900
(£36,350 – £5,000) = £31,350 × 28%	8,778
	9,678

WORKINGS

(1) Gift of painting

	£
Proceeds (MV)	20,000
Less: cost	(2,100)
Capital gain	17,900

Gain cannot exceed $\frac{5}{3}$ × (£20,000 – £6,000) = £23,333

Therefore gain	17,900

(2) Shares in Wolf plc

	£
Proceeds (MV) (W3)(20,000 × 331p)	66,200
Less: cost (£55,275 × 20,000/30,000)	(36,850)
Gain	29,350

(3) Lower of

¼ up = 330 + ¼ (334 – 330) = 331p

Mid-marked bargain = (331 + 337)/2 = 334p

(b) IHT on transfers chargeable as a result of Bill's death

1 June 2010 – Gift to discretionary trust

	£	£
Value		384,000
Nil rate band in September 2014	325,000	
Less: gross chargeable transfers since 1.2.03	–	
Nil rate band remaining		(325,000)
Excess over nil rate band		59,000
Inheritance tax @ 40%		23,600
Taper relief (4 – 5 years) @ 60%		14,160
Less: tax already paid (W)		(11,800)
Additional tax payable		£2,360

5 July 2012 – Cash gifts to grandchildren
All exempt as covered by small gifts exemption

18 August 2013 – Gift of painting

	£	£
Value		20,000
Less fall in value (£20,000 – £18,000)		(2,000)
		18,000
Less: marriage exemption		(5,000)
Less: annual exemptions – 2013/14		(3,000)
– 2012/13		(3,000)
Transfer of value		7,000
Nil rate band in September 2014	325,000	
Less: gross chargeable transfers since 18.8.06	(384,000)	
Nil rate band remaining		(–)
Excess over nil rate band		7,000
Inheritance tax @ 40% (no taper relief)		£2,800

9 March 2014 – Gift of shares

		£
Value (from part (a))		66,200
Nil rate band in September 2014	325,000	
Less: gross chargeable transfers since 9.3.07 (£384,000 + £9,000)	(393,000)	
Fall in value relief is ignored in the cumulation		
Nil rate band remaining		–
Excess over nil rate band		66,200
Inheritance tax @ 40% (no taper relief)		£26,480

Inheritance tax on the death estate

		£
Value of estate		1,200,000
Less: CGT payable for 2013/14 (part (a))		(9,678)
Nil rate band in September 2014	325,000	
Less: gross chargeable transfers in the 7 years prior to death		
£384,000 + 9,000 + 66,200	(459,200)	
Nil rate band remaining		–
Excess over the nil rate band		1,190,322
Inheritance tax @ 40%		£476,129

WORKING

1 June 2010 – Gift to discretionary trust, lifetime tax

	£	£
Value		390,000
Less: annual exemptions (2010/11 and 2009/10)		(6,000)
Transfer of value		384,000
Nil rate band in June 2010	325,000	
Less: gross chargeable transfers since 1.6.03	–	
Nil rate band remaining		(325,000)
Excess over nil band		59,000
Inheritance tax payable @ 20%		£11,800

Marks

(a) Gain on painting ... ½
Chattels restriction ... ½
Conclusion ... ½
MV of shares ... 1½
Cost of shares ... ½
Net gains ... ½
AEA ... ½
CGT liability ... <u>1½</u>

6

(b) *Lifetime tax (W)*
    AE's ... ½
    NRB at gift ... ½
    GCT's previous 7 years ... ½
    IHT ... ½
IHT as a result of death
Gift to discretionary trust
    Value ... ½
    NRB at death ... ½
    GCT's previous years ... ½
    IHT ... ½
    Taper relief ... ½
    Less lifetime tax ... ½
    Additional tax payable ... ½
Gift of cash to grandchildren
    Exempt as small gifts ... 1
Gift of painting
    Value ... 1
    Fall in value relief ... 1
    Marriage exemption ... 1
    AE's ... ½
    NRB ... ½
    GCT's previous 7 years ... ½
    IHT ... ½
Gift of shares
    Value ... 1
    NRB at death ... ½
    GCT's in previous 7 years ... ½
    IHT ... ½
Death estate
    CGT liability ... 1
    Value of estate less NRB ... ½
    IHT ... <u>½</u>

<u>16</u>
<u>22</u>

17 Megan (M12)

	£	£
CLT – 31 December 2000		
More than 7 years pre death – no additional IHT due on death		
PET – 1 February 2007		
Gift		185,000
Less AE 2006/7		(3,000)
Less AE b/f 2005/06		(3,000)
Gross chargeable transfer		179,000
Nil rate band remaining		
Nil rate band at death (W1)	406,250	
Less gross chargeable transfers since 1.02.00 (W2)	(244,000)	
Taxed at 0%		(162,250)
Taxed at 40%		16,750
Death tax		6,700
Taper relief 6-7 years (80% relief or 20% chargeable)		(5,360)
No lifetime tax paid		–
Death tax due		1,340

Death estate	£	£
Land		245,000
Cash etc		415,000
Less funeral costs		(6,337)
		653,663
Less exempt transfer to charity		(200,000)
		453,663
Less nil rate band at death (W1)	406,250	
Less gross chargeable transfers since 1 January 2007	(179,000)	
		(227,250)
		226,413
IHT due at 36%		81,509

(£200,000/£426,413 is greater than 10% so IHT rate is 36% not 40%. £653,663 – £227,250 = £426,413)

WORKINGS

(1) Nil rate band	£
Own nil rate band	325,000
Unused portion of spouse's nil rate band	
(£312,000 – £234,000)/ £312,000 = 25%	
25% × nil rate band at death	81,250
	406,250

(2) CLT December 2000 gross chargeable transfer	£
Gift of cash to a discretionary trust	248,000
Less AE 2000/01 and 1999/2000 b/f	(6,000)
Chargeable transfer	242,000
Nil rate band at date of gift	(234,000)
Taxed at 20/80	8,000
Lifetime tax	2,000
Gross chargeable transfer = £242,000 + £2,000	244,000

Marks

CLT on 31 December 2000

– No IHT on death	½
– AE	½
– Nil band	½
– Tax @ 20/80	½
– GCT	½

PET on 1 February 2007

– AE	½
– NRB at death	½
– GCT in previous 7 years	½
– IHT @ 40%	½
– Taper relief and no lifetime tax deduction	1

Death Estate

– Land	½
– Cash	½
– Funeral costs	½
– Exempt transfer to charity	1
– NRB at death	½
– GCT's in previous 7 years	½
– IHT @ 36%	1

NRB (W1)

–Own NRB	½
– Unused proportion of husband's	1
– Unused proportion × NRB at death	½
	__12__

18 Tina Chang (J12)

(a) **IHT on lifetime gifts**

15 May 2008: Gift to discretionary trust

	£	£
Transfer of value		344,000
Less: Annual exemptions – 2008/09		(3,000)
– 2007/08		(3,000)
		338,000
Nil rate band in May 2008	312,000	
Less: gross chargeable transfers in the previous 7 years	–	
		(312,000)
Excess over the nil rate band		26,000
Inheritance tax payable £26,000 × 20%		5,200

IHT as a result of death

15 May 2008: Gift to discretionary trust

	£	£
Transfer of value		338,000
Less: fall in value relief £(344,000 – 302,000)		(42,000)
		296,000
Nil rate band in November 2013	325,000	
Less: gross chargeable transfers in the previous 7 years	–	
		(325,000)
Excess over the nil rate band		Nil

No IHT on death and no refund for lifetime tax

Death estate	£	£
House	790,000	
Less: mortgage	(145,000)	
		645,000
Shares in WMK plc (W1)		
1,000 × 103p [lower value chosen]		1,030
Land:		
£149,000 × $\dfrac{31,000}{31,000+75,000}$		43,575
Insurance policy		120,000
Cash		250,000
Chattels		92,000
Less: exempt legacy to spouse		(250,000)
		901,605
Nil rate band in November 2013	325,000	
Less: chargeable transfers in the previous 7 years	(338,000)	
		–
Excess over the nil rate band		901,605
Inheritance tax at 40%		360,642

WORKINGS

(1)   Shares in WMK plc

Lower of:

¼ up = 103p + $\dfrac{(106-103)p}{4}$ = 103.75p

Mid-marked bargain = 100p + 106p /2 = 103p

(b) **Shares in Lynch Ltd**

Capital gains tax liability: 2013/14

	£
Proceeds	15,650
Less: selling costs	(480)
	15,170
Less: Cost (probate value)	(3,900)
Gain	11,270

Compare to: 5/3 × (£15,650 – 6,000) = £16,083

Therefore the chargeable gain is [choose lower]	11,270
Less: annual exempt amount	(10,900)
Taxable gain	370

Capital gains tax liability: £370 × 18%   67

Therefore the number of shares that can be purchased =

$$\frac{£(15,170-67)}{9} = 1,678 \text{ shares}$$

Marking guide

		Marks
(a)	*Gift to discretionary trust – lifetime tax*	
	Value less AE's	½
	NRB	1
	IHT	½
	Gift to discretionary trust - tax as a result of death	
	Transfer value	½
	Fall in value relief	1
	NRB	1
	IHT	½
	Death estate	
	House less mortgage	1
	Shares in WMK plc (W1)	1½
	Land	1
	Insurance policy	1
	Cash and chattels	½
	Exempt gift to spouse	1
	NRB	1½
	IHT	½
		13
	Max	12
(b)	Net sale proceeds	½
	Cost	½
	Chattels comparison	1
	AEA	½
	CGT liability	½
	Number of shares to purchase	1
		4
		16

19 Felicity Sharp (M13)

Capital gains tax liability

	£
Shares in Legato plc (W1)	15,733
Painting (W3)	20,800
Shares in Staccato Ltd (W4)	13,000
Gains	49,533
Less: annual exempt amount	(10,900)
Capital gain	38,633
Capital gains tax liability:	
(£32,010 – (£22,745 - £9,440)) = £18,705 × 18%	3,367
(£38,633 – £18,705) = £19,928 × 28%	5,580
	8,947

WORKINGS

(1) Shares in Legato plc

	£
Proceeds (2,000 × £10.50)	21,000
Less: cost (W2)	(5,267)
Gain	15,733

(2) Share pool

	Number	Cost £
June 2009 – Acquisition	4,800	9,200
March 2011 – Rights issue 1:4 @ £5.50	1,200	6,600
	6,000	15,800
2013/14 - Disposal	(2,000)	(5,267)
	4,000	10,533

(3) Gift of painting

	£
Proceeds (MV)	25,900
Less: cost	(5,100)
Capital gain	20,800

Gain cannot exceed $\frac{5}{3} \times (£25,900 - £6,000) = £33,167$

Therefore gain	20,800

(4) Shares in Staccato Ltd

	£
Proceeds	55,000
Less: MV82	(42,000)
Gain	13,000

Marking guide

	Marks
AEA	½
BRB remaining	1
CGT liability	1
Shares in Legato plc (W1)	1½
Share pool (W2)	2
Gain on painting (W3)	½
Chattel restriction	1
Shares in Staccato Ltd (W4)	½
	8

20 Delia Major (M13)

1 April 2007 – Gift to discretionary trust – CLT
No death tax due as more than seven years before death

	£	£
1 March 2008 – Gift to Bernard – PET		
Transfer of value		50,000
Less: Annual exemptions – 2007/08		(3,000)
– 2006/07 b/f		–
		47,000
Nil rate band in December 2014	325,000	
Less: gross chargeable transfers in the previous 7 years (W1)	(291,250)	
		(33,750)
Excess over the nil rate band		13,250
IHT @ 40%		5,300
Less: taper relief £6,300 × 80% (6-7 yrs)		(4,240)
		1,060

18 June 2008 – Gifts to grandchildren
Covered by small gifts exemption   nil

£10,000 school fees
This is exempt as it constitutes normal expenditure out of income   nil

Death estate	£	£
Estimated value		1,700,000
Brightlights share		300,000
Argyle Towers		230,000
Less: to charity		(1,000,000)
Chargeable estate		1,230,000
Nil rate band in December 2014	325,000	
Less: gross chargeable transfers in the previous 7 years	(47,000)	
		(278,000)
Excess over the nil rate band		952,000
Inheritance tax payable £952,000 × 36%		342,720

(more than 10% of estate bequeathed to charity)

WORKINGS

(1) Lifetime tax on gift to discretionary trust

	£	£
Transfer of value		296,000
Less: Annual exemptions – 2006/07		(3,000)
– 2005/06 b/f		(3,000)
		290,000
Nil rate band on 1 April 2007	285,000	
Less: gross chargeable transfers in the previous 7 years	–	
		(285,000)
Excess over the nil rate band		5,000
Inheritance tax payable £5,000 × 20/80		1,250
Gross chargeable transfer £290,000 + £1,250		291,250

Marks

Gift to discretionary trust – April 2007

No death tax ½

Gift to Bernard

Value less AE's ½

NRB 1

IHT ½

Taper ½

Working – lifetime tax

Value less AE's ½

NRB ½

IHT ½

GCT ½

Gifts to grandchildren 1

School fees 1

Death estate

Assets 1½

Gift to charity 1

NRB ½

IHT <u>1</u>

<u>11</u>

21 Preparation question: capital allowances

(a) **Capital allowances**

Plant and machinery

	FYA £	Main pool £	Special rate pool £	Private use asset (90%) £	Allowance £
10 m/e 31/3/14					
Additions					
10.3.14 Refrigeration equipment	25,000				
FYA @ 100%	(25,000)				25,000
	—				
	═══				
30.1.14 Computer equipment		5,000			
2.3.14 Plant		79,844			
2.3.14 Plant			151,840		
AIA (£250,000 × 10/12)		(56,493)	(151,840)		208,333
1.2.13 Cars		10,000		32,000	
		38,351	–	32,000	
WDA @ 18% × 10/12		(5,753)			5,753
WDA @ 8% × 10/12			–	(2,133) × 90%	1,920
TWDV c/f		32,598	–	29,867	
Allowances					241,006

(b) **Expenditure on office accommodation**

Rent payable is allowable as a trading expense. A lease premium, to the extent that it is taxable income of the landlord, will be divided into yearly deductions depending on the length of the lease. Office equipment, including certain fixtures such as carpets, does attract capital allowances as plant. Repairs are deductible expenses unless disallowed as capital expenditure.

22 Preparation question: adjustment of profits

Adjusted trading income – year ended 30 June 2014

	£	£
Net profit as per accounts		9,173
Add:		
Lease premium adjustment (W)		22,524
		31,697
Less:		
Stock adjustment re trendy clothing (£3,590 – £2,650)	940	
Fixed rate deduction for business use of home (11 × £10) + (1 × £18)	128	
Loss on Archer's withdrawal of stock at selling price		
(£100 – £95) (Note below)	5	
		(1,073)
Adjusted trading profit		30,624
Less: Capital allowances		(11,960)
Trading income		18,664

Note: The withdrawal of goods for personal use must be added back in the adjusted profit computation at their retail market value.

Lease premium deduction

	£
The landlord will be assessed to property income on:	

$$£\,24{,}000 \times \frac{50-(10-1)}{50} =$$ <u>19,680</u>

The annual allowable deduction for Archer is:

$$\frac{£19{,}680}{10}$$ <u>1,968</u>

As the lease was taken out on 1 October 2013 the deduction for the period to 30 June 2014 is:

$$\frac{9}{12} \times £1{,}968$$ <u>1,476</u>

As the full premium has been deducted now add back (£24,000 – £1,476) <u>22,524</u>

23 Preparation question: change of accounting date

		£
2012/13:	CYB y/e 30 November 2012	<u>24,000</u>
2013/14:	CYB y/e 30 November 2013	<u>40,500</u>
2014/15:	Year of change	
	Two accounting periods ending in the tax year	
	Y/e 30 November 2014	25,500
	4 m/e 31 March 2015	<u>14,000</u>
		39,500
	Less overlap profits	
	$\frac{4}{4} \times £11{,}500$	<u>(11,500)</u>
		<u>28,000</u>

24 Preparation question: cash basis of accounting for small businesses

Taxable trading profits for the year ended 31 March 2014

	£	£
Net profit (receipts) per accounts		15,280
Add: Disallowable expenditure:		
Goods for own consumption (Note 2)	400	
Private element of expenses (W1)	1,433	
Legal and professional fees (relate to capital which is not plant and machinery)	650	
Van – motor expenses (W2)	281	
Car – motor expenses (W2)	1,400	
Sundry expenses (W3)	<u>30</u>	
		<u>4,194</u>
		19,474
Less: Fixed rate mileage allowance for car (W2)		(3,150)
Adjustment expense (Note 3)		<u>(800)</u>
Taxable trading profit		<u>15,524</u>

Notes:

(1) No adjustments are required for the proceeds from the sale of the equipment and the purchase of the weighing scales. Both are items of plant and machinery and receipts therefrom are taxable when received and payments are deductible from trading profits when made.

(2) Goods for own consumption: Under the cash basis of accounting a 'just and reasonable' amount (eg the cost of the goods) must be added to the trading profit. There is no requirement to add back the market value of the goods as required for accrual accounting traders.

(3) Adjustment expense is deductible from trading profits in the first year in which cash accounts are prepared.

WORKINGS

(1) **Private element of expenses**

	£
Light and heat	1,850
Rent	2,250
Telephone	200
	4,300
Private use element (1/3)	1,433

Note:

It would not be beneficial for Mr Hainey to claim the fixed rate monthly adjustment for private use of business premises as the adjustment added back to trading profits would be £6,000 (£500 × 12) rather than £1,433.

(2) **Motor expenses**

Mr Hainey cannot claim the fixed rate mileage allowance in respect of the van as he has already claimed capital allowances.

	£	Disallow £
Expenditure per accounts re van	1,125	
Less: Private use (1,000/4,000 = 25%)	(281)	281
Allowable	844	

A fixed rate mileage rate allowance (FRMA) may be claimed in respect of the hire car. The actual costs are disallowed and the FRMA is £3,150 (7,000 miles, being the visits to clients and potential clients, at 45p).

(3) **Sundry expenses – amounts disallowed**

	£
Cash donations to national charities	5
Subscriptions to golf club	25
	30

25 Elinor (J09)

(a) **VAT registration**

Elinor's cumulative turnover to the end of May 2014 added to her taxable turnover for June 2014 means she has exceeded the VAT registration threshold of £79,000 at the end of June under the historic test. Note that both sales to EU customers are taxable sales (W1).

Therefore, Elinor has until 30 July 2014 to notify HMRC of her need to register for VAT.

W1 – VAT treatments of June 2014 contracts

Sales to EU VAT-registered customer – zero rated
Sales to EU non-VAT registered customer – standard rated

(b) Keeping the money permanently in full knowledge of the facts would constitute theft and would be a criminal offence. The chartered accountant should inform Elinor of this.

The engagement letter should be checked to see whether it authorises disclosure of the error to HMRC. If not, then permission to disclose the error is required from Elinor. If she refuses, the chartered accountant should resign.

Having ceased to act, the chartered accountant should inform HMRC of this, but should not disclose the error without first taking legal advice.

Unless Elinor makes repayment in full, her actions may constitute money laundering. The chartered accountant would have a duty to report this.

(c) (i) *Year ended 31 December 2014*

	£
Adjusted trading profit	89,000
Less:	
Salary for assistant (£1,280 × 9)	(11,520)
Childcare payments (£50 × 9)	(450)
Employer's Class 1A on provision of van benefit	
£3,000 × 2/12 × 13.8%	(69)
Employer's Class 1 NI	
£(1,280 – 641) × 9 × 13.8%	(794)
	76,167
Less: capital allowances on van	
£13,000 × 5/6 × 100% (AIA)	(10,833)
Revised adjusted trading profits	65,334

(ii)

		£
2013/14	Actual: 1.1.14 – 5.4.14	
	3/12 × £65,334	16,334
2014/15	Year ended 31 December 2014	65,334
	Overlap profits	16,334

Marking guide

				Marks
(a)		Historic test	2	
		30 July	1	
		EU VAT reg – zero	½	
		EU non-VAT reg – standard	½	
				4
(b)		Theft	½	
		Inform client	½	
		Check engagement letter	1	
		Permission to disclose	½	
		Resign	1½	
		Money laundering	½	
			4½	
		Max		4
(c)	(i)	Adjusted trading profit		
		Salary	1	
		Childcare	1	
		NICs	2	
		CAs on van	1	
				5
	(ii)	2013/14	1	
		2014/15	1	
		Overlap profits	1	
				3
				16

26   Jose Cranem (S09)

(a)

		£
Adjusted trading profit		62,090
Less: capital allowances (W1)		(7,130)
		54,960

WORKING

(1)   Capital allowances

	Main pool £	Jose's car £	Total £
TWDV b/f	17,190	13,000	
Less: disposal	(12,100)	(7,900)	
Balancing allowance	5,090		5,090
		5,100 × 40%	2,040
Total allowances			7,130

(b) **Trading income assessment**

	£
2013/14	
Year ended 30 June 2013 + 6 months ended 31 December 2013	
£93,800 + £54,960	148,760
Less: overlap relief	(2,700)
	146,060

(c) **Income tax computation**

	Non savings £	Savings £	Dividends £
Trading income assessment	146,060		
Bank interest (£1,200 × 100/80)		1,500	
Dividends (£8,900 × 100/90)			9,889
	146,060	1,500	9,889
Less: personal allowance (Note 1)	(nil)		
Taxable income	146,060	1,500	9,889

Income tax on:	
£32,160 × 20% (W1)	6,432
£115,400 × 40%	46,160
£2,590 × 32.5%	842
£150,150	
£7,299 × 37.5%	2,737
Income tax liability	56,171
Less: Tax credit on dividend	(989)
Tax credit on interest	(300)
Income tax payable	54,882

WORKING

W1 – Extended basic rate and higher rate limits (Note 2)

Basic rate threshold	32,010
Add: Extension due to Gift Aid (£120 × 100/80)	150
	32,160
Higher rate threshold	
Add: Extension due to Gift Aid	150,000
	150
	150,150

Notes:

(1)   The personal allowance is fully abated once adjusted net income reaches £118,880.

(2)   An additional rate tax payer is entitled to 25% additional tax relief on Gift Aid contributions. In order to achieve this it is necessary to gross up the Gift Aid donation by 100/80 and then add this gross amount on to both the basic rate band and the higher rate band limits.

(d) Taxable gains

	£	£
Gain on goodwill		
Consideration	80,000	
Less: cost	–	
Gain		80,000
Gain on factory		
Consideration	160,000	
Less: cost	(140,000)	
		20,000
Total gain		100,000
Less: annual exempt amount		(10,900)
Taxable gain		89,100

No gain on plant and machinery

Marking guide

			Marks
(a)	Disposals	1	
	Balancing allowances	1½	
	Adjusted profit less CAs	½	
			3
(b)	Y/e 30 June 2013	½	
	6 m/e 31 December 2013	½	
	Overlap relief	1	
			2
(c)	Net income	2½	
	PA	1	
	IT liability	1½	
	Extension of BR and higher rate limits	2	
	Tax credits	1	
			8
(d)	Gains on business assets	3	
	AEA	1	
			4
			17

27 George (D10)

(a)

	£
Adjusted trading profit	220,873
Less:	
Reverse disallowing gift of samples to customers	(1,000)
Plus:	
Add back incorrectly deducted VAT (include in capital allowances)	3,600
Add back profit on goods taken for own use	45
	223,518
Less: capital allowances (W1)	(138,998)
Tax adjusted trading profit	84,520

(W1) Capital allowances

	Main pool £	Special rate pool £	Private use asset (65%) £	Allowance £
16 m/e 30 April 2014				
Additions			21,600	
May 2013 Car £18,000 × 6/5				
Jan 2013 Equipment	21,500			
Aug 2013 Electrical system		24,000		
May 2013 Furniture	92,000			
AIA (max £250,000 × 16/12 = £333,333)	(113,500)	(24,000)		137,500
	–	–	21,600	
WDA @ 8% × $\frac{16}{12}$			(2,304) × 65%	1,498
TWDV c/f	–	–	19,296	
Allowances				138,998

(b) Trading income assessments

		£
2012/13	Actual: 1.1.13 – 5.4.13	
	3/16 × £84,520	15,848
2013/14	No period of account ending in tax year	
	Use tax year: 6.4.13 – 5.4.14	63,390
	12/16 × £84,520	
2014/15	Twelve months to accounting date	
	1.5.13 – 30.4.14	
	12/16 × £84,520	63,390
	Overlap profits = 11 months	
	1.5.13 – 5.4.14	58,108

28 Paula Petrova (D11)

(a) (i)

Tax adjusted trading profit for the 14 months to 31 March 2014	£
Adjusted profit (W1)	88,620
Less: capital allowances (W2)	(10,196)
Tax adjusted trading profit	78,424

(W1)	£
Profit for the period	80,915
Add: Depreciation	3,925
New water heating system	3,300
No other repair add backs	–
Private expenses on cars (£4,700 × 40%)	1,880
Less: Employer's NI on part-time assistant	–
Bank interest	(1,400)
Adjusted profit	88,620

(W2) Capital allowances

14 m/e 31 March 2014	Main pool £	Fiat (60%) £	Toyota (60%) £	Special rate pool £	Allowance £
TWDV b/f	3,180	14,800		600	
Additions					
Water heating system				3,300	
AIA				(3,300)	3,300
Office furniture	1,800				
AIA	(1,800)				1,800
Toyota car			18,000		
Disposals		(10,100)			
	3,180	4,700		600	
Balancing allowance		(4,700)ₓ₆₀%			2,820
WDA @ 18% × 14/12	(668)				668
WDA @ 8% × 14/12			(1,680)ₓ₆₀%		1,008
Write off of special rate pool				(600)	600
TWDV c/f	2,512	–	16,320	–	
Allowances					10,196

(a) (ii)

		£
2013/14	14 months to 31 March 2014	78,424
	Less: 2 months of overlap profit	(6,286)
		72,138

ICAEW

(b)

Income tax payable: 2013/14

	Non savings £	Dividends £	Total £
Salary (£45,000 × 10/12) + 7,000	44,500		44,500
Use of car:			
£(21,000 – 2,500) × 13% × 9/12	1,804		1,804
Fuel benefit: £21,100 × 13% × 9/12	2,057		2,057
General expense allowance	900		900
	49,261		49,261
Less: no claim for entertaining expenses	Nil		Nil
	49,261		49,261
Income from the REIT (£2,400 × 100/80)	3,000		3,000
UK dividends (£18,000 × 100/90)		20,000	20,000
	52,261	20,000	72,261
Less: Personal allowance	(9,440)	–	(9,440)
Taxable income	42,821	20,000	62,821

Income tax on: (W1)		
£42,821 × 20%		8,564
£4,189 × 10%		419
£47,010		
£15,811 × 32.5%		5,139
Income tax liability		14,122
Less:		
Tax credit on UK dividend £20,000 × 10%		(2,000)
Tax credit on REIT income £3,000 × 20%		(600)
PAYE		(9,300)
Income tax payable		2,222

(W1)	£
Basic rate band	32,010
Add: pension contributions £12,000 × 100/80	15,000
	47,010

Class 1 National insurance

	£
Tap Shoes Ltd: £(37,500 +900) /10 = £3,840 per month	
£(3,454 – 646) × 12% × 10mth	3,370
£(3,840 – 3,454) × 2% × 10mth	77
	3,447
Ice Ltd: £7,000 × 2%	140

			Marks
(a)	(i)	Deduction of capital allowances	½
		Adjustment of profit (W1)	
		Profit for period	½
		Adjustments (½ each)	3
		Capital allowances (W2)	
		TWDV b/f	½
		Water heating	1
		AIA on water heating	1
		Office furniture and AIA	1
		Car	½
		Disposal	½
		Balancing allowance (restricted)	1
		WDA on main pool	1
		WDA on Toyota car (restricted)	1½
		Write off of special rate pool balance	1
			13
	(ii)	2013/14 14 months to 31 March 2014	1
		Less overlap profits	1
			2
(b)		Salary	1½
		Car benefit	1½
		Fuel benefit	1
		General expense allowance	½
		No expense deduction	½
		REIT	1
		Dividends	1
		PA	1
		Extension of BRB (W1)	1
		Income tax liability	1½
		Tax credits	1½
		National insurance	3
			15
			30

29 Kirsty (M12)

(a) (i)

Adjusted profits	£
Trading profit	36,000
Client entertaining	842
Staff costs – Class 1A NIC (W1)	(501)
Depreciation	3,846
Property costs	28,000
Lease premium – deemed additional rent (W2)	(5,060)
Allowable rent (£3,000 × 15/12)	(3,750)
	59,377
Less capital allowances (AIA)	(16,500)
	42,877

No other adjustments (need not be stated)

WORKINGS

(1) Class 1A NIC

	£	£
Leased van + private fuel		3,564
Computer – significant private use as exceeds 40%		
Usage of employer asset = £750 × 20%	150	
Less actual business use = £150 × 55%	(83)	
Taxable benefit		67
Vouchers – subject to Class 1 not 1A NIC		0
Private use of a mobile telephone		0
		3,631
Class 1A NIC = £3,631 × 13.8%		501

(2) Lease premium

£22,000 × [(50 - 4) / 50] = £20,240 / 5 = £4,048

	£
£4,048 × 15/12	5,060

(a) (ii)

Kirsty's trading income assessments

		£
2012/13	Commencement to next 5 April ie 1.1.13 – 5.4.13 = 3/15 × £42,877	8,575
2013/14	12 months to accounting date ie 1.4.13 – 31.3.14 = 12/15 × £42,877	34,302

(b)

Kirsty's capital gains

	£
Total gains	28,905
Less AEA	(10,900)
Taxable gains	18,005
£7,450 @ 18%	1,341
£10,555 @ 28%	2,955
Total CGT due	4,296

(W1) BRB remaining

	£
Total income	34,000
Less PA	(9,440)
Taxable income	24,560
BRB remaining £32,010 – £24,560	£7,450

Marks

(a) (i) Adjusted profits
Client entertaining ½
Class 1A NIC (own figure) ½
Depreciation ½
Property costs ½
Lease premium deduction ½
Allowable rent 1
Capital allowances 1
No other adjustments ½
Class 1A NIC (W1)
Van benefit and fuel benefit 1½
Use of computer 2
Vouchers ½
Private use of mobile phone ½
Class 1A @ 13.8% ½
Lease premium deduction – annual figure (W2) 1½
Deduction × 15/12 ½
‎ 12

(ii) 2012/13 1
2013/14 1
‎ 2

(b) Total gains ½
AEA ½
CGT liability 1
BRB remaining 1
‎ 3
‎ 17

30 Preparation question: income tax

(a) Income tax computation

	Non-savings £	Savings £	Dividend £	Total £
Trading income	14,000			
Property income (W)	24,200			
Dividend (£2,700 × 100/90)			3,000	
Bank interest (£2,240 × 100/80)		2,800		
Net income	38,200	2,800	3,000	44,000
Less: personal allowance (Note)	(9,440)			(9,440)
Taxable income	28,760	2,800	3,000	34,560

	£
Tax on non-savings income	
£28,760 × 20%	5,752
Tax on savings income	
£2,800 × 20%	560
Tax on dividend income	
£450 ×10%	45
£2,550 × 32.5%	829
	7,186
Less: married couples' allowance (Note)	(304)
Tax liability	6,882
Less: tax suffered on bank interest £2,800 × 20%	(560)
tax credit on dividends £3,000 × 10%	(300)
Tax payable	6,022

WORKING

Property income

	£
Property profits	7,800
Lease premium	
$£20,000 \times \dfrac{50-(10-1)}{50}$	16,400
	24,200

Note: Although Sean was born between 6 April 1938 and 5 April 1948, his net income of £44,000 will cause the age personal allowance of £10,500 to be reduced to the basic personal allowance of £9,440, and the married couples' allowance of £7,915 (based on Grainne's age) to be reduced to £3,040.

(b) The Gift Aid payment has two effects:

(1) For the purposes of calculating the age personal allowance and married couples' allowance, net income is reduced by the gross Gift Aid payment of £10,000 ($£8,000 \times \dfrac{100}{80}$)

	£
Original net income	44,000
Less: Gift Aid	(10,000)
	34,000

The allowances are now:

	£	£
Personal allowance		10,500
Less: reduction		
½ (£34,000 – £26,100)	3,950	
restricted to	(1,060)	(1,060)
Remaining reduction	2,890	
		9,440
Married couples' allowance		7,915
Less: remaining reduction		(2,890)
		5,025
Tax relief @ 10%		503

(2) The gross Gift Aid payment of £10,000 extends the basic rate band to £42,010 (£32,010 + £10,000). As a result there will be no income in the higher rate band.

31 Preparation question: benefits

Taxable income

	Non-savings £
Salary	40,000
Less occupational pension (4%)	(1,600)
	38,400
Benefits (W)	2,871
Less additional expenses (W)	(800)
General earnings	40,471
Pension	1,500
Net income	41,971
Less personal allowance	(9,440)
Taxable income	32,531

WORKING

Benefits

	£	£
Computer equipment (insignificant private use)		-
Loan benefit £50,000 × (4% – 1.5%) × $^5/_{12}$		521
Photocopier – use 20% × £4,000 × $^6/_{12}$		400
Photocopier – transfer		
Higher of		
(i) MV at transfer, and	270	
(ii) MV when first provided	4,000	
Less previous benefits		
2011/12 20% × £4,000	(800)	
2012/13 20% × £4,000	(800)	
2013/14 (above)	(400)	
	2,000	
ie	2,000	
Less price paid	(50)	
		1,950
		2,871
Statutory mileage rate scheme		
Income received £12,000 × 35p		4,200
Less allowable expense		
10,000 × 45p	4,500	
2,000 × 25p	500	
		(5,000)
Additional allowable expense		800

ICAEW

32   Preparation question: pensions

(a) As Tom's earnings are £350,000, all of the contributions of £275,000 qualify for tax relief.

He will have paid £220,000 (£275,000 less 20%) to the pension company.

(b) Higher rate tax relief will be given by extending Tom's basic rate tax band for 2013/14 to £307,010 (32,010 + 275,000). The higher rate limit will similarly be increased by £275,000 to £425,000.

However, there will be a tax charge on the excess of his contributions above the annual allowance of £50,000.

Tom does not have any unused annual allowance brought forward as his annual pension contributions for the previous three tax years have exceeded £50,000.

His income tax liability for the tax year 2013/14 is therefore:

	£
Trading profit	350,000
Personal allowance (W1)	(9,440)
Taxable income	340,560
Income tax:	
£307,010 at 20%	61,402
£33,550 at 40%	13,420
	74,822
Excess contribution charge (W2)	
	97,028
Tax liability	171,850

WORKING 1

Tom's adjusted net income for the purposes of the restricting of the personal allowance is:

Trading profit	350,000
Less personal pension contribution	(275,000)
Adjusted net income	75,000

Tom is therefore entitled to the full personal allowance as his adjusted net income is less than £100,000.

> **Tutorial note:**
>
> When calculating adjusted net income in order to determine if there would be any available personal allowance, only those pension contributions paid net of basic rate tax would be included. Therefore as Tom has paid all his contributions net of tax into a personal pension scheme, the gross value of these contributions are deducted from net income in order to calculate adjusted net income. This is then used to determine the availability of the personal allowance.

WORKING 2

	£
Excess contributions (£275,000 − £50,000)	225,000
Annual allowance charge	
(£425,000 − £340,560) £84,440 × 40%	33,776
(£225,000 − £84,440) £140,560 × 45%	63,252
	97,028

(c) Adrienne will receive tax relief (mostly at the additional rate of 45%) on the pension contributions as they are less than her earnings of £210,000. This will be done by extending her basic rate tax band and increasing her higher rate limit by £77,500 (£62,000 × 100/80). As the higher rate limit will be increased to £227,500 she will be a higher rate taxpayer for the year instead of an additional rate taxpayer.

As her total gross contributions of £77,500 for the year exceed the annual allowance of £50,000 she may be subject to an annual allowance charge. This charge would tax her excess contributions at her marginal rate of tax. However any unused annual allowance from the previous three tax years can be carried forward and used to increase the available annual allowance for the current tax year. If this is at least £77,500 then there will be no annual allowance charge.

Adrienne has had annual pension contributions of £37,500 for each of the tax years 2008/09, 2009/10, 2010/11, 2011/12 and 2012/13. She has £12,500 unused annual allowance from each of these tax years. However as unused annual allowance can only be carried forward for three years she is no longer able to utilise the amounts from 2008/09 and 2009/10.

Annual allowance 2013/14	£50,000
Unused annual allowance from 2010/11	£12,500
Unused annual allowance from 2011/12	£12,500
Unused annual allowance from 2012/13(balance)	£2,500
Total annual allowance to be used in 2013/14	£77,500
Unused annual allowance carried forward to 2014/15:	
2012/13 (£12,500 − £2,500)	£10,000

Tutorial note:

The adjusted net income will be £210,000 - £77,500 = £132,500. The pension contribution does not affect the restricting of the personal allowance which will be £nil.

33 Preparation question: trust income tax

(a) **Income tax payable**

	Non-savings £	Savings £	Dividend £
Bank interest (£12,000 × 100/80)		15,000	
Dividend (£27,000 × 100/90)			30,000
Property income	14,500		
Taxable income	14,500	15,000	30,000

	£
Tax on non-savings income	
£1,000 × 20% (basic rate)	200
£13,500 × 45% (trust rate)	6,075
Tax on savings income	
£15,000 × 45% (trust rate)	6,750
Tax on dividend income	
£30,000 × 37.5% (trust dividend rate)	11,250
Tax liability	24,275
Less: tax suffered on bank interest £15,000 × 20%	(3,000)
tax credit on dividends £30,000 × 10%	(3,000)
Tax payable	18,275

(b) **Tax pool**

	£
Balance b/f	1,500
Add 2013/14 tax:	
Tax paid at 20%	200
Tax paid at 45% (£6,075 + £6,750)	12,825
Tax paid at 37.5% − 10% (£11,250 − £3,000)	8,250
Less: required to cover tax credit on payment of £20,000 (× 100/55 × 45%)	(16,364)
Balance c/f	6,411

Note: As there is sufficient tax to cover the tax credit on the payment to the beneficiary there is no additional tax due from the trustees.

(c) **Form R185**

	Net £	Tax credit £
Non-savings	20,000	16,364

Note: Income payments from discretionary trusts are always treated as non-savings income in the hands of the beneficiary.

34 Preparation question: overseas aspects of income tax

Income tax payable

Income	Non-savings Income £	Savings Income £	Total £
Employment income – UK	25,000		25,000
Property income – overseas	42,000		42,000
Pension income – overseas (90% taxable)	5,400		5,400
Interest × 100/80		4,000	4,000
Total income	72,400	4,000	76,400
Personal allowance	(9,440)		(9,440)
Taxable income	62,960	4,000	66,960

Tax	£
£32,010 @ 20%	6,402
£34,950 @ 40%	13,980
	20,382
Less: DTR (W1)	(7,200)
Income tax liability	13,182
Less: tax deducted at source	
Via PAYE	(7,379)
On interest: £4,000 × 20%	(800)
Income tax payable	5,003

WORKING 1 – DTR

Excluding the overseas property income, UK income tax would be:

Taxable income	20,960	4,000	24,960

Tax	£
£24,960 @ 20%	4,992
Income tax liability	4,992

Thus UK income tax on the overseas income is £20,382 – £4,992 = £15,390

DTR is the lower of the actual overseas tax of £7,200 and the UK tax on the overseas income, ie the DTR is the overseas tax of £7,200.

35 Stefan Blitzburger

Income tax payable

	Non-savings Income £	Savings Income £	Dividend Income £	Total £
Employment income	250,000			250,000
UK dividend income × 100/90			21,500	21,500
Interest × 100/80		12,000		12,000
Property income – exempt as not remitted				–
Overseas dividends (W1) (Note)	11,961			11,961
Total income	261,961	12,000	21,500	295,461
Personal allowance – (no PA as claimed remittance basis)	Nil			Nil
Taxable income	261,961	12,000	21,500	295,461

Tax		£
£32,010 @ 20%		6,402
£117,990 @ 40%		47,196
£111,961 @ 45%		50,382
£12,000 @ 45%		5,400
£21,500 @ 37.5%		8,063
		117,443
Less: DTR (W2)		(1,615)
Income tax liability		115,828
Less: tax deducted at source		
Via PAYE		(87,948
On UK dividends: £21,500 × 10%		(2,150)
On interest: £12,000 × 20%		(2,400)
On overseas dividends (W1)		(1,196)
		22,134
Add: remittance basis charge (resident for at least 12 out of last 14 tax years)		50,000
Tax payable		72,134

Note: The overseas dividends are taxable as they have been remitted to the UK. They are treated in the same way as UK dividends, ie they come with a 10% notional tax credit. However, remitted income loses its 'nature' and is taxed as non savings income, so the dividend tax rate does not apply to these dividends.

WORKINGS

(1) **Taxable overseas dividend**

		£
Net overseas dividend	9,150	
Add overseas withholding tax: £9,150 × 15/85	1,615	
Gross overseas dividend		10,765
Add UK tax credit: £10,765 × 10/90		1,196
Taxable foreign dividend		11,961

(2) **Double taxation relief**

DTR is the lower of the actual overseas tax of £1,615 and the UK tax on the overseas income (excluding the notional tax credit of 10%) of £4,186 (£11,961 × 45% – £1,196), ie the DTR is the UK tax of £1,615.

Marking guide

	Marks
Employment income	½
Gross up UK dividend income	1
Gross up interest income	1
Property income not taxable as not remitted	1
Overseas dividends	
Taxable as remitted	1
Taxed as non savings income	1
Amount of dividend	1
No PA	1
Tax liability	2½
Deduct DTR	½
DTR amount	1
Deduct tax credits/ suffered	2
Remittance basis charge and reasoning	1½
	15

36 The Breville Trust

(a) **Income tax payable**

	Non-savings £	Savings £	Dividend £
Bank interest (£3,000 × 100/80)		3,750	
Dividend (£9,000 × 100/90)			10,000
Property income (£12,000 – £4,300)	7,700		
Less: trust expenses (£1,575 × 100/90)			(1,750)
Taxable income	7,700	3,750	8,250

	£
Tax on non-savings income	
£500 × 20% (basic rate, note)	100
£7,200 × 45% (trust rate)	3,240
Tax on savings income	
£3,750 × 45% (trust rate)	1,688
Tax on dividend income	
£1,750 × 10% (basic rate as used to pay expenses)	175
£8,250 × 37.5% (trust dividend rate)	3,094
Tax liability	8,297
Less: tax suffered on bank interest £3,750 × 20%	(750)
tax credit on dividends £10,000 × 10%	(1,000)
Tax due	6,547
Add: additional tax liability (W)	2,703
Tax payable	9,250

Note: the basic rate band is divided by the number of settlements made by Barry ie £1,000/2.

WORKING

Tax pool

	£
Balance b/f	Nil
Add 2013/14 tax:	
Tax paid at 20%	100
Tax paid at 45% (£3,240 + £1,688)	4,928
Tax paid at 37.5% – 10% (£3,094 – £825)	2,269
Total tax credits	7,297
Less: required to cover tax credits on payments of 2 × £5,000 (£10,000 × 100/55 × 45%)	(8,182)
Additional tax due from trustees	(885)
Balance c/f	Nil

Note: As there is insufficient tax in the pool to cover the 45% tax credit for the payments to the beneficiaries, the trustees must pay over the shortfall to HMRC.

(b) **Form R185 for each beneficiary**

	Net £	Tax credit £
Non-savings	5,000	4,091

Marks

(a)   IT payable
      Gross up interest and dividends   2
      Rental income   1
      Deduct expenses from dividends   ½
      Basic rate tax on first £500   1
      Trust rate on savings and non-savings income   1
      Basic rate on dividends use to pay expenses   ½
      Trust dividend rate   ½
      Deduct tax credits/tax suffered   1
      Tax pool
      Tax paid at basic and trust rate entering the pool   1
      Tax paid at trust dividend rate entering the pool   1
      Deduct tax credit required for payments to beneficiaries   1
      Additional tax due   ½
                                                                             ──
                                                                             11

(b)   R185
      Net non-savings income   1
      Tax credit   1
                                                                             ──
                                                                              2
                                                                             ──
                                                                             13
                                                                             ══

37   The Oyster Trust

(a)   (i)   **Income tax payable**

	Non-savings £	Savings £	Dividend £
Bank interest (£4,000 × 100/80)		5,000	
Dividend (£10,800 × 100/90)			12,000
Property income (£16,200 − £6,800)	9,400		
Taxable income	9,400	5,000	12,000
Tax @ 20%/20%/10%	1,880	1,000	1,200
Less credits	nil	(1,000)	(1,200)
Tax due	1,880	nil	nil

Note: There is no relief for trust expenses incurred by interest in possession trustees.

(ii) **Form R185**

	Net £	Tax credit £
Non-savings (W)	7,520	1,880
Savings (W)	4,000	1,000
Dividend (W)	9,700	1,078

Tax credit on dividend = £9,700 × 100/90 × 10% = £1,078

WORKING

Net distributable income

	Non-savings £	Savings £	Dividend £
Gross	9,400	5,000	12,000
Less: tax	(1,880)	(1,000)	(1,200)
Less: trust expenses			(1,100)
Net distributable income	7,520	4,000	9,700

Note: The amount of income actually received by the life tenant is irrelevant. He is taxable on all of the income received by the trust, so it must be shown in full on the R185.

(b) Capital gains tax liability

	£
House (W1)	30,800
Shellac plc (W3)	11,000
Necklace – exempt chattel (both cost and proceeds below £6,000)	–
	41,800
Annual exempt amount	(5,450)
Taxable gains	36,350
Capital gains tax liability @ 28%	10,178

WORKINGS

(1) House

	£
Gain	350,000
Less: PPR relief (W2) £350,000 × 114/125	(319,200)
Chargeable gain	30,800

(2) PPR periods

	Total	Exempt	Chargeable
16.5.03 – 15.11.09 – actual occupation	78	78	
16.11.09 – 15.10.10 – no occupation	11		11
16.10.10 – 15.10.13 – last 36 months	36	36	
	125	114	11

(3) Shellac plc shares

	£
Proceeds	15,000
Less: Cost (W4)	(4,000)
Gain	11,000

(4) Cost of shares

	No. of shares	Cost £
June 2004 – purchase	400	1,500
October 2009 – purchase	1,100	4,500
	1,500	6,000
February 2014 – disposal	(1,000)	(4,000)
Pool c/f	500	2,000

Marks

(a)(i) Income tax payable
Gross up interest and dividend	2	
Property income	1	
Tax liability	1½	
Deduct tax credit/ suffered	1	
No relief for trust expenses	½	
		6

(ii) Form R185
Net non-savings	1	
Net savings	1	
Net dividend	1½	
Tax credit on dividend	½	
		4

(b) CGT liability
House – gain after relief	1	
PPR periods	1½	
Gain on Shellac plc shares	1	
Cost of shares (W4)	2	
Necklace – chattel exemption	1	
AEA	1	
CGT liability	½	
		8
		18

38 William Pembroke (J09)

(a) (i) **Car: Income tax**

Taxable benefit:

$£(37{,}000 + 1{,}000 - 2{,}300) = £35{,}700 \times [11\% + (175 - 95)/5\,] = £9{,}639$

Tutorial note: The cost of the accessories increases the list price in the benefit calculation but is reduced by the capital contribution made by William.

The fuel benefit is: $£21{,}100 \times 27\% = £5{,}697$

Income tax: $£(£9{,}639 + 5{,}697) \times 40\% = \underline{£6{,}134}$

Car: National insurance

There are no NI contributions for William of the car arrangements.

(ii) **Salary**

	£
Income tax: £8,000 × 40%	3,200
Class 1 primary national insurance: £8,000 × 2%	160

(b) Income tax liability 2013/14

	Non savings £	Savings £	Dividends £
Salary £(59,000 + 8,000)	67,000		
Loan benefit – £7,000 × 10/12 × [4% – 3%]	58		
Staff suggestion scheme award – exempt as less than £5,000	–		
Use of computer – exempt	–		
IT advice – no marginal cost	–		
Total employment income	67,058		
Property income (W2)	15,960		
Building society interest (£220 × 100/80)		275	
Dividend income (£225 × 100/90)			250
Net income	83,018	275	250
Less: Personal allowance	(9,440)		
Taxable income	73,578	275	250
Income tax on:			
£39,130 × 20% (W1)			7,826
£34,723 × 40% (including savings income)			13,889
£250 × 32.5%			81
Income tax liability			21,796

WORKINGS

W1   Extended basic rate band

Basic rate threshold	32,010
Add: Gift Aid (£320 × 100/80)	400
Personal pension contribution (£448 × 12 × 100/80)	6,720
Revised BR threshold	39,130

W2   Property income

	£
Rent: £14,400 × 11/12	13,200
Lease premium:	
$£3,000 \times \dfrac{50-(5-1)}{50}$	2,760
Property income	15,960

---

39 Lea Oswald (J10)

Income tax liability 2013/14

	Non savings £	Dividends £
Salary (£48,000 × 10/12)	40,000	
Car benefit:		
£32,000 × [11% + $\frac{(160-95)}{5}$]× 10/12	6,400	
Fuel benefit: £21,100 × 24% × 10/12	4,220	
Accommodation benefit: £1,750 × 10	17,500	
Use of laptop: £2,900 × 20% × 80% × 9/12 (first provided on 30 April 2013)	348	
Purchase of laptop:		
Greater of:		
£800 and		
£(2,900 – 348) = £2,552	£2,552	
Less: price paid	£(300)	
	2,252	
Dividends (£4,000 × 100/90)		4,444
Net income	70,720	4,444
Less: Personal allowance	(9,440)	–
Taxable income	61,280	4,444
Income tax on:		
£32,760 (W1) × 20%		6,552
£28,520 × 40%		11,408
£4,444 × 32.5%		1,444
Income tax liability		19,404

WORKINGS

(1) **Extension of BRB**

Basic rate limit	£32,010
Add: Gift Aid £600 × 100/80	£750
Revised limit	£32,760

Marking guide

	Marks
Salary	½
Car benefit	1
Fuel benefit	½
Accommodation benefit	½
Use of laptop	1
Purchase of laptop	1½
Dividends	1
Personal allowance	1
Income tax liability	1½
Extension of BRB (W1)	½
	9

40 Violet (D10)

(a) Income tax liability 2013/14

	Non savings £	Savings £	Dividend £
Employment income (W1)	65,488		
Rental income (W2)	3,176		
Interest Direct Saver account received gross		1,500	
National Savings Certificates exempt		–	
Dividend = £10,800 × 100/90			12,000
Less qualifying interest £32,000 × 4.25%	(1,360)		
Net income	67,304	1,500	12,000
Less personal allowance	(9,440)		
Taxable income	57,864	1,500	12,000

Non- savings income	£32,010	× 20%	6,402
Extend BRB by PPS = £800 × 100/80	£1,000	× 20%	200
	£24,854	× 40%	9,942
	£57,864		
Savings income	£1,500	× 40%	600
Dividend income	£12,000	× 32.5%	3,900
Income tax liability			21,044

WORKINGS

(1) Employment income

Salary			62,050
Company car	£16,450 × 10% × 11/12		1,508
Fuel	£21,100 × 10% × 11/12		1,934
Excess SMRS	Claimed 52p × 2,800	1,456	
	Permitted 45p × 2,800	(1,260)	
			196
Cost of holiday voucher			1,800
Employer pension contribution *(need not be explicitly stated)*			Nil
			67,488
Employee occupational pension contribution			(2,000)
			65,488

(2) Rental income

Rent		10,400
Mortgage interest		(2,800)
Agent fee	£1,040 × 1.20	(1,248)
		6,352
		3,176

Split 50:50 as no declaration regarding actual ownership made

(b) National Insurance contributions

	£
Earnings	
Salary	62,050
Excess SMRS	196
Holiday voucher	1,800
Total	64,046

Class 1 NIC is due on cash and vouchers exchangeable for cash, goods or services

	£
Employee	
Class 1 primary NIC [(£41,450 − £7,755) × 12%] + [(£64,046 − £41,450) × 2%]	4,495

	£
Employer	
Class 1 employer NIC (£64,046 − £7,696) × 13.8%	7,776
Class 1A NIC (£1,508 + £1,934) = £3,442 × 13.8%	475
	8,251

Marks

(a) Employment income (W1)

Salary	½
Car benefit	1
Fuel benefit	½
SMRS	1½
Holiday voucher	1
Employer pension contribution *(not need to state)*	½
Employee pension contribution	1

Rental income (W2)

Mortgage interest	½
Agent fee	½
Split 50:50	½
Direct Saver account interest	½
NS Certificates	½
Dividends	½
Loan interest	1
Personal allowance	1
Extension of BRB	1
Income tax liability	1½
Total income tax liability	½
	14

(b)

Earnings	1
Employee NIC	2
Employer NIC – Class 1	1
Employer NIC – Class 1A	1
	5
	19

41 Mary Queen (M11)

(a) (i) **Employment income**

	£
Salary (£74,200 × 5/12)	30,917
Bonus	1,000
Company car (£24,000 × 16% × 4/12)	1,280
Mileage allowance (less than 45p per mile)	nil
Entertaining allowance	340
Loan written off (no benefit re duration of loan of under £5,000)	3,500
Gifts – exempt (less than £250 per donor)	nil
	37,037
Less: deduction for approved mileage allowance (35p – 45p) × 500	(50)
Less: claim for client entertaining	(270)
Employment income	36,717

(ii) **Adjusted trading profits for the 8 months ending 30 April 2014**

	£
Revenue	48,000
Less: costs	
Running costs of the car (£3,175 × 60%)	(1,905)
Rent on the office (£1,100 × 8)	(8,800)
Deduction for lease premium (W)	(512)
Other allowable costs	(2,900)
	33,883
Less: capital allowances	
Car: £20,200 × 18% × 60% × 8/12	(1,454)
Computer equipment: £6,100 (AIA)	(6,100)
Adjusted trading profit	26,329

WORKINGS

Income element of lease premium paid

$$£2,400 × \frac{50-(3-1)}{50} = £2,304$$

Deduction available = £2,304/3 × 8/12 = £512

(iii) **Income tax liability for 2013/14**

	Non savings £	Dividends £
Employment income (part i)	36,717	
Trading income (£26,329 × 7/8) (part ii)	23,038	
ISA interest - exempt		
Dividends (£1,600 × 100/90)		1,778
	59,755	1,778
Less: Personal allowance	(9,440)	–
	50,315	1,778
Income tax on:		
£50,315 × 20%	10,063	
£ 445 × 10%	45	
£50,760 (W)		
£ 1,333 × 32.5% (£1,778 − £445)		433
Income tax liability		10,541

WORKINGS

Basic rate band	32,010
Add: pension contribution (£15,000 × 100/80)	18,750
Revised basic rate band	50,760

(iv) *Mary's national insurance contributions for 2013/14*

As an employee, Mary pays Class 1 contributions on her earnings including the bonus, but not on any benefits.

Once Mary becomes self-employed, Class 2 NICs will be payable at a fixed rate of £2.70 per week.

Class 4 contributions are payable on her tax-adjusted trading profits.

(b) Albert would be working for two competing businesses which poses a potential conflict of interest.

He should evaluate the threat, taking into account whether this is insignificant, as well as considering how his being married to Mary affects the situation.

The threats are not clearly insignificant and therefore safeguards should be considered and applied including:

- Notifying both parties of the fact that their interests are in conflict
- Obtaining consent from both parties to continue acting if they wish it
- Ensuring confidentiality is maintained

Here, the fundamental principles of objectivity and confidentiality are subject to self-interest and familiarity threats because he is married to Mary.

If the threats cannot be eliminated or reduced to an acceptable level, Albert should conclude that it is not appropriate to act for both parties. Ceasing to act for Mary may be the best course of action in this situation. [Any other sensible conclusion, eg work on the tender being handled by other advisers.]

Marking guide

				Marks
(a)	(i)	**Employment income**		
		Salary	½	
		Bonus	½	
		Car benefit	1½	
		Mileage allowance	½	
		Entertaining allowance	1	
		Loan write off	1	
		Gifts	1	
		Mileage deduction	½	
		Client entertaining deduction	½	
				7
	(ii)	**Adjusted trading profits**		
		Revenue	½	
		Running costs of car	1	
		Rent	1	
		Lease premium (W)	2	
		Allowable costs	½	
		CA on car	2	
		CA on computer equipment	1	
				8
	(iii)	**Income tax liability**		
		Employment income	½	
		Trading income	1	
		ISA	½	
		Dividends	1	
		PA	1	
		Extended BRB	1	
		Income tax liability	1	
				6
	(iv)	**NIC**		
		Class 1	1½	
		Class 2	½	
		Class 4	1	
				3
(b)		Conflict of interest	½	
		Evaluate the threat	1	
		Consider safeguards and examples	2	
		Fundamental principles/threats	2	
		Conclusion	1	
		Max	6½	
				5
				29

42 Henry Brocard (J11)

(a) **Income tax liability 2013/14**

	Non savings £	Savings £	Dividends £
Salary	110,000		
Less: qualifying expenses	(1,230)		
Subscription to dining club (Note)	Nil		
Car benefit: £45,000 × 15%	6,750		
Insurance and repairs (Note)	Nil		
Fuel benefit: £21,100 × 15%	3,165		
Medical insurance (Note)	780		
Costs of medical treatment	Nil		
Bank interest (£960 × 100/80)		1,200	
Dividends (£10,800 × 100/90)			12,000
Net income	119,465	1,200	12,000
Less: Personal allowance (W1 & W2)	(607)	-	-
Taxable income	118,858	1,200	12,000

Income tax on:	
£47,010 × 20% (W3)	9,402
£71,848 × 40%	28,739
£ 1,200 × 40%	480
£12,000 × 32.5%	3,900
£132,058	
Income tax liability	42,521

WORKINGS

(1) **Net income**

Net income	132,665
Less: Pension contributions (£1,000 × 12 × 100/80)	(15,000)
Adjusted net income	117,665

> **Tutorial note:**
>
> When calculating adjusted net income in order to determine if there would be any available personal allowance, only those pension contributions paid net of basic rate tax would be included. Therefore as Henry has paid all his contributions net of tax into a personal pension scheme, the gross value of these contributions are deducted from net income in order to calculate adjusted net income. This is then used to determine the availability of the personal allowance (W2).

(2) **Personal allowance**

Personal allowance	9,440
Less: (£117,665 − £100,000) × ½ (W2)	(8,833)
Personal allowance available	607

(3) **Extension of BRB**

Basic rate limit	32,010
Add: Pension contributions (£1,000 × 12 × 100/80)	15,000
Revised limit	47,010

> **Tutorial note:**
>
> Where a question asks you to clearly show your treatment of all items, this is the level of detail that is required.

(b) Pensions

The maximum tax free lump sum for Meg is £1,500,000 × 25% = £375,000

The balance of the fund up to the lifetime allowance (£1,500,000 − £375,000) = £1,125,000 is available to provide pension income benefits. These will be taxable on receipt.

The excess over the lifetime allowance (£1,850,000 − £1,500,000) ie £350,000 is taken as a lump sum.

Meg's lifetime allowance charge is £350,000 × 55% = £192,500

The scheme administrator pays Meg £350,000 − £192,500 = £157,500

(Alternatively: The scheme administrator pays Meg £375,000 + £350,000 − £192,500 = £532,500)

Marking guide

		Marks
(a)	Salary	½
	Travel expenses	1
	Subscription to dining club	½
	Car benefit	1
	Insurance and repairs	½
	Fuel benefit	1
	Medical insurance	1
	Medical costs	½
	Bank interest	1
	Dividends	1
	Adjusted net income (W1)	1
	PA (W2)	1
	Income tax liability	2
	Extension of BRB (W3)	1
		13
(b)	Lifetime allowance	1
	Tax free lump sum – 25%	1
	Balance taxable when received as pension	1
	Excess	1
	Lifetime allowance charge	1
	Payment to Meg by scheme administrator	1
		6
	Max	5
		18

43 Paola (S11)

Income tax computation

	Non savings £	Savings £	Dividend £
Employment income (W1)	163,265		
Bank interest (£2,500 × 100/80)		3,125	
Treasury stock interest received gross		250	
Dividends (£11,970 × 100/90)			13,300
Net income	163,265	3,375	13,300
Less: personal allowance	(Nil)		
Taxable income	163,265	3,375	13,300

Income tax on:		
£42,635 × 20%		8,527
£117,990 × 40%		47,196
£160,625		
£2,640 × 45%		1,188
£3,375 × 45%		1,519
£13,300 × 37.5%		4,988
Income tax liability		63,418

Primary NIC liability

Primary NIC is not due on taxable benefits

Salary + loan write off	161,650
(£41,450 − £7,755) × 12%	4,043
(£161,650 − £41,450) × 2%	2,404
	6,447

WORKINGS

1 Employment income

Salary		86,500
Company car (£26,900 + £200 − £5,000) × (3% + 17%)		4,420
Loan write off		75,150
Laptop use (£3,400 × 20% × 6/12)		340
Gift of laptop – higher of:		
MV now	1,800	
MV at first use	3,400	
Less taxable benefits (£3,400 × 20% × 18/12)	(1,020)	
		2,380
Employer pension contribution		nil
		168,790
Employee occupational pension contribution (£86,500 × 5%)		(4,325)
GAYE		(1,200)
		163,265

2 Extended tax limits

Both limits extended by:	
(£8,000 + £500) × 100/80	10,625
Basic rate limit (£32,010 + £10,625)	42,635
Higher rate limit (£150,000 + £10,625)	160,625

Income tax – the income tax computation   145

	Marks
Salary	½
Car	2
Loan write off	½
Laptop	1
Gift of laptop	2½
Employer pension contribution	½
Employee occupational pension contribution	1
GAYE	1
Bank interest	½
Treasury stock interest	½
Dividends	½
Personal allowance	1
Extended tax limits	2
Income tax liability	2
NIC liability	
Salary and loan	1
NIC @ 12%	1
NIC @ 2%	1½
	19

44   Kristina Grey (J12)

(a)   (i)   Tax adjusted trading profit

Two months ended 30 June 2013

	£
Adjusted trading profit	22,770
Less: cessation costs	
Statutory redundancy costs	(2,200)
Compensation for loss of office	(4,800)
	15,770
Less: Capital allowances (W1)	(390)
Tax-adjusted trading profits	15,380

WORKINGS

Capital allowances

	Main pool	Car (special rate)		Total
	£	£		£
TWDV b/f	5,800	4,250		
Disposal – Kristina's car		(5,100)		
- Derek's car	(3,900)			
- Plant and machinery	(1,000)			
No WDAs	900	(850)		
Balancing allowance	(900)			900
Balancing charge		850	X60%	(510)
Total allowances				390

(ii)   Trading income assessments

		£
2012/13	Year ended 30 April 2012	46,910
2013/14	1 May 2012 – 30 June 2013	
	£(67,030 + 15,380)	82,410
	Less: overlap profits	(8,170)
		74,240

(b) (i) **Income tax computation – 2013/14**

	Non savings £	Dividends £
Trading income (part aii)	74,240	
Salary: (£95,000 × 8/12)	63,333	
Company car: £25,000 × [11% + 3% + $\dfrac{(165-95)}{5}$] × 7/12	4,083	
Fuel: £21,100 × 28% × 7/12	3,446	
[*No deduction for fuel contribution of £100 × 7*]		
Bonus not paid in the tax year		
Dividends: £39,000 × 100/90		43,333
	145,102	43,333
Less: qualifying interest on loan to purchase shares		
£22,000 × 7% × 5/12	(642)	
Net income	144,460	43,333
Less: Personal allowance (fully abated)	-	
Taxable income	144,460	43,333

Income tax liability:	£
£47,010 × 20% (W1)	9,402
£97,450 × 40%	38,980
£144,460	
£20,540 × 32.5%	6,676
£165,000	
£22,793 × 37.5%	8,547
Income tax liability	63,605

WORKINGS

(1) **Extended BR and HR limits**

	£
Basic rate limit	32,010
Add: PPC	15,000
Extended BR limit	47,010

	£
Higher rate limit	150,000
Add: PPC	15,000
Extended HR limit	165,000

(ii) National insurance contributions

Class 1 contributions:	£
£(95,000/12 – 641) × 13.8% × 8	8,032

Class 1A contributions:	
£(4,083 + 3,446) × 13.8%	1,039

(iii) Pension contributions

The maximum amount of contributions attracting tax relief each tax year is the higher of £3,600 and 100% earnings.

	Deemed annual allowance	Allowance utilised	Unused	Tax relief
	£	£	£	£
2011/12	50,000	15,000	35,000	
2012/13	50,000	15,000	35,000	
2013/14	50,000	15,000	35,000	
2014/15	50,000	50,000	nil	50,000 + 7,000 (11/12) = 57,000
2015/16	50,000	50,000	nil	50,000 + 7,000 (12/13) = 57,000
2016/17	50,000	50,000	nil	50,000 + 35,000 (13/14) = 85,000

Marking guide

			Marks
(a)	(i)	Trading profit	½
		Redundancy	½
		Compensation for loss of office	½
		Deduction of CA's	½
		CA's (W1)	
		TWDV b/f	½
		Disposal value – Kristina's car	½
		Disposal value – Derek's car	1
		Disposal value – plant	½
		No WDA	1
		BA	½
		BC @ 60%	1
			7
	(ii)	2012/13	1
		2013/14	1
		Deduct overlap profits	1
			3
(b)	(i)	Trading income	½
		Salary	½
		Car benefit	1½
		Fuel benefit	1
		Bonus	½
		Dividends	1
		Qualifying loan interest	1½
		PA	½
		Income tax liability	1½
		Extension BR and HR limits	1½
			10
	(ii)	Class 1	1
		Class 1A	1
			2
	(iii)	*Pension tax relief*	
		2014/15	1
		2015/16	1
		2016/17	1
		No extra relief given in 2016/17	1
		Comparison between £3,600 and 100% earnings	½
			4½
		Max	4
			26

National insurance contributions

45 Cagney and Lacey

Cagney

Earnings	£
Salary	63,000
Excess SMRS (15,000 × (50p – 45p))	750
Total	63,750

Employee	£
Class 1 primary NIC [(£41,450 – £7,755) × 12%] + [(£63,750 – £41,450) × 2%]	4,489

Employer	
Class 1 employer NIC (£63,750 – £7,696) × 13.8%	7,735

Tutorial note:

When calculating earnings for national insurance contributions the excess mileage is always calculated by reference to 45p irrespective of how many business miles have been travelled.

Lacey

Earnings	£
July to November; January to March	
Salary (monthly)	3,500
December	
Salary	3,500
Bonus	6,000
Total	9,500

Employee	£
Class 1 primary NIC	
[(£3,500 – £646) × 12%] × 8	2,740
[(£3,454 – £646) × 12%] + [(£9,500 – £3,454) × 2%]	458
	3,198

Employer	
Class 1 employer NIC	
[(£3,500 – £641) × 13.8%] × 8	3,156
[(£9,500 – £641) × 13.8%]	1,223
	4,379

Tutorial note:

As Cagney has been employed for the whole of 2013/14 and has had the same salary every month it is possible to calculate her national insurance contributions on an annual basis using the annual primary and secondary thresholds and upper earnings limit.

Lacey has not worked for Angels Ltd for the whole of 2013/14 and did not receive the same income every month as she received a bonus in December. The national insurance contributions must therefore be calculated on a monthly basis using the monthly primary and secondary thresholds and upper earnings limit.

Marks

Cagney	
SMRS included in earnings	1
Class 1 primary	2
Class 1 secondary	1
Lacey	
Earnings (include bonus in one month)	1
Class 1 primary – 8 months	1
Class 1 primary – December	1½
Class 1 secondary	1½
	9

46 Diana

National Insurance Contributions payable

Class 1 primary and secondary contributions are calculated on cash earnings and childcare vouchers received in excess of £55 per week ie £35,000 (£33,800 + £1,200 (W1)).

	£
Class 1 primary contributions	
(£35,000 – £7,755) × 12%	3,269
Class 1 secondary contributions	
(£35,000 – £7,696) × 13.8%	3,768

Class 1A contributions

- Calculated on the cash equivalent value of the benefits in Diana's income tax computation.
- No class 1A NIC on computer benefit as it is exempt for income tax purposes.
- No class 1A NIC on purchase of car by Diana as this results in a benefit of zero.
- Other non-cash benefits are assessable as follows

	£
Car benefit (W2)	17,000
Fuel benefit (£21,100 × 34%)	7,174
Medical insurance	240
	24,414
Class 1A (£24,414 × 13.8%)	3,369

WORKINGS

(1) **Childcare vouchers**

The first £55 per week of childcare vouchers are exempt from income tax and national insurance contributions (NIC). Income tax and NICs are payable on the excess of £1,200 [48 × (£80 – £55)]. As Diana was in her employers' scheme prior to 6 April 2011 the £55 per week limit applies irrespective of her level of earnings.

(2) **Car benefit**

CO_2 emissions 212 g/km, petrol engine, available all year.

Appropriate % = (210 – 95)/5 = 23 + 11% = 34%

	£
Car (34% × £50,000)	17,000

	Marks
NIC	
Earnings	1
Class 1 primary	1
Class 1 secondary	1
Class 1A	2
Childcare vouchers (W1)	1
Car benefit (W2)	1½
Fuel benefit	½
	__8__

47 Jim

National Insurance Contributions payable

Class 1 primary and secondary contributions are calculated on cash earnings (salary). Jim is contracted out.

	£
Class 1 primary contributions	
(£7,755 – £5,668) × 1.4% rebate	(29)
(£40,040 – £7,755) × 10.6%	3,422
(£41,450 – £40,040) × 12%	169
(£54,000 – £41,450) × 2%	251
	3,813
Class 1 secondary contributions	
(£7,696 – £5,668) × 3.4% rebate	(69)
(£40,040 – £7,696) × 10.4%	3,364
(£54,000 – £40,040) × 13.8%	1,926
	5,221

Class 1A – applied to Jim's non-cash benefits (ie car)

Paid by employer only (£2,013 × 13.8%) — 278

CO_2 emissions 158 g/km, petrol engine, available for 3 months.

Appropriate % = (155 – 95)/5 = 12% + 11% = 23%

Car benefit (£35,000 × 23%) × 3/12 — 2,013

Note: There is no fuel benefit assessable on Jim as he himself pays for **all** of his private petrol.

Due dates for payment

Class 1 contributions

Class 1 NICs will be paid monthly under the PAYE system by the 19th day of the next calendar month (ie 14 days after the end of each tax month) or 22nd if paid electronically.

Class 1 A

Due date is 19 July 2014 (22nd July 2014 if paid electronically)

	Marks
Earnings (exclude dividends)	1
Employee NIC	
Rebate	1
Contracted out element	1
Part at 12%	1
Part at 2%	1
Employer NIC	
Rebate	1
Contracted out element	1
Part at 13.8%	1
Due dates	
Class 1	1
Class 1A	1
	10

48 Alexander

Alexander

	£
Class 2	
£2.70 × 52	140
Class 4	
Assessed on profits for the year ended 31 December 2013 (CYB)	
[(£41,450 − £7,755) × 9%] + [(£47,000 − £41,450) × 2%]	3,144
Total	3,284

Gareth

	£
Class 2	
Accounting profits for the tax year 6.4.13 to 5.4.14 are compared to the small earnings exception	
(£3,000 × 7/10) + (£6,300 × 5/12) = £4,725. This is less than £5,725 so no Class 2 NIC payable	Nil
Class 4	
(£8,250 (W) − £7,755) × 9%	45
Total	45

WORKING

	£
Assessable profits	
2013/14	
First 12 months of trading	
10 m/e 31 October 2013	5,000
2 m/e 31 December 2013 (2/12 × £19,500)	3,250
	8,250

Harry

	£
Class 2	
Age 69 on 10 January 2013. As over 65 no Class 2 payable	Nil
Class 4	
Age 69 at the start of the tax year therefore no Class 4 payable	Nil
Total	Nil

	Marks
Alexander	
Class 2	1
Class 4	2
Gareth	
Class 2	2
Calculation of assessable profits (W)	2
Class 4	1
Harry	
Class 2	1
Class 4	1
	10

49 Preparation question: short accounting period

(W) Capital allowances for period ending 31 March 2014

	FYA £	Main pool £	Allowances £
Energy efficient car (N1)	14,500		
	(14,500)		14,500
	–		
Van		8,800	
Computer		3,200	
AIA (N2)		(12,000)	12,000
Car for salesman (N1)		9,667	
WDA 18% × 9/12		(1,305)	1,305
TWDV c/f		8,362	
Allowances			27,805

Note 1: There is no restriction for private use where the asset is owned by a company. An asset used by an employee is never a private use asset. Cars are not eligible for the AIA.

Note 2: The AIA would have been restricted to £187,500 (£250,000 × 9/12).

Corporation tax computation

	£	£
Trading profits	374,000	
Less: research and development (125% × £20,000)	(25,000)	
CAs (W)	(27,805)	
Trading income		321,195
Non-trading loan relationships		1,950
		323,145
Less: qualifying charitable donation		(11,000)
Taxable total profits		312,145

Limits

£300,000 × 9/12 = £225,000
£1,500,000 × 9/12 = £1,125,000

Marginal rate applies

£312,145 × 23%	71,793
Less: 3/400 × £(1,125,000 – 312,145)	(6,096)
CT payable	65,697

50 Preparation question: marginal relief

Corporation tax computation for the year ended 31 December 2013

	£	£
Trading income		220,000
Property income		103,000
Non-trading loan relationships		6,000
Capital gains (£32,500 + £5,500)	38,000	
Less: capital losses brought forward	(24,000)	
		14,000
		343,000
Less: qualifying charitable donation		(4,000)
Augmented profits = Taxable total profits		339,000

	£
Corporation tax	
FY 2012: £339,000 × 3/12 × 24%	20,340
FY 2013: £339,000 × 9/12 × 23%	58,478
Less marginal relief:	
FY2012: (£1,500,000 – 339,000) × 1/100 × 3/12	(2,903)
FY2013: (£1,500,000 – 339,000) × 3/400 × 9/12	(6,531)
Corporation tax payable	69,384

51 Preparation question: long period of account

Jasmine Ltd

Corporation tax computations

15 months ended 30 June 2014

	Year ended 31 March 2014 £	3 months ended 30 June 2014 £
Adjusted trading profit before capital allowances (prorate 12:3)	260,000	65,000
Less capital allowances (W)	(15,200)	(1,476)
	244,800	63,524
Chargeable gain (allocated based on date – 10 June 2013)	265,000	
Qualifying charitable donation (allocated based on date – each April)	(4,000)	(4,000)
Taxable total profits	505,800	59,524
Franked investment income (£10,800 × $\frac{100}{90}$) – allocated based on date	12,000	–
Augmented Profits	517,800	59,524
Limits		
Upper limit (12 months : 3 months)	1,500,000	375,000
Lower limit	300,000	75,000
	marginal company	small company
Taxable total profits @ 23%/20%	116,334	11,905
Less: marginal relief		
$\frac{3}{400}$ (£1,500,000 – 517,800) × $\frac{505,800}{517,800}$	(7,196)	–
Corporation tax payable	109,138	11,905

WORKING

Capital allowances – separate computation for each AP

	Pool	Allowances
	£	£
Y/e 31 March 2014		
TWDV b/f	40,000	
Additions – 4 Dec 2013	8,000	
AIA	(8,000)	8,000
	40,000	
WDA @ 18%	(7,200)	7,200
		15,200
3 m/e 30 June 2014	32,800	
WDA @ 18% × $^3/_{12}$	(1,476)	1,476
TWDV c/f	31,324	

52 Preparation question: capital gains

(a) **The office building**

	£
Proceeds	400,000
Less cost	(130,000)
Unindexed gain	270,000
Less indexation allowance	
$\dfrac{250.6 - 101.8}{101.8} = 1.462 \times £130,000$	(190,060)
Chargeable gain	79,940

(b) **The Shoot plc shares**

	Shares	Cost	Indexed Cost
		£	£
The s.104 pool			
May 1984 acquisition	4,000	8,000	8,000
Indexation to April 1985: £8,000 × 0.065			520
$\dfrac{94.78 - 88.97}{88.97} = 0.065$			8,520
Indexed rise to March 1988:			
$\dfrac{104.1 - 94.78}{94.78} \times £8,520$			838
March 1988 acquisition	4,000	10,000	10,000
	8,000	18,000	19,358
Indexed rise to July 2013:			
$\dfrac{251.7 - 104.1}{104.1} \times £19,358$			27,447
			46,805
July 2013 disposal	(8,000)	(18,000)	(46,805)
	–	–	–

	£
Sale proceeds	48,000
Less: cost	(18,000)
	30,000
Less: indexation allowance £(46,805 – 18,000)	(28,805)
Chargeable gain	1,195

Total chargeable gains for the year are £79,940 + £1,195 = £81,135.

Corporation tax payable thereon is £81,135 × 23% = £18,661.

53 Atlantis Ltd (J04)

(a) **Atlantis Ltd**

Corporation tax computation – y/e 30 November 2013

	£
Trading income (W1)	122,974
Non-trading loan relationships (W2)	5,740
Overseas property income (£24,200 × 100/82)	29,512
Chargeable gain (W3)	137,511
	295,737
Less: Qualifying charitable donation	(2,000)
Taxable total profits	293,737

Corporation tax (W4)

	£
FY2012: £293,737 × 24% × 4/12	23,499
FY2013: £293,737 × 23% × 8/12	45,040

Less   marginal relief

$$FY2012: \frac{1}{100} \times (£750,000 - £303,626) \times \frac{293,737}{303,626} \times 4/12 \qquad (1,439)$$

$$FY2013: \frac{3}{400} \times (£750,000 - £303,626) \times \frac{293,737}{303,626} \times 8/12 \qquad (2,159)$$

	£
	64,941
Less DTR (W6)	(5,312)
Corporation tax payable	59,629

WORKINGS

(1) **Trade profits**

	Tutorial notes	£
Net profit per accounts		635,566
Add Depreciation		10,060
Debenture interest to Kennedy Ltd	(i)	12,900
Costs of debenture issue	(i)	3,200
Interest on overdue tax	(ii)	268
Charitable donation		2,000
Research equipment (capital)		11,500
		675,494
Less: Bank interest receivable (loan relationships)		(22,108)
Rent receivable (overseas property business profits)		(24,200)
Profit on sale of investment property (capital gain)		(202,900)
Dividends received (exempt income, but FII)		(8,900)
Additional R&D relief (see answer to part (b))		(44,050)
Adjusted profit before capital allowances		373,336
Less: Capital allowances (W5)		(250,362)
Trading income		122,974

> **Tutorial notes:**
>
> These notes (including the explanations in brackets above) were not requested but are included here to better explain the answer for tutorial purposes. They would have received no marks.

(i)   The debentures were issued for a non-trade purpose, therefore the debenture interest payable and associated costs of issue are loan relationship debits. They are not allowable trading deductions and must be added back in the adjustment to profits computation.

(ii) Interest on overdue tax is an allowable loan relationship debit for companies. It is not allowable for trade profits and therefore must be added back in the adjustment to profits computation.

(2) **Non-trading loan relationships**

	£
Bank interest receivable	22,108
Debenture interest to Kennedy plc	(12,900)
Costs of debenture issue	(3,200)
Interest on overdue tax	(268)
Non-trading loan relationship credit	5,740

(3) **Sale of Apollo Place – September 2013**

	£
Sale proceeds (September 2013)	814,300
Less: Cost (May 2000)	(420,085)
Enhancement expenditure (June 2001)	(34,100)
Legal fees for extension (June 2001)	(2,980)
	357,135

Indexation allowance from May 2000 to September 2013

$$\frac{253.1 - 170.7}{170.7} = 0.483 \times £420,085 \qquad (202,901)$$

Indexation allowance from June 2001 to September 2013

$$\frac{253.1 - 174.4}{174.4} = 0.451 \times (£34,100 + £2,980) \qquad (16,723)$$

Chargeable gain	137,511

(4) **Corporation tax rates – y/e 30 November 2013**

	£
Taxable total profits	293,737
FII (£8,900 × 100/90)	9,889
Augmented profits	303,626

	FY2012/FY2013 £
Upper limit (£1,500,000 ÷ 2)	750,000
Lower limit (£300,000 ÷ 2)	150,000

Marginal relief applies

(5) **Capital allowances – y/e 30 November 2013**

	FYA £	Main pool £	Special rate pool £	Allowances £
TWDV b/f		9,800		
Lift			277,600	
AIA ((£25,000 × 1/12) + (£250,000 × 11/12)) not restricted as post 1 January 2013 expenditure			(231,250)	231,250
Research equipment	11,500			
FYA @ 100%	(11,500)			11,500
Car			26,750	
		9,800	73,100	
WDA @ 18%		(1,764)		1,764
WDA @ 8%			(5,848)	5,848
TWDV c/f	–	8,036	67,252	
Total allowances				250,362

(6) **DTR**

	£
Lower of:	
Overseas tax on property income (18% × £29,512)	5,312
UK tax on the overseas property income	
64,941/293,737 = 22.109% × £29,512	6,525

(b) **Treatment of staff costs**

The pension contributions paid into the group registered occupational pension scheme in the period are allowable deductions for trade purposes.

The directors' remuneration is allowable for trade purposes provided it is paid within nine months of the end of the chargeable accounting period.

Treatment of research and development costs

Qualifying research and development (R&D) expenditure is allowable against trading profits, and as a small company 225% of the expenditure incurred is allowable.

To qualify for the relief the expenditure must be revenue, not capital, and must relate to the company's trade.

The research equipment is capital expenditure and not eligible for R&D relief (but see below). However, the payments to Gemini Ltd are allowable as they are made to a connected subcontractor in respect of qualifying R&D and the staff costs are allowable.

R&D expenditure of £46,740 has been charged in the accounts.

The cost of the research equipment (£11,500) must be added back in the adjustments to profit computation, and a 100% FYA will be available for this expenditure.

An additional deduction of £44,050 [(£46,740 – £11,500) × 125%] is therefore available.

Marking guide

			Marks
(a)		CT computation	
		Overseas property income	½
		Qualifying charitable donation	½
		CT	1
		Marginal relief	2
		DTR	½
	Working 1	– Add backs	3
		Deductions	2½
		Capital allowances	½
	Working 2	– Each item ½ mark	2
	Working 3	– Unindexed gain	1½
		Indexation (2 × ½)	1
	Working 4	– Augmented profits	½
		Limits	1
	Working 5	– Car (special rate pool)	½
		FYA	½
		Lift (special rate pool) and AIA	1
		WDA	2
	Working 6	– Overseas tax	1
		UK tax on overseas income	1
		Lower of	½
			23

(b)	Staff costs	
	Pension contributions	½
	Directors' remuneration	½
	R&D costs	
	225%	½
	Capital allowances	½
	Amount of deduction	1
		3
		26

54 Argus Ltd group (S09)

(a) Corporation tax computations

	Y/e 31 December 2013 £	3 m/e 31 March 2014 £
Trading income before capital allowances (W1) (12/15:3/15)	274,800	68,700
Less: capital allowances (W2)	(4,852)	(12,658)
Trading income	269,948	56,042
Non-trading loan relationship (W3)	1,920	100
Chargeable gains (W4)	Nil	80,700
Qualifying charitable donation	(700)	Nil
Taxable total profits	271,168	136,842

Corporation tax liability (W5)

FY2012: £271,168 × 24% × 3/12	16,270	
FY2013: £271,168 × 23% × 9/12	46,776	
Less: marginal relief		
FY2012: 1/100 × (£750,000 – £271,168) × 3/12	(1,197)	
FY2013: 3/400 × (£750,000 – £271,168) × 9/12	(2,693)	
£136,842 × 23%		31,474
	59,156	31,474

WORKINGS

(1)	**Trading income**	£
	Trading income before capital allowances	350,000
	Less: Patent royalties payable	(3,600)
	Interest payable	(2,900)
	Trading income before capital allowances	343,500

(2)	**Capital allowances**	Main pool £	Allowances £
	Year ended 31 December 2013		
	WDV b/f	29,055	
	Disposal	(2,100)	
		26,955	
	Less: WDA @ 18%	(4,852)	4,852
	WDV c/f	22,103	
	3 months ended 31 March 2014		
	Additions	11,663	
	Less: AIA (max is £62,500, ie £250,000 × 3/12)	(11,663)	11,663
		22,103	
	WDA @ 18% × 3/12	(995)	995
		21,108	
			12,658

(3)	Non-trading loan relationships	Y/e 31 December 2013	3 m/e 31 March 2014
		£	£
	Interest receivable (£2,400 × 12/15:3/15)	1,920	480
	Interest payable	–	(380)
	Non-trading loan relationships income	1,920	100

(4)	Chargeable gains		£
	Proceeds		150,830
	Less: cost		(55,000)
			95,830
	Less: indexation allowance 0.226 × £55,000		(12,430)
	Gain		83,400
	Less capital loss b/f		(2,700)
	Chargeable gain		80,700

(5)	Corporation tax limits	Y/e 31 December 2013	3 m/e 31 March 2014
	No of associates	2	3
	Upper limit	£750,000	£125,000
	Lower limit	£150,000	£25,000

(b) Bank loan

The interest payable is deductible as a trading expense.

Issue of shares

There are no corporation tax consequences for Unicorn Ltd of the share issue. Any costs in connection with the issue are not deductible for corporation tax purposes.

Sale of Ark Ltd shares

The shares will qualify under the substantial shareholding exemption and therefore no chargeable gain will arise.

This is because the shareholding was at least 10% and would have been held for a continuous period of twelve months in the two years prior to sale.

Marking guide

		Marks
(a)	Trading income (W1)	1
	Capital allowances (W2)	
	y/e 31.12.13	2
	3 m/e 31.3.14	2
	Non-trading loan relationships (W3)	2
	Chargeable gains (W4)	
	Gains	1
	Capital loss b/f	1
	Limits (W5)	2
	Split of trading income pre CAs	1
	Chargeable gain in 3 m/e 31.3.14	½
	Qualifying charitable donation in y/e 31.12.13	1
	Corporation tax liability:	
	y/e 31.12.13	3
	3 m/e 31.3.14	½
		17
(b)	Bank loan	1
	Issue of shares	1
	Sale of Ark Ltd shares	2
		4
		21

55   Zita Ltd (D10)

(a) **Corporation tax computation: year ended 31 December 2013**

	£
Adjusted trading profit (W1)	1,185,575
Less: Capital allowances – R&D Capex (£125,000 + £25,000)	(150,000)
Less: Capital allowances	(205,831)
Trading Profits	829,744
Rental income (W2)	24,000
Non-trading loan relationships (W3)	7,983
Taxable total profits	861,727
FII (£1,440,000 × 100/90)	1,600,000
Augmented profits	2,461,727

Corporation tax payable:

	£
FY2012: £861,727 × 24% × 3/12	51,704
FY2013: £861,727 × 23% × 9/12	148,648
	200,352

WORKINGS

(1) **Adjusted profits**

		£
Trading profit		3,288,558
Less:		
	Additional R&D revenue expenditure (£450,000 × 30%)	(135,000)
	Rental income	(108,000)
	Interest receivable (£52,150 + £3,333)	(55,483)
	Receipts on investment in Zuppa Ltd	(2,000,000)
Plus:		
	Loss on disposal of 5% loan stock	27,500
	Rented portion of security & utilities (£1.2m × 10%)	120,000
	Interest relating to rented office space (£200,000 × 10%)	20,000
	Accrued pension costs	28,000
		1,185,575

(2) **Rental income**

	£
Rent receivable	144,000
Less: cost of security & utilities	(120,000)
	24,000

(3) **Non-trading loan relationships**

	£
Interest receivable	55,483
Less: loss on disposal of 5% loan stock	(27,500)
Less: interest payable on rented out portion of office	(20,000)
	7,983

(4) **Gain on disposal of shares in Zuppa Ltd**

Exempt as SSE applies	£Nil

	Total input VAT £	Taxable £	Exempt £
Input VAT	386,975	355,242	31,733
Van (£7,596 × 1/6)	1,266	1,266	

Non-attributable input VAT

$$\text{Recoverable amount} = \frac{6,455,879}{(6,455,879 + 301,548)}$$

= 96% (round up)

Unattributable input VAT			
= £189,390 + £400 (ie fuel £2,400 × 1/6)	189,790		
Relating to taxable supplies = £189,790 × 96%		182,198	
Relating to exempt supplies = £189,790 × 4%			7,592
	578,031	538,706	39,325

The exempt input VAT is clearly not *de minimis* and therefore not recoverable

	£
Output VAT collected = £6,455,879 × 20%	1,291,176
Fuel scale charge	87
Less recoverable input VAT (taxable only)	(538,706)
Payable to HMRC	752,557

Marking guide

			Marks
(a)	Adjustment to profits (W1)		
	R&D	1	
	Rental income	½	
	Interest receivable	1	
	Receipts from investment in Zuppa Ltd	½	
	Loss on loan stock	½	
	Utilities	½	
	Interest relating to office space	½	
	Accrued pension costs	½	
	No other adjustments (patent royalties and overdraft interest)	1	
	CA's on R&D	1	
	CA's	½	
	Rental income (W2)	1	
	Non-trading loan relationships (W3)	2½	
	Chargeable gain (W4)	1	
	FII	1	
	CT payable	1	
			14
(b)	VAT on van	1	
	Recoverable amount calculation	1	
	Round up %	½	
	VAT on fuel and added on to unattributable VAT	1	
	Unattributable VAT – taxable supplies	½	
	Unattributable VAT – exempt supplies	½	
	De minimis	½	
	Output VAT	½	
	Fuel scale charge	½	
	Less recoverable VAT	½	
	Payable to HMRC	½	
			7
			21

ICAEW

56 Sylon Ltd (M11)

(a) Corporation tax computation: Year ended 31 December 2013

	£
Adjusted trading profit (W1)	1,325,657
Interest receivable (W3)	1,340
Property income (W4)	26,400
Chargeable gains (W5 and W6) £(56,680 + 5,396)	62,076
Taxable total profits	1,415,473

	£
Corporation tax payable	
FY2012: £1,415,473 × 24% × 3/12	84,928
FY2013: £1,415,473 × 23% × 9/12	244,169
	329,097

WORKINGS

(1) Adjusted trading profit

	£
Trading profit	1,603,300
Less: interest payable	
– interest on loan to purchase machinery	(4,160)
– interest on loan to purchase Biers House (80% × £12,800)	(10,240)
Less: capital allowances	
– plant and machinery (W2)	(263,243)
Adjusted trading profit	1,325,657

(2) Plant and machinery

	Main pool £	Special rate pool £	Allowances £
TWDV b/f	70,670	18,900	
Rewiring		162,900	
Machinery	91,000		
AIA (maximum £250,000, allocated to SRP first)	(87,100)	(162,900)	250,000
Disposal	(9,400)		
	65,170		
WDA @ 18%/8%	(11,731)	(1,512)	13,243
	53,439	17,388	
TWDV c/f			263,243

(3) Non-trading loan relationships

	£
Interest receivable	6,800
Interest on loan on Biers House (20% × £12,800)	(2,560)
Interest on loan to purchase Pegasus plc loan stock	(2,900)
Non-trading loan relationship credit	1,340

(4) Property income

	£
Biers House	20,400
Buck Mews premises 2 × £3,000	6,000
Total	26,400

(5) Gain on Brook Avenue

	£
Proceeds	150,600
Less: cost	(80,000)
	70,600
Less: indexation	

$$\frac{252.6 - 215.1}{215.1} = 0.174 \times £80,000$$

	£
	(13,920)
	56,680

(6)   Gain on Pegasus plc shares

	£
Proceeds	29,089
Less: Cost (W7)	(19,575)
	9,514
Less: Indexation allowance (£23,693 – 19,575)	(4,118)
Gain	5,396

(7)   Pegasus plc shares

	No. of shares	Cost	Indexed cost
	£	£	£
Jan 2007: Purchase	1,000	22,500	22,500
Indexation to May 2009:			
$\dfrac{212.8 - 201.6}{201.6} \times £22,500$			1,250
May 2009: Rights issue @ £18	200	3,600	3,600
	1,200	26,100	27,350
Indexation to January 2013:			
$\dfrac{245.8 - 212.8}{212.8} \times £27,350$			4,241
			31,591
January 2013: Disposal (900/1,200) (to W6)	(900)	(19,575)	(23,693)
C/f	300	6,525	7,898

(b)   After tax cost:

	£
Staff entertaining	55,000
General expense allowance	20,000
Net cost of the laptop (£5,000 – 2,000)	3,000
	78,000
Less: tax relief £78,000 × 23%	(17,940)
	60,060
Add: disallowable costs	
Client entertaining	32,000
Food hampers	1,650
Total cost	93,710

ICAEW

(b)

Staff entertaining	1
Expense allowance	1
Net cost of laptop	1
Tax relief	1½
Client entertaining	1
Food hampers	1
Total cost	½
	$\frac{7}{22}$

57 Bryde Ltd (J11)

(a) **Corporation tax payable for year ended 31 December 2013**

	£
Trading profit (W1)	187,307
Property income	14,000
Chargeable gains	2,380
Non-trading loan relationships (W3)	400
Taxable total profits	204,087
FII (£34,000 × 100/90)	37,778
Augmented profits	241,865

Corporation tax liability	£
FY2012 and FY2013: £204,087 × 20%	40,817

WORKINGS

(1) *Adjustment of profits*

	£
Profit for the year	248,230
Add:	
Depreciation	13,100
Interest on the loan to purchase shares in Euclid plc	2,000
Legal fees re loan to purchase shares in Euclid plc	1,100
Less:	
Profit on the sale of the investment property	(4,970)
Rental income (£1,500 + £12,500)	(14,000)
UK dividends received (FII)	(34,000)
Bank interest receivable	(3,500)
	207,960
Less: capital allowances (W2)	(20,653)
Trading profit	187,307

(2) **Capital allowances**

	FYA £	Main pool £	Allowances £
WDV b/f		12,890	
Acquisitions – FYA			
Low emission car	15,000		
FYA @ 100%	(15,000)		15,000
Acquisitions – AIA			
Computer			
£4,000 × 100/120		3,333	
AIA		(3,333)	3,333
		12,890	
WDA @ 18%		(2,320)	2,320
WDV c/f	—	10,570	
Total allowances			20,653

(3) **Non-trading loan relationships**

	£
Bank interest receivable	3,500
Less: Interest payable on loan to fund the purchase of Euclid plc	(2,000)
Less: legal fees on the loan to fund the purchase of Euclid plc	(1,100)
Profit on non-trading loan relationships	400

(b) (i) **Loan**

The interest payable on the loan will be deductible as a debit on a non-trading loan relationship.

For the year ended 31 December 2014 a deduction of (£85,000 × 6% × 6/12) = £2,550 will be available against the interest income, estimated at £3,000.

There will be a profit on non-trading loan relationships of £450.

(ii) **Sale of shares on 1 July 2014**

A chargeable gain will arise in Bryde Ltd as follows:

	£	£
Proceeds		51,000
Less: cost		
(£15,300 × 9/30)	4,590	
indexation update		
$\dfrac{260.4 - 252.6}{252.6} \times £4,590$	142	
		(4,732)
Chargeable gain		46,268

No substantial shareholding exemption is available as the shares in Garfield Ltd have not been held for 12 months out of the previous 24 months.

Sale of the shares in September 2014

If sold in September 2014, the substantial shareholding exemption will apply such that the disposal will be exempt from tax.

Marking guide

		Marks
(a)	Trading profit	½
	Property income	½
	Chargeable gains	½
	NTLR	½
	FII	1
	CT liability	1
	Trading profits (W1)	
	Profit for the year	½
	Deductions (½ each)	2
	Additions (½ each)	1½
	CA's	½
	CAs (W2)	
	FYA on car	1
	Computer net of VAT	½
	AIA	½
	WDA	1
	NTLR (W3)	
	Bank interest	½
	Interest on loan to buy Euclid plc	½
	Legal fees re loan to buy Euclid plc	½
		13

(b)	(i)	NTLR debit	½	
		Calculation of interest	1	
		Offset against interest income	½	
				2
	(ii)	*Sale on 1 July 2014*		
		Proceeds	½	
		Cost	½	
		IA (no rounding)	½	
		Chargeable gain	½	
		No SSE	½	
		Sale in September 2014		
		SSE applies	1	
			3½	
		Max		3
				18

58 HEP Ltd group (D11)

(a) **Corporation tax computation: year ended 30 June 2014**

	£
Adjusted trading profit (W1)	371,697
Non-trading loan relationships (W2)	11,920
Rental income	40,400
Chargeable gains (W3)	20,800
Taxable total profits	444,817
Corporation tax payable:	
FY2013/FY2014: £444,817 × 23%	102,308

WORKINGS

(1) **Adjusted profits**

	£
Draft adjusted trading profit	478,900
Less:	
Bank overdraft interest	(240)
R&D revenue expenditure (£56,150 – £15,500) × 225%	(91,463)
FYA on laboratory equipment	(15,500)
	371,697

(2) **Non-trading loan relationships**

	£
Bank interest	12,800
Debenture interest	4,000
Less: interest on overdue corporation tax	(450)
Less: interest payable to purchase debentures	(2,800)
Less: interest payable to purchase a rental property	(1,630)
	11,920

(3) **Chargeable gains**

The sale of the shares in Crusha Ltd is exempt under the substantial shareholding exemption.

River Plaza:

	£
Proceeds	408,089
Less: Cost	(260,100)
	147,989
Less: indexation (258.1 – 173.3/173.3) = 0.489 × £260,100	(127,189)
Chargeable gain	20,800

(4) **Limits**

    4 associates

    Upper limit: £1,500,000/4 = £375,000

    Lower limit: £300,000/4 = £75,000

(b) If HEP Ltd is large in the year ended 30 June 2015 it will need to pay corporation tax in instalments.

Bringing forward capital expenditure will reduce profits (possibly below the upper limit so instalments are avoided), and that is a legal method of tax avoidance.

For corporation tax purposes the deduction for directors' bonuses can only be made if paid within 9 months of the end of the accounting period ie by 31 March 2016. The group finance director has stated that they will not be paid until May 2016. The submission of a return with incorrect bonuses deducted would be tax evasion, and may constitute money laundering.

Roberto should consider

- Whether his objectivity is compromised.

- There is an intimidation threat that he should evaluate, as the group finance director has suggested that his expense claims will be put through with no questions asked.

- There is a self-interest threat that he should evaluate, as he will benefit from agreeing to the group finance director's demands.

- Documenting the relevant facts, relevant parties and the ethical issues involved.

- Whether he should contact the ICAEW ethics helpline service.

- Whether confidentiality issues prevent him from contacting HMRC.

Marking guide

			Marks
(a)	Adjustment to profits (W1)		
	Trading profit	½	
	Bank interest	½	
	R&D	2	
	FYA	1	
	NTLR (W2) (½ each)	2½	
	Rental income	½	
	Gain on Crusha Ltd shares exempt	1	
	Gain on River Plaza (W3)		
	Proceeds	½	
	Cost	½	
	Indexation	1	
	CT payable	1	
	Limits (W4)	<u>1</u>	
			12
(b)	Instalments	½	
	Bringing forward CAPEX is legal	1	
	Bonus rule	½	
	Submission of incorrect return is tax evasion	1	
	Money laundering	½	
	Objectivity	½	
	Intimidation threat	1	
	Self-interest threat	1	
	Documentation	1	
	ICAEW ethics helpline	1	
	Confidentiality	<u>1</u>	
		9	
	Max		<u>8</u>
			<u><u>20</u></u>

59 Red Ltd (M12)

Capital allowances

Year ended 31 March 2014	Main pool £	Special rate pool £	SLA £	(a) £
TWDV b/f	888,150	431,500		
Additions				
SLA election for IT equipment			43,000	
Air conditioning		82,000		
Plant and machinery	175,000			
AIA	(168,000)	(82,000)		250,000
	895,150	431,500	43,000	
WDA @ 18%	(161,127)			168,867
WDA @ 8%		(34,520)	(7,740)	34,520
TWDV c/f	734,023	396,980	35,260	
Total capital allowances				453,387

SLA election

As the IT equipment will be sold within eight years for nil value it would be beneficial to make a SLA election. This means that on disposal it will receive a balancing allowance rather than receiving WDA in perpetuity (ie after it had actually been sold) if it were added to the main pool.

AIA

This is allocated against the special rate pool item first, since it will receive a WDA of only 8% otherwise. Then the remainder is set against main-pool items. If there was any remaining AIA it would be set against the SLA last as this will receive a balancing allowance on disposal in any event.

Marking guide

	Marks
Air conditioning in SRP	½
WDA @ 18%	½
WDA @ 8%	½
Total allowances	½
SLA	
SLA election as sold < 8 years	½
Balancing allowance	½
Allowances in perpetuity in main pool	½
AIA	
SRP first	½
Then main pool	½
Finally SLA	½
	5

60 Alpha Ltd (M12)

(a) (i) **Shares in X Ltd**

The gain on the shares in X Ltd is exempted from tax by the substantial shareholding exemption.

Property	£
Proceeds	150,000
Less cost	(195,000)
Allowable loss	(45,000)

(ii) **Disposal on 31 December 2014**

A gain on the disposal of a 6% shareholding from what was a substantial shareholding for at least 12 months in the past two years is exempted as a substantial shareholding.

A disposal on 31 December 2014 must have been substantial (>10%) for at least 12 months in the period from 1 January 2013 to 31 December 2014.

Up until the disposal on 1 January 2014 Alpha Ltd held a 13% holding, therefore a disposal on 31 December 2014 means that it qualifies under the 12 months in the past two years rule.

Disposal on 31 March 2015

A disposal on 31 March 2015 must have been substantial (>10%) for at least 12 months in the period from 1 April 2013 to 31 March 2015.

The disposal of 7% of the shares on 1 January 2014 means that this is not satisfied as the period from 1 April 2013 to 1 January 2014 is less than 12 months. Therefore a chargeable gain/allowable loss will arise when the shares are sold on 31 March 2015.

(b) (i) **Shares held in E Ltd**

	Purchased	Bonus Issue	Rights Issue	Total
1 January 1980 – 1982 pool	1,000	500	300	1,800
1 January 1990 – s.104 pool	2,000	-	400	2,400
	3,000	500	700	4,200

(ii)

Shares in the s.104 pool	2,400
Shares in the 1982 pool	1,600
	4,000

(iii)

S.104 pool	No.	Cost £	Indexed cost £
1 January 1990 – purchase	2,000	10,000	10,000
Indexed rise January 1990 to January 1995 [(146.0 – 119.5) / 119.5] × £10,000			2,218
Rights 1:5 @ £6	400	2,400	2,400
			14,618
Indexed rise January 1995 to February 2014 [(257.0 – 146.0) / 146.0] × £14,618			11,114
	2,400	12,400	25,732
Disposal	(2,400)	(12,400)	(25,732)
c/f	NIL	NIL	NIL

Gain on s.104 pool	£
Disposal proceeds 2,400/4,000 × £260,000	156,000
Less: indexed cost	(25,732)
Chargeable gain	130,268

1982 pool

	No.	Cost £	31.3.82 MV £	Rights £
January 1980	1,000	2,000	3,000	
January 1985 – Bonus issue	500			
January 1995 – Rights 1 for 5 @ £6	300			1,800
	1,800	2,000	3,000	1,800
February 2014	(1,600)	(1,778)	(2,667)	(1,600)
c/f	200	222	333	200

Gain on 1982 pool – use MV82 as clearly higher

	£
Disposal proceeds 1,600/4,000 × £260,000	104,000
Less: 31.3.82 MV	(2,667)
Rights	(1,600)
Unindexed gain	99,733
Less: indexation allowance on original shares	
$[(257.0 - 79.44) / 79.44] = 2.235 \times £2,667$	(5,961)
indexation allowance on rights shares	
$[(257.0 - 146.0) / 146.0] = 0.760 \times £1,600$	(1,216)
Gains	92,556

(c) **Taxable total profits for year ended 31 March 2014**

	£
Trading income (W1)	50,700
Non-trading loan relationships	42,000
Property income	5,800
Net gains (W2)	159,424
	257,924
Less qualifying donation	(2,100)
Taxable total profits	255,824
CT liability :	
£255,824 × 20%	51,165

WORKINGS

(1) **Trading income**

Trading profit	78,200
Additional 125% relief for R&D expenditure as a SME	(27,500)
	50,700

(2) **Net gains**

Shares in X Ltd	–
Shares in E Ltd (£130,268 + £92,556)	222,824
	222,824
Less current year capital loss	(45,000)
Less brought forward capital loss	(18,400)
Net gains	159,424

				Marks
(a)	(i)	Shares in X Ltd	1	
		Loss on property	1	
				2
	(ii)	*Disposal on 31 December 2014*		
		Over 10%	1	
		1 Jan 2013 to 31 Dec 2014	1	
		Disposal qualifies	1	
		Disposal on 31 March 2015		
		Qualifying period needed	½	
		1 April 2013 to 1 January 2014 not satisfy	1	
			4½	
		Max		4
(b)	(i)	1982 pool	1	
		s.104 pool	½	
		Total	½	
				2
	(ii)	Shares in s.104 pool	½	
		Shares in 1982 pool	½	
				1
	(iii)	*s.104 pool*		
		Indexed rise to rights issue	½	
		Rights issue	½	
		Indexed rise to disposal	1	
		Disposal proceeds	½	
		Indexed cost	1	
		1982 pool		
		Disposal in pool	1½	
		Proceeds	½	
		Cost	½	
		Indexation on original shares	½	
		Indexation on rights issue	½	
				7
(c)		Non trading loan relationships	½	
		Property income	½	
		Qualifying donation	½	
		CT liability	1	
		Trading income (W1)		
		R&D deduction	1	
		Net gains (W2)		
		Shares in E Ltd	½	
		Less current year loss	½	
		Less b/f capital loss	½	
				5
				21

61 Coe Ltd group (J12)

(a) **Corporation tax computation: year ended 31 March 2014**

	£
Tax adjusted trading profit (W1)	43,304
Property income (£78,000 × 1/12)	6,500
Chargeable gains (W3)	43,597
Taxable total profits	93,401
Corporation tax liability (W4):	
£93,401 × 20%	18,680

WORKINGS

Adjusted profit

(1) Adjusted trading profit — 179,674

Less:

Lease costs for car	(8,100)
Gift of samples	(120)
Patent royalties	(20,000)
Deduction for lease premium (W2)	(750)
	150,704
Less: capital allowances (15,000 + 92,400)	(107,400)
	43,304

(2) **Lease premium**
Amount of premium taxed as rent on the landlord:

$$£5,000 \times \frac{50-5}{50} \qquad 4,500$$

Deduction for Ovett Ltd: £4,500/6 — 750

(3) **Gain on building**

	£
Proceeds	525,900
Less: Cost	(307,000)
	218,900
Less: Indexation allowance	(162,403)

$$\frac{250.0-163.5}{163.5} = 0.529 \times £307,000$$

Gain	56,497
Less capital loss b/f	(12,900)
Chargeable gain	43,597

(4) **Corporation tax limits**
£300,000/3 = £100,000
£1.5m/3 = £500,000

(b) **Corporation tax computation: year ended 31 March 2014**

	£	£
Adjusted trading profits per the question		400,190
Add:		
Interest on a loan to purchase P&M	–	
Interest on a loan to purchase shares	790	
		790
Less:		
Research and development (£40,000 × 225%)	90,000	
Bank interest receivable	2,845	
		(92,845)
		308,135
Less: Capital allowances (W1)		(23,060)
Tax adjusted trading profit		285,075
Non-trade loan relationships (2,845 – 790)		2,055
Taxable total profits		287,130
Corporation tax liability:		
£287,130 × 23%		66,040
Less marginal relief		
3/400 × (£500,000 – £287,130)		(1,597)
		64,443

Intra-group dividend of £10,000 is not taxable

WORKINGS

(1) **Capital allowances**

	Main pool £	Allowances £
TWDV b/f	17,000	
Additions: Lorry	20,000	
Less: AIA	(20,000)	20,000
	17,000	
WDA @ 18%	(3,060)	3,060
TWDV c/f	13,940	
Total allowances		23,060

(c) The accountant does not currently work for Blake or his wife, nor for Coe Ltd. The accountant should consider whether their skills make them competent to provide the advice required as the advice needed here is very different from the corporation tax work carried out for Cram Ltd.

No work should be commenced without proper contact with Blake's wife, carrying out money laundering checks (including asking for ID) and a signed engagement letter. The engagement letter should make clear the scope of services, whether preparing the full tax return or just advising on disclosure of the royalty income.

There is a self-interest threat to the accountant's objectivity, since Blake is offering future work if the accountant assists on this occasion.

The accountant should feel under no pressure to accept the engagement, and it may well be best to refuse.

Marks

(a) Adjusted profit (W1)

Adjusted profit	½
Lease costs	1
Samples	1
Royalties	½
Lease premium	½
CA's	½
Lease premium (W2)	2
Gain (W3)	
Proceeds less cost	½
IA	1
Capital loss b/f	1
CT limits	1
Property income	1
CT liability	½

11

(b)

Adjusted trading profits	½
Interest on loan to buy P&M	1
Interest on loan to buy shares	1
R&D	1
Bank interest	1
CA's	½
Omit intra group dividend	1
CT liability	2
CA's (W1)	
Additions	1
AIA	1
WDA	1

11

(c)

Does not work	½
Competence	½
Contact client	½
Money laundering checks	1
Engagement letter	1½
Self-interest threat/ objectivity	1½
Conclusion	½

6

Max   5

27

62   Reaper Ltd (D12)

Corporation tax computation: year ended 31 March 2014

	£
Trading profit (W1)	517,098
Credit on non-trading loan relationships (W3)	10,200
Taxable total profits	527,298
Add: FII £1,100 × 100/90	1,222
Augmented profits	528,520

Corporation tax:	
£527,298 × 23%	121,279
Less: marginal relief	
3/400 × (750,000 – 528,520) × 527,298/528,520	(1,657)
Corporation tax liability	119,622

Corporation tax limits:
£1.5m/2 = £750,000
£300,000/2 = £150,000

WORKINGS

(1) **Adjusted trading profit**

	£
Profit for the year	640,070
Add:	
Depreciation	3,600
Loss on disposal of plant and machinery	5,900
Legal costs relating to acquisition of the lease	380
No adjustment for other legal fees	-
No adjustment for patent royalties	-
No adjustment for amortisation of goodwill	-
Abortive costs of trying to raise loan finance	600
Interest payable on loan to purchase shares in Butcher Ltd	4,900
Less:	
Lease cost of the van £8,000 × 6/12	(4,000)
Class 1A NI on van	
£(3,000+564) × 13.8% × 6/12	(246)
Bank interest	(15,700)
Dividends	(30,600)
Capital allowances (W2)	(87,806)
Trading profit	517,098

(2) **Capital allowances**

	Main pool £	Special rate pool £	Total £
TWDV b/f	73,100	13,970	
Additions:			
Plant and machinery = £60,000 × 5/6	50,000		
Thermal insulation = £23,100 × 20/21		22,000	
AIA	(50,000)	(22,000)	72,000
Car		28,500	
Disposals £5,000 × 5/6	(4,167)		
	68,933	42,470	
WDA@ 18%	(12,408)		12,408
WDA@ 8%		(3,398)	3,398
TWDV c/f	56,525	39,072	
			87,806

(3) **Non-trading loan relationships**

	£
Bank interest receivable	15,700
Less:	
Interest on loan to purchase shares in Butcher Ltd	(4,900)
Abortive costs of raising loan finance	(600)
	10,200

Marks

Adjusted profit (W1)	
Profit for year	½
Depreciation	½
Loss on disposal	½
Legal costs re lease	1
No adjustment – legal fees, royalties, amortisation	1
Abortive costs	1
Interest on loan – Butcher Ltd	½
Lease costs	1
Class 1A on van	2½
Bank interest	½
Dividends	½
CA's	½
Capital allowances (W2)	
TWDV b/f	½
Plant	1
Thermal insulation	1½
AIA	1
Car	1
Disposal	1
WDA's	1
NTLR (W3)	
Bank interest receivable	½
Interest on loan – Butcher Ltd	½
Abortive costs	½
NTLR	½
FII	1
CT limits	½
CT liability	<u>1½</u>
	<u><u>22</u></u>

63 Rex Wood (J12)

(a) (i) **Capital gains tax on sale of building**

Gain on the building

	£
Proceeds	394,000
Less: Cost	(161,000)
Total taxable gain	233,000
CGT liability	
£233,000 × 28%	65,240

(ii) **VAT treatment of sale**

Because Rex opted to tax the building, VAT will be payable on the building at 20%.

As there is no provision in the sale and purchase agreement for VAT, the purchase price of £394,000 will be deemed to be VAT inclusive.

Rex will then have to account for VAT of £394,000 × 20/120 = £65,667.

(b) **VAT payable for quarter ended 31 May 2014**

	£
Output tax:	
UK customers: £25,900 × 20%	5,180
VAT-registered EU customers	nil
This is a zero-rated supply	
Non-VAT registered EU customers: £3,670 × 20%	734
This is a standard-rated supply	
Sale of machinery: £2,000 × 20%	400
	6,314
Input tax:	
Expenses related to the UK business: £870 × 1/6	(145)
Expenses related to the other EU business: £2,900 × 1/6	(483)
Purchase of car: Irrecoverable VAT	nil
Purchase of computer: £890 × 1/6 × 70%	(104)
Purchase of plant: £3,910 × 1/6	(652)
VAT payable to HMRC	4,930

(c) This would be tax evasion, not avoidance, and illegal.

Deliberately false information would be supplied to HMRC.

At best, if discovered, HMRC would seek the extra tax with interest. There may also be a penalty for error. Possible penalties would be affected by Esther's behaviour in terms of disclosure and cooperation with HMRC.

Serious cases of fraud are the subject of criminal prosecution, resulting in fines and/or imprisonment.

This would constitute money laundering at the point too little income tax was paid.

				Marks
(a)	(i)	Gain on building	1	
		CGT @ 28%	1	
				2
	(ii)	VAT on building	1½	
		Purchase price VAT inclusive	1	
		VAT to pay to HMRC	½	
				3
(b)		*Output tax*		
		UK customers	½	
		VAT – registered EU customers	1½	
		Non VAT – registered EU customers	1½	
		Machinery	½	
		Input tax		
		Expenses related to UK business	1	
		Expenses related to other EU business	1	
		Car	1	
		Computer	1	
		Plant	½	
		VAT payable	½	
				9
(c)		Tax evasion and illegal	1½	
		False information	1	
		Extra tax and interest	1	
		Penalties affected by disclosure	1	
		Prosecution, fines, imprisonment	1½	
		Money laundering	1	
			7	
		Max		6
				20

64 Apollo Ltd (M11)

	£
Output tax:	
UK sales: £48,300 × 20/120	8,050
VAT-registered customers in EU: zero-rated	nil
Non VAT-registered customers in EU: £8,400 × 20/120	1,400
Lease premium: £6,000 × 20%	1,200
Rent: £1,800 × 20%	360
	11,010
Input tax:	
Costs: £13,700 × 20%	(2,740)
VAT payable	8,270

Marks

Output VAT	
UK sales	1
EU VAT-registered	1
EU non VAT-registered	1
Lease premium	1
Rent	1
Input VAT	
Costs	½
VAT payable	½
	6

65 Artifex Ltd

(a) Artifex Ltd paid VAT of £70,000 (£420,000 × 20/120) in January 2011.

Artifex Ltd will initially recover £42,000 (60% × £70,000) in the first interval to March 2011.

In the interval to March 2012 additional input tax can be claimed as taxable usage has increased:

(£70,000/10) × (75% − 60%) = £1,050

In the interval to March 2013 input tax is payable as taxable usage has decreased:

(£70,000/10) × (40% − 60%) = £1,400 repayable

In the interval to March 2014 the building is sold. There is the usual annual adjustment. As taxable usage had remained at 40% this will be £1,400 repayable to HMRC (as in the previous year).

There is also an adjustment on disposal. This is calculated based on 100% taxable use for any remaining intervals of the adjustment period as it was a taxable sale. As this is a building the adjustment period is ten intervals and six intervals remain to be adjusted for:

(£70,000/10) × (100% − 60%) × 6 intervals = £16,800 recoverable.

(b) If a supply cannot be split into two components, there is a composite supply to which only one rate of VAT must be applied. The rate used will depend on the nature of the supply involved as a whole.

If there is a composite supply one element is likely to be merely incidental to the main element.

Air travel, is a composite supply as the two parts of the supply (the flight and the meals) would not be the subject of separate negotiation and choice. The in-flight meals are incidental to the supply as a whole. The supply will be zero rated as a supply of air travel.

Marks

(a) *Building*

VAT on purchase	1
Adjustments in y/e 31 March 2011	1
Adjustments in y/e 31 March 2012	1½
Adjustments in y/e 31 March 2013	1½
Adjustments in y/e 31 March 2014	1
Adjustment on sale	2
	8

(b)

Identification of composite supply	1
One rate applied to the whole supply	1
One part of the supply is incidental	1
Application to air travel	1
	4
	12

66 Crescent Ltd

(a) **Input tax recoverable**

	£
Related to standard rated supplies	1,832
Related to zero-rated supplies to Brooke SA	680
Related to supplies to non-registered customers in France	676
Non-attributable input tax =	
$£1,060 \times \dfrac{£31,500+£6,769+£3,555}{£31,500+£6,769+£3,555+£3,960} = 92\%$ (rounded up) $\times £1,060$	975
Other recoverable input tax (W2)	1,015
Total	5,178

WORKING

(1) **Simplified partial exemption tests**

Total monthly input tax is greater than £625 per month on average and therefore simplified Test one is not met. The value of exempt supplies is not more than 50% of the value of all supplies but both parts of the test have to be satisfied for Test one to be met.

The total input tax less input tax directly attributable to taxable supplies is £1,990 (£930 + £1,060). This is more than £625 per month on average. Therefore s.implified Test two is not met. Again, the value of exempt supplies is not more than 50% of the value of all supplies but both parts of the test have to be satisfied for Test two to be met.

A partial exemption calculation is therefore needed for the period.

(2) **Other recoverable input tax**

Total irrecoverable input tax [£930 + (£1,060 – £975)] = £1,015

which is not more than 50% of total input tax and not more than £625 per month on average.

Note: Supplies to Brooke SA are zero-rated as Brooke SA is VAT registered

(b) **Crescent Ltd**

   (i) **Taxable total profits**

	£
Trading income (W1)	550,705
Property income (W2)	43,175
Non-trading loan relationships (W3)	4,250
Chargeable gain (W4)	51,692
Taxable total profits	649,822

WORKINGS

    (1) **Trading income**

	£
Adjusted trading income before adjustments	563,590
Interest payable on loan for new factory (£201,000 × 6%)	(12,060)
Interest on Lyttelton Place (£110,000 × 6% × 1/12)	(550)
Repairs to Lyttelton Place (£3,300 × 1/12)	(275)
	550,705

    (2) **Property income**

	£
Rent receivable (11 × £4,200)	46,200
Less: Repairs and maintenance (£3,300 × 11/12)	(3,025)
	43,175

    (3) **Non trading loan relationships**

	£
Debenture interest receivable (£10,200 + £3,400)	13,600
Less: Interest payable	
Purchase of shares/debentures (£55,000 × 6%)	(3,300)
Purchase of Lyttelton Place (£110,000 × 6% × 11/12)	(6,050)
	4,250

    (4) **Gain on sale of Dingly House**

	£
Sales proceeds	156,000
Less: Cost	(73,250)
Unindexed gain	82,750
Indexation (March 2014 – April 2003)	

$$\frac{258.1 - 181.2}{181.2} = 0.424 \times £73,250 \qquad (31,058)$$

	£
Chargeable gain	51,692

  (ii) **Stamp duty and stamp duty land tax**

Stamp duty and stamp duty land tax are payable by the purchaser ie Crescent Ltd.

Stamp duty land tax (SDLT) is payable on the new factory. This will be a percentage on the purchase price. At £201,000, the SDLT payable will be at 1% or £2,010. This will be an allowable cost for capital gains purposes but not an allowable expense for corporation tax purposes.

Stamp duty will be payable on the acquisition of the shares, but not the debentures. Stamp duty on shares is payable at 0.5% of the value of the shares.

SDLT is also payable on the acquisition of leasehold property. However, the lease premium of £110,000 is chargeable at 0% as it is less than £150,000.

Marks

(a) Input tax recoverable

Standard-rated	½	
Zero rated	1	
Non-registered French customers	1	
Non-attributable working	2	
Consideration of simplified Test one	1	
Consideration of simplified Test two	1	
W2 De minimis test	1½	
Brookes SA treatment	1	
		9

(b) (i) Taxable total profits

TTP	½	
Working 1 – Trading income	4	
Working 2 – Property income	1½	
Working 3 – Non-trading loan relationships	3	
Working 4 – Gain	2	
		11

(ii) SDLT/SD

Factory	2	
Shares	1	
Lease	1	
		4
		24

67 Crista (D12)

Under the historic test, Crista is required to register if her taxable supplies in the previous 12 months exceed the registration threshold of £79,000. That threshold is exceeded at the end of July 2014.

The exempt supplies are not included in this test as they are not taxable.

Therefore Crista should have notified HMRC of the need to register by 30 August 2014 and VAT should have been charged from 1 September 2014.

VAT on standard rated supplies in September and on the sale of plant and machinery should have been charged, ie £(10,400 + 3,700) × 20% = £2,820

However, as these amounts have already been charged it is unlikely that the extra VAT can be reclaimed from the customers, in which case the amounts received will be deemed to be inclusive of VAT and £(10,400 + 3,700) × 1/6 = £2,350 will be payable from the revenue/proceeds already received.

As the failure to notify HMRC was not deliberate the maximum penalty is 30% x potential lost revenue ie £705 (30% × £2,350). However this could be reduced to nil as Crista gave unprompted disclosure within 12 months.

	Marks
Date historic test exceeded	1
Exclude exempt supplies	1
Date notify HMRC	½
Date registration effective	½
VAT due for September	1
Reclaim VAT from customers	1
Amounts deemed inclusive of VAT	1
Maximum penalty	1
Reduction for unprompted disclosure	1
	8

68 Bactrian Ltd (M13)

	£
VAT – quarter ended 28 February 2014	
Output tax	
UK supplies £39,500 × 20%	7,900
Supplies to non-registered EU customers £12,900 × 20%	2,580
Computer advice (reverse charge) £190 × 20%	38
Fuel scale charge £450 × 1/6	75
Input tax	
Materials £8,100 × 20%	(1,620)
Computer advice £190 × 20%	(38)
Car acquisition – irrecoverable as private use, add to CAs comp	–
Car £1,750 × 20%	(350)
VAT payable	8,585

	Marks
UK supplies	½
EU supplies	1
Computer advice – reverse charge	½
Fuel scale charge	1
Materials	½
Computer advice	½
Car acquisition	½
Car	½
VAT payable	½
	5½
	5

69 Dave Eaton

(a) UK resident

Dave does not meet the automatic overseas tests because he spent 16 days or more in the UK in 2013/14 (and was resident in at least one (in fact, all) of the three tax years prior to this) and he did not work full time overseas. He does meet one of the automatic UK tests, as he spent at least 183 days of the tax year in the UK and so he was UK resident.

(b) 2013/14 income tax and CGT liability

	£
Income tax liability (W1)	27,366
Capital gains tax liability (W2)	70,700
Remittance basis charge (resident for at least 12 out of previous 14 tax years)	50,000
Total liability	148,066

WORKINGS

(1) Income tax liability

	Non savings £	Savings £	Dividend £	Total £
Employment income (W3)	79,695			79,695
Bank interest: £3,000 × 100/80		3,750		3,750
UK dividends: £1,080 × 100/90			1,200	1,200
Total income	79,695	3,750	1,200	84,645
Less: personal allowance – lost as claiming remittance basis	(Nil)			(Nil)
Taxable income	79,695	3,750	1,200	84,645
Non savings income	£32,010	@ 20%		6,402
	£47,685	@ 40%		19,074
Savings income	£3,750	@ 40%		1,500
Dividend income	£1,200	@ 32.5%		390
Income tax liability				27,366

(2) CGT liability

	£
Flat (W4)	Nil
Rifle – exempt wasting chattel	Nil
Killian plc shares (W6)	52,500
Land in Whereatania (W8)	200,000
Total gains	252,500
Less: annual exempt amount – lost as claiming remittance basis	(Nil)
	252,500
Tax @ 28%	70,700

(3) Employment income

	£	
Salary:		
UK: 9 × £6,250	56,250	
Overseas: 3 × £7,750	23,250	
Total salary		79,500
Accommodation – exempt		–
Dave's flights – both exempt		–
Karen's flights – 2 exempt		195
Employer pension contributions – exempt		–
Total employment income		79,695

(4) **Flat**

	£
Proceeds	382,000
Less: cost	(225,000)
Gain before reliefs	157,000
Less: PPR relief (W5)	
132/152 × £157,000	(136,342)
	20,658

Less: letting relief:

Lower of
(i)   PPR relief
(ii) Gain in let period: 20/152 × £157,000
(iii) £40,000

	£
	(20,658)
Gain	Nil

(5) **PPR relief**

	Reason	Months	Absent	Actual/deemed occupation
1 July 2001 – 31 August 2001	Concession	2		2
1 September 2001 – 31 August 2002	Occupied	12		12
1 September 2002 – 31 August 2005	3 years for any reason	36		36
1 September 2005 – 30 April 2007	Let	20	20	
1 May 2007 – 28 February 2011	Occupied	46		46
1 March 2011 – 28 February 2014	Last 36 months	36		36
		152	20	132

(6) **Killian plc shares**

	£
Proceeds: £16.50 × 5,000	82,500
Less: cost (W7)	(30,000)
Gain	52,500

(7) **Share pool**

	No of shares	Cost £
Purchase 11/04	6,000	18,000
Rights issue 9/09: 2:1 @ £7.50	12,000	90,000
Total	18,000	108,000
Disposal 10/13	(5,000)	(30,000)
C/f	13,000	78,000

(8) **Whereatanian land**

	£
Proceeds	625,000
Less: part disposal cost	
$\dfrac{625,000}{625,000 + 1,050,000} \times £207,800$	(77,537)
Gain	547,463
Taxable on the remittance basis	200,000

Note: As the gain exceeds the amount remitted during the year, only the amount actually remitted is taxable.

ICAEW

Marks

(a)

Automatic overseas tests	1½	
Automatic UK tests and conclusion	1½	
		3

(b)

Employment income		
Salary	1	
Accommodation – exempt	½	
Dave's flights – exempt	½	
Karen's flights – 2 exempt	1	
Employer pension contributions – exempt	½	
IT liability		
Bank interest grossed up	1	
Dividends grossed up	1	
No PA as remittance basis claimed	½	
Tax liability	2	
CGT liability		
Gain on disposal of flat	1	
PPR relief	3	
Letting relief	1½	
Rifle – exempt wasting chattel	1	
Gain on Killian plc shares	1	
Share matching	1	
Rights issue	1	
Gain on disposal of Whereatanian land – part disposal	2	
Only remittance basis gain chargeable	1	
No AEA as remittance basis claimed	½	
		21
		24

70 Amanda (S09)

(a) (i) **Educational course options**

		Income tax	National insurance
	Option One	No IT payable (tutorial note: the marginal cost of the benefit is nil)	No NI for Amanda
	Option Two	IT payable on the beneficial loan £5,500 × 4% × 40% = £88	No NI for Amanda
	Option Three	IT on £3,000 × 40% = £1,200	Class 1 NI payable £3,000 × 2% = £60

(ii) *Employment income 2013/14*

	£
Salary	68,000
Computer	nil
Medical insurance	420
Childcare payments (£80 – 28) × 52 weeks (Note)	2,704
Education choice (option 1)	nil
Cycle allowance	200
Car benefit: £(15,000 – 500) × [11% + $\frac{145 - 95}{5}$]	3,045
	74,369
Less: Amanda's occupational pension contributions (£68,000 × 5%)	(3,400)
Total employment income	70,969

Employer pension contributions are an exempt benefit.

> **Tutorial note:**
>
> As Amanda has basic earnings at the higher rate level and has joined the childcare scheme on or after 6 April 2011, she will only receive the first £28 per week of employer-supported childcare tax free.

(b) **Property income**

	£
Rent – old tenants (£1,200 × 7)	8,400
Rent – new tenants (£10,000 × 4/12)	3,333
Lease premium: income element $\frac{50-(5-1)}{50} \times £2,100$	1,932
Less: repairs	(200)
	13,465
Less: property losses b/f	(1,100)
Net property income	12,365

(c) Amanda is subject to:

- Self-interest threats
- Familiarity threats
- Intimidation threats

The business interests and/or relationships between Amanda and Kenneth may give rise to a conflict of interest.

There is unlikely to be an engagement letter between Amanda and Kenneth, as she undertook the work for free.

Amanda should tell Kenneth in writing that:

- He should not be claiming expenses that he has not incurred
- He will be exposed to interest and penalties

If Kenneth does not agree to amend his return, Amanda should consider

- Her position as she may be committing a money laundering offence, even if she has in no way facilitated the evasion

- Reporting the money laundering offence to SOCA

- Ceasing to act for Kenneth

(d) **IHT on Amanda's estate**

	£	£
Residence		644,070
17 Appian Road		280,500
Shares in Windsor Ltd		33,930
Chattels and cash		40,710
		999,210
Less: liabilities		(11,100)
Chargeable estate		988,110
Less: Amanda's nil rate band	325,000	
Cyd's unused nil rate band (100% × £325,000)	325,000	
		(650,000)
		338,110
IHT payable: £338,110 × 40%		£135,244

				Marks
(a)	(i)	Option 1	1½	
		Option 2	1½	
		Option 3	1	
				4
	(ii)	Salary	½	
		Computer	½	
		Medical insurance	½	
		Childcare	1½	
		Education option	1	
		Cycle allowance	1	
		Car benefit	1½	
		Pension contributions	1½	
				8
(b)		Rent	2	
		Lease premium	1	
		Repairs	½	
		Losses b/f	½	
				4
(c)		Threats	1½	
		Conflict of interest	1	
		Lack of engagement letter	1	
		Advise Kenneth	1	
		Action if Kenneth does not amend returns	1	
		Money laundering	1½	
			7	
		Max		6
(d)		Chargeable estate	2½	
		NRB	2	
		IHT	½	
				5
				27

71 Wentworth Ltd (M10)

(a) (i) *Corporation tax payable for year ended 31 December 2013*

	£
Draft adjusted trading profit	346,700
Add: Capital R&D costs – computer hardware	5,800
Less: Additional relief for R&D £(31,000 + 1,900) × 125%	(41,125)
Less: Capital allowances (W1)	(57,798)
Trading profits	253,577
Non-trading loan relationships	1,230
Chargeable gains (W2)	52,970
	307,777
Less: qualifying charitable donation	(13,570)
Taxable total profits	294,207
Add: FII £4,860 × 100/90	5,400
Augmented profits	299,607

Corporation tax liability:	£
FY2012: £294,207 × 24% × 3/12	17,652
FY2013: £294,207 × 23% × 9/12	50,751
Less: marginal relief	
FY2012: 1/100 × (£375,000 – 299,607) × 294,207/299,607 × 3/12	(185)
FY2013: 3/400 × (£375,000 – 299,607) × 294,207/299,607 × 9/12	(416)
Corporation tax liability	67,802

WORKINGS

(1) Capital allowances

	FYA £	Main Pool £	Special rate pool £	MD's car £	Total £
TWDV b/f		26,900		23,000	
Additions:					
Furniture		35,900			
Computer equipment		8,100			
AIA		(44,000)			44,000
Computer h/w - R&D	5,800				
FYA @ 100%	(5,800)				5,800
Car			13,000		
Disposals					
Plant and machinery		(2,000)			
Car		(2,910)			
		21,990	13,000	23,000	
WDA @ 18%		(3,958)			3,958
WDA @ 8%			(1,040)		1,040
WDA max £3,000				(3,000)	3,000
TWDV c/f	–	18,032	11,960	20,000	
Total allowances					57,798

(2) Chargeable gains

17 Harville Road

	£
Proceeds (May 2013)	612,880
Less : Cost (Jun 2003)	(390,000)
Less: Indexation allowance to May 2013	(147,810)

$$£390,000 \times \frac{250.0 - 181.3}{181.3} = 0.379$$

	£
Gain	75,070
Less capital losses brought forward	(22,100)
Chargeable gain	52,970

Shares in Benwick Ltd

The gain on the sale of the shares in Benwick Ltd is exempt under the substantial shareholding exemption as the following conditions are met:

- Sold from at least a 10% holding
- Owned for 12 months out of last 24 months
- Unquoted trading company

(3) Non-trading loan relationships

	£
Debenture interest receivable	8,000
Loss on the sale of debentures	(5,570)
Interest on the loan to buy debentures	(1,200)
Non-trading loan relationships	1,230

(4) Corporation tax

Corporation tax limits:
£300,000/4 = £75,000
£1,500,000/4 = £375,000

ICAEW

(a) (ii) **Stamp taxes implications**

17 Harville Road
The purchaser of the 17 Harville Road property would have been subject to stamp duty land tax at 4%.
£612,880 × 4% = £24,515

Lyme Court
Russell Ltd will have been subject to stamp duty land tax on the purchase of Lyme Court. This would have been at 3%.
£327,868 × 3% = £9,836

Shares in Benwick Ltd
If the transfer of the shares were by a stock transfer form, the purchaser of the shares in Benwick Ltd would have been subject to 0.5% stamp duty.
£17,400 × 0.5% = £87
The stamp duty is rounded up to the nearest multiple of £5 = <u>£90</u>

If the transfer was electronic, the purchase would have been subject to 0.5% stamp duty reserve tax ie £87 (no rounding).

(b) **VAT issues**

EU supplies

The supply of goods to VAT registered EU customers will be zero rated for VAT purposes provided the customer's VAT number is quoted on the invoice and the supplier holds evidence that the goods were delivered to another member state.

The supply of goods to non-VAT registered EU customers will be standard rated for VAT purposes.

Purchases

- Newspapers – zero rated
- Stamps - exempt
- Wages – no VAT as outside the scope
- Insurance premium – exempt
- Stationery – standard rated
- Books – zero rated

Marks

(a) (i) Draft adjusted trading profit ½
Computer hardware 1
R&D 1½
CAs ½
Chargeable gains ½
NTLR ½
Qualifying charitable donation ½
FII 1
CT liability 2
CAs (W1)
– TWDV b/f ½
– Additions and AIA 1
– R&D and FYA 1
– Car and WDA 1
– Disposals ½
– WDA 2
Chargeable gains (W2)
– Gain 2½
– Capital losses b/f 1
– Benwick Ltd shares 2½
Non-trading loan relationships (W3) 2
CT limits (W4) 1
_____
23

(ii) 17 Harville Road 1½
Lyme Court 1½
Shares in Benwick Ltd 3
___
6
Max 5

(b) VAT
EU supplies 2
Purchases (each item ½ mark) 3
___
33
===

72 Alec Ealing (M10)

(a) Adjusted trading profit

	£
Adjusted trading profit	117,000
Less: extra deductions	
Salary (£450 × 3)	(1,350)
Allowable lease payments (£635 × 3 × 85%)	(1,619)
Class 1 NIC – employer's contributions (W1)	–
Class 1A NIC (W2)	(152)
Tax adjusted trading profit	113,879

WORKINGS

(1) There will be no secondary NI contributions as the monthly salary to Alec does not exceed the secondary earnings threshold.

(2) Car benefit: $£19,200 \times [11\% + \dfrac{155 - 95}{5}] \times 3/12 = 1,104$

Class 1A NIC: £1,104 × 13.8% = £152

Note: The secondary earnings threshold does not apply for the purposes of Class 1A NIC. In other words, the fact that Alec's salary is below £7,696 has no effect on the amount of Class 1A NIC due.

(b) **Assessable property income**

	£
Rental income	27,000
Less:	
Allowable costs	(3,490)
Rent payable	(1,200)
Deduction for part of the premium paid (W)	(4,493)
Capital allowances:	
£3,100 × 100% (AIA)	(3,100)
Property income	14,717

WORKING

Lease premium
Income element of the lease premium paid to the landlord:

$$£216,000 \times \frac{50 - 24}{50} = £112,320$$

Trading deduction for Alec against the rental income:
£112,320/25 = £4,493 pa

Note: this is a furnished holiday letting

(c) **Income tax computation 2013/14**

	Non savings £	Savings £	Dividends £
Salary (part (a))	1,350		
Car benefit (part (a))	1,104		
Property income (part (b))	14,717		
Bank interest (£240 × 100/80)		300	
Dividends (£36,000 × 100/90)			40,000
	17,171	300	40,000
Less: personal allowance	(9,440)	-	-
Taxable income	7,731	300	40,000

Income tax on:	£
£7,731 × 20%	1,546
£ 300 × 20%	60
£24,729 × 10%	2,473
£32,760 (W1)	
£15,271 × 32.5%	4,963
Income tax liability	9,042

WORKING

(1) Basic rate band	32,010
Add: Gift Aid extension (£50 × 12 × 100/80)	750
Revised basic rate band	32,760

(d) **VAT payable for the three months to 31 March 2014**

	£
Output tax: £62,000 × 20%	12,400
Input tax:	
UK customers: £33,920 × 20%	(6,784)
Relating to Contract Two: £7,920 × 20%	(1,584)
Additional recovery of input tax (W)	(1,905)
VAT payable	2,127

WORKING

Partial exemption calculation
Neither simplified test is met and therefore the full partial exemption calculation is required.

Recoverable input tax: $\dfrac{£(62,000+15,000)}{£(62,000+15,000+26,000)} = 75\% \times £12,700 \times 20\%$ 1,905

Note: percentage rounded as non-attributable input tax less than £400,000 per month

Non-recoverable non-attributable input tax: £(12,700 × 20%) − £1,905	635
Input tax relating to exempt supplies: £11,700 × 20%	2,340
Total non-recoverable input tax	2,975

De minimis limit:
The non-recoverable input tax is > £625 per month on average and therefore not recoverable.

(e)

	£
Option One	
£20,000 × 5/6	16,667
Less: CT saving £16,667 × 20%	(3,333)
Cost	13,334
Option Two	
Salary	13,000
NI £(13,000 − 7,696) × 13.8%	732
	13,732
Less: CT saving £13,732 × 20%	(2,746)
Less: relief for capital allowances: £[(3,900 − £1,000] × 5/6 × 100% × 20%	(483)
Loss on plant and machinery £(3,900 − 1,000) × 5/6	2,417
	12,920

Marks

(a)	Salary	½	
	Lease deduction	1	
	Class 1	½	
	Class 1A	1	
	Car benefit	1	
			4
(b)	Rental income	½	
	Allowable costs	½	
	Rent payable	½	
	Premium	2	
	CAs	1½	
	FHL	1	
		6	
	Max		5
(c)	Salary and car benefit	½	
	Property income	½	
	Bank interest	1	
	Dividends	1	
	PA	1	
	Income tax liability	1	
	Extension of BRB	1	
			6
(d)	Output tax	½	
	Input tax	1½	
	Partial exemption (W)		
	– Simplified tests	1	
	– Recoverable input tax	1½	
	– Non recoverable input tax	1	
	De minimis limit	½	
		6	
	Max		5
(e)	Option 1	1	
	Option 2		
	Salary and NI	1½	
	CT saving	½	
	CA's	2	
	Loss on plant and machinery	1	
			6
			26

73   Rosa Gergiev (M10)

(a) (i)   **Trading income assessments**

		£
2012/13	1.6.12 – 5.4.13	
	£28,800 + 1/12 × £69,140	34,562
2013/14	Year ended 28.02.14	69,140
Overlap profits	1.3.13 – 5.4.13	
	1/12 × £69,140	5,762

(ii) **Capital gains tax payable**

	£
Gain on jewellery (W1)	12,000
Gain on shares (W2)	41,800
Total gains	53,800
Less: Annual exempt amount	(10,900)
	42,900
Capital gains tax @ 28% × £42,900	12,012

WORKINGS

(1) *Sale of jewellery in June 2013*

	£
Proceeds	15,000
Less: Probate value	(3,000)
Capital gain	12,000

Gain is the lower of £12,000 and 5/3 (£15,000 – 6,000) = £15,000 ie £12,000.

(2) *Sale of shares in July 2013*

	£
Proceeds	87,800
Less: Cost = MV at time of gift	(46,000)
Capital gain	41,800

(b) **Threats**

Self interest: Valerie is financially reliant on income from work for Rosa and other family members.

Familiarity: There is both a professional and a family relationship here.

Fundamental principles breached if Valerie prepares an incorrect return

Integrity: A chartered accountant should not prepare a return containing a false statement.

Objectivity: Valerie should not let family ties influence her judgement.

Professional behaviour: Part of professional behaviour expected of a chartered accountant is compliance with the law, and deliberately assisting tax evasion would be illegal.

Marking guide

				Marks
(a)	(i)	Trading income assessments		
		2012/13	1	
		2013/14	1	
		Overlap profits	1	
				3
	(ii)	AEA	1	
		CGT @ 28%	1	
		Gain on sale of jewellery (W1)	2	
		Gain on sale of shares (W2)	1	
				5
(b)		Threats		
		Self interest	1	
		Familiarity	1	
		Fundamental principles		
		Integrity	1	
		Objectivity	1	
		Professional behaviour	1	
				5
				13

74 Charlie Schott

(a) (i)

	Y/e 31 March 2014 £
Trading profit (W1)	nil
Non-trading loan relationships (W4)	500
Property income	17,900
Chargeable gains (W5)	-
Taxable total profits	18,400
Corporation tax liability £18,400 × 20% (W6)	3,680

WORKINGS

(1) Adjustment of profits

	£
Loss for the year	(306,466)
Add:	
Depreciation	7,910
Loss on sale of Penn House	70,800
Lease amortisation	2,400
Bonus payment	-
Interest payable on loan to purchase Penn House – 20% × £13,000 (W4)	2,600
Less:	
Bank interest receivable (W4)	(3,100)
Rental income	(17,900)
UK dividends received (FII)	(11,700)
Deduction for part of lease premium paid (W2)	(2,208)
	(257,664)
Less: capital allowances (W3)	(80,020)
Trading loss	(337,684)

(2) Lease premium

Income element of lease premium paid:

$$£12,000 \times \frac{50-(5-1)}{50} = £11,040$$

Deduction available = £11,040/5 = £2,208

(3) Capital allowances

	FYA £	Main pool £	Special rate pool £	Allowances £
WDV b/f		46,900	1,980	
Acquisitions – FYA				
Low emission car	13,000			
FYA @ 100%	(13,000)			13,000
Acquisitions – AIA				
Electrical systems			4,710	
Machinery		52,890		
AIA		(52,890)	(4,710)	57,600
Acquisitions – car			14,300	
Disposals		(1,800)		
		45,100	16,280	
WDA @ 18%		(8,118)		8,118
WDA @ 8%			(1,302)	1,302
WDV c/f	-	36,982	14,978	
Total allowances				80,020

(4) Non-trading loan relationships

	£
Bank interest receivable	3,100
Less: Interest payable on loan to purchase Penn House	
20% × £13,000	(2,600)
Non-trading loan relationship income	500

(5) Chargeable gain on Penn House

	£
Proceeds	590,000
Less: Cost	(600,400)
Allowable loss	(10,400)

(6) Limits

£300,000/2 = £150,000
£1,500,000/2 = £750,000

(a) (ii)   Stamp duty land tax

Lease of warehouse

SDLT is payable on both the lease premium and the net present value of the lease rentals as follows:

On the grant of a non-residential lease for a premium between £0 and £150,000, where the annual rent exceeds £1,000 the SDLT is (1% × £12,000) = £120.

On the net present value of the lease rentals (ignoring discounting), where the NPV exceeds £150,000 the SDLT is [(£36,000 × 5) – £150,000] × 1% = £300

A land transaction form must be submitted to HMRC and the associated SDLT paid by Lincoln Ltd within 30 days of the lease agreement.

(b)   Sale of Abe House

	£	£
Proceeds		350,000
Less: cost		
-original cost		(197,500)
Less: Indexation allowance		
$\dfrac{260.0 - 165.2}{165.2}$ = 0.574 × £197,500		(113,365)
Chargeable gain		39,135

Sale of the shares in Kennedy Ltd

The sale of the shares will result in a gain in Lincoln Ltd in June 2014 as follows:

	£
Proceeds	350,000
Less: cost	(8,000)
	342,000
Less: Indexation allowance	
$\dfrac{260.0 - 181.6}{181.6}$ × £8,000	(3,454)
Chargeable gain	338,546

The substantial shareholding exemption does not apply as Kennedy Ltd is not a trading company.

(c)

Part of the accountant's professional behaviour involves complying with relevant laws. The accountant should tell Charlie that the corporation tax return must be prepared correctly, with the bonus either paid earlier, or otherwise not claimed for until the following year.

The accountant must not become involved in the preparation or submission of a return which deliberately gives any false information, and must not assist tax evasion.

If Charlie persists in wishing to submit an incorrect return, the accountant should consider ceasing to act.

If the engagement is terminated, the accountant must notify Charlie. HMRC should also be told that the accountant is no longer acting, but not the reason, as it would be a breach of confidentiality.

If the accountant also prepares Charlie's personal tax returns, this engagement should probably also be terminated.

Marking guide

				Marks
(a)	(i)	Corporation tax computation		
		Trading profit	½	
		NTLR income	½	
		Property income	½	
		CT liability	1	
		Adjustment of profits (W1)		
		Loss	1	
		Additions (½ each including for non adjustment re bonus)	2½	
		Deductions for interest, rental income and dividends	1½	
		Lease premium deduction (W2)	1½	
		CAs (own figure)	½	
		Capital allowances (W3)		
		TWDV b/f	½	
		FYA 100%	½	
		Electrical equipment (special rate pool)	1	
		Machinery	½	
		AIA	1	
		Car in special rate pool	½	
		Disposals	½	
		WDAs	1	
		Non trading loan relationships (W4)	1	
		Gain on Penn House (W5)	1	
		CT limits	1	
				18
	(ii)	Stamp duty land tax		
		SDLT on premium	1	
		SDLT on rentals	1	
		Due date	1	
				3
(b)		Sale of Abe House		
		Gain in Kennedy Ltd	½	
		Cost	½	
		IA to June 2014	1	
		Sale of shares in Kennedy Ltd		
		Gain in Lincoln Ltd	½	
		Gain	1	
		No SSE	½	
				4
(c)		Comply with relevant laws	½	
		Tell Charlie how to treat bonus	1	
		Accountant must not become involved	2	
		Cease to act	3	
		Terminate engagement if prepare personal tax returns	1	
			7½	
		Max		6
				31

75 Martina McQueen (J10)

(a) Martina will be required to register for VAT if:

- At the end of any month, her taxable supplies in the previous 12 months have exceeded the registration threshold or

- At any point, she expects that taxable supplies in the next 30 days alone will exceed the registration threshold.

In the first case, HMRC must be notified of the need to register within 30 days from the end of the month in which the registration limit is exceeded.

In the second case, HMRC must be notified of the need to register by the end of the 30 day period during which she anticipates that the limit will be exceeded.

The sales to EU VAT registered customers are zero-rated and those to non VAT registered customers should be treated as standard-rated. Both are therefore taxable supplies and count towards the turnover test for registration.

(b) (i) **Trading profit: year ended 31 December 2014**

	£
Sales of glassware	86,060
Less:	
Tax deductible expenses (£12,200 × 5/6)	(10,167)
Client entertaining	–
Capital allowances:	
Car: £11,500 × 18% × 30%	(621)
Computer: £3,900 × 5/6 (AIA)	(3,250)
	72,022

(ii) **Trading income assessments**

		£
2013/14	1.1.14 – 5.4.14	
	3/12 × £72,022	18,006
2014/15	Year ended 31 December 2014	72,022
Overlap profit	1.1.14 – 5.4.14	
	3/12 × £72,022	18,006

(c)

Cost of employing assistant

	£
Salary	12,900
Employer's Class 1 national insurance:	
£(12,900 – 7,696) × 13.8%	718
Leasing cost of van	7,200
Class 1A national insurance on van benefit:	
£3,000 × 13.8%	414
	21,232
Less: income tax and Class 4 NI saving @ 47% × £21,232	(9,979)
Cost to the business of employing assistant	11,253

Cost of employing her husband

	£
Salary	7,000
Childcare vouchers (£160 × 52)	8,320
Mileage allowance (5,000 miles × 50p)	2,500
Employer's Class 1 national insurance on earnings (W1)	692
	18,512
Less: income tax and Class 4 NI saving @ 47% × £18,512	(8,701)
Cost to the business of employing husband	9,811

WORKING

(1) Class 1 earnings

	£
Salary	7,000
Childcare vouchers – (£160 – £55) × 52	5,460
Mileage allowance – 5,000 × (50p – 45p)	250
	12,710
Less secondary threshold	(7,696)
	5,014
Class contributions @ 13.8%	692

Marking guide

				Marks
(a)		Historic test	1½	
		Future test	1½	
		Sales outside of the UK	2	
			5	
		Max		4
(b)	(i)	Sales	½	
		Deductible expenses	½	
		Client entertaining	½	
		CAs		
		Car	1½	
		Equipment	1	
				4
	(ii)	2013/14	1	
		2014/15	1	
		Overlap profit	1	
				3
(c)		Cost of employing assistant		
	–	Salary	½	
	–	Employer NI	1	
	–	Lease costs	½	
	–	Class 1A NI	1	
	–	IT and NI saving	1	
		Cost of employing husband		
	–	Salary	½	
	–	Childcare	1	
	–	Mileage allowance	1	
	–	Employer NI	2	
	–	IT and NI saving	1	
			9½	
		Max		9
				20

76 Yelena, Katya and Alina (S10)

(a) (i) **Adjusted trading profit**

	£
Adjusted profit before capital allowances	72,900
Less: capital allowances (W1)	(14,801)
Tax adjusted trading profit	58,099

W1 – Capital allowances

	Pool £	BMW £	Toyota £	Total £
TWDV b/f	15,870	14,600		
Acquisition (AIA)				
Computer: £3,965 × 5/6	3,304			
AIA	(3,304)			3,304
Toyota car			15,000	
FYA @ 100%			(15,000) × 40%	6,000
Disposal - BMW		(8,000)		
		6,600		
Balancing allowance		(6,600) × 40%		2,640
	15,870			
WDA @ 18%	(2,857)			2,857
Total allowances				14,801
TWDV c/f	13,013			

(ii) **Allocation of partnership profit**

	Total £	Yelena £	Katya £	Alina £
Year ended 30 June 2014				
Salary	78,500	37,000	41,500	-
PSR 1:1:1	(20,401)	(6,800)	(6,800)	(6,801)
	58,099	30,200	34,700	(6,801)

The reallocation of the profit is as follows:

	£
Yelena: [£30,200 / (30,200 + 34,700)] × £58,099	27,035
Katya: [£34,700 / (30,200 + 34,700)] × £58,099	31,064

Alina will have a trading income assessment of NIL

(b) **Trading income assessment**

		£
2014/15	Year ended 30 June 2014 + 6 months ending 31 December 2014	
	£(27,035 + 33,417)	60,452
	Less: overlap profits	(2,900)
		57,552

(c) **Money laundering**

Yelena is engaged in money laundering if she possesses, deals in or conceals the proceeds of crime. This includes situations where Yelena:

- Conceals, disguises, converts or transfers criminal property, or
- Acquires, uses or has possession of criminal property.

Criminal property includes the proceeds of tax evasion or any other crime.

The actions that the chartered accountant should take are:

- Report the suspicion of money laundering to the Serious Organised Crime Agency (SOCA) using a suspicious activity report (SAR)

- Consider taking legal advice

- Retain records of client identification and relevant transactions for at least five years

- Avoid 'tipping off' Yelena as this would constitute an offence.

Marks

(a) (i) Computer (net of VAT)   ½
         AIA   ½
         Toyota   1½
         Balancing allowance on BMW   1½
         WDA @ 18%   ½
         Deduction from adjusted profit   ½
         5

     (ii) Salary   ½
         PSR   ½
         Reallocation to Yelena   1
         Reallocation to Katya   1
         3

(b) Adjusted profits   1
     Overlap   1
     2

(c) Examples of concealing proceeds of crime   1
     Tax evasion   1
     Actions
     Report to SOCA using SAR   2
     Legal advice   ½
     Retain records   ½
     Avoid tipping off   1
     6
     16

77 Quark Ltd (S10)

(a) (i) **Tax adjusted trading loss**

	£
Loss for the year	(60,940)
Add:	
Depreciation	13,200
Interest on the loan to purchase Hadron House: £2,900 × 20%	580
Less:	
Profit on sale of Hadron House	(137,200)
Rent receivable	(8,400)
UK bank interest receivable	(1,430)
Less: capital allowances (W1)	(12,900)
Adjusted loss	(207,090)

No adjustment for: other interest, legal & professional fees or closure costs

W1 – capital allowances

	Main pool £	Special rate pool £	Total £
TWDV b/f	24,800	900	
Less: disposals	(12,800)	-	
	12,000	900	
Balancing allowance	(12,000)		12,000
Balancing allowance		(900)	900
Total allowances			12,900

(ii) **Spin Ltd corporation tax liability**

	£
Trading profit	Nil
Rental income	8,400
Interest receivable (W1)	850
Chargeable gains (W2)	95,600
Taxable total profits	104,850

	£
Corporation tax liability (W3):	
£104,850 × 23%	24,116
Less: marginal relief	
3/400 (£166,667 – £104,850)	(464)
	23,652

WORKINGS

(1) **Interest receivable**

	£
Bank interest receivable	1,430
Less: interest on loan taken out to purchase Hadron House	
£2,900 × 20%	(580)
	850

2 **Chargeable gains**

	£
Proceeds	210,000
Less: cost	(104,000)
	106,000
Less: indexation (10% × £104,000)	(10,400)
Chargeable gain	95,600

3 **Limits**

£1,500,000/3 × 4/12 = £166,667
£300,000/3 × 4/12 = £33,333

(iii) **Stamp duty land tax**

Stamp duty land tax would have been payable by Quark Ltd at 1%
£200,000 × 1% = £2,000

(b) **Option One**

	£
No cost of providing the accommodation	nil
Class 1A NICs (W1)	3,229
Less: corporation tax relief (£3,229 × 20%)	(646)
Cost of Option One	2,583

Option Two

	£
Allowance £1,000 × 12 months	12,000
Class 1 NICs (£12,000 × 13.8%)	1,656
	13,656
Less: corporation tax relief (£13,656 × 20%)	(2,731)
Cost of Option Two	10,925

W1

	£
Accommodation benefit for Michelle:	
Annual value	17,000
Additional charge	
£(235,000 – 75,000) × 4%	6,400
	23,400
Class 1A contributions;	
£23,400 × 13.8%	£3,229

(c) Reducing pension contributions

	£
Cash saved:	
£(1,400 − 600) × 12 × 80%	7,680
Less: additional tax as a result of reduced extension to basic rate band	
£(1,400 − 600) × 12 × 20%	(1,920)
Cash saving	5,760

Sale of painting

Proceeds:	8,200
Less: capital gains tax (W1)	(644)
Cash generated	7,556

Sale of vintage car – exempt from CGT

Proceeds generated	£7,600

W1 – Chargeable gain

	£
Proceeds	8,200
Less: Cost	(5,900)
Gain	2,300

Restricted to max: 5/3 × (8,200 − 6,000) = £3,667 *(or statement that normal gain is clearly smaller)*

CGT: £2,300 × 28% = £644

Marking guide

				Marks
(a)	(i)	Loss	½	
		Depreciation	½	
		Loan interest	1	
		Deductions	1	
		No adjustment for other costs (does not need to be shown)	2	
		Deduction of capital allowances	½	
		Capital allowances (W1)	1½	
				7
	(ii)	Rental income	½	
		Taxable total profits	½	
		Interest receivable (W1)	1½	
		Chargeable gains (W2)	1½	
		CT liability	1½	
		Limits (W3)	1½	
				7
	(iii)	SDLT	1	
				1
(b)	Option 1	– Cost of accommodation	1	
		Class 1A NICs (W1)	2½	
		CT saving	1	
	Option 2	– Allowance	1	
		Class 1 NICs	½	
		CT saving	1	
				7
(c)	*Reduced pension contributions*			
		Cash saved	1	
		Extra tax due to BRB no longer extended	1	
		Sale of painting		
		Capital gains tax (W1)	2	
		Cash generated	½	
		Sale of car		
		Exempt	1	
		Proceeds generated	½	
				6
				28

78 Murray and Carla Gellman (S10)

(a) **Income tax computation**

	Non savings £	Savings £	Dividends £
Trading income assessment	18,560		
Rental income ((£19,500 × 9/12) − £1,200)	13,425		
Bank interest (£6,200 × 100/80)		7,750	
Dividends (£2,070 × 100/90)			2,300
	31,985	7,750	2,300
Less: personal allowance (W1)	(9,440)	–	–
Taxable income	22,545	7,750	2,300

Income tax on:	
£22,545 × 20%	4,509
£7,750 × 20%	1,550
£1,715 × 10%	172
£(2,300 − 1,715) = 585 × 32.5%	190
Income tax liability	6,421
Less: Tax credit on dividend (£2,300 × 10%)	(230)
Tax credit on interest (£7,750 × 20%)	(1,550)
Income tax payable	4,641

W1 – Personal allowance

Age allowance (born between 6 April 1938 and 5 April 1948)	10,500
Less: restriction ½ × (42,035 − 26,100) = £1,060 max	(1,060)
	9,440

(b) **IHT on transfers chargeable as a result of Murray's death**

12 June 2013: Gift of Baryon Ltd shares

	£	£
Value		41,000
Less: annual exemptions – 2013/14		(3,000)
– 2012/13		(3,000)
Transfer of value		35,000
Nil rate band in February 2014	325,000	
Unused nil rate band from Carla	325,000	
Less: gross chargeable transfers since 12.6.06	(635,000)	
		(15,000)
Excess over nil rate band		20,000
Inheritance tax @ 40% *(No taper relief less than 3 years)*		£8,000

Inheritance tax on the death estate

	£	£
Value of the estate:		
Principal private residence		670,000
Rental property		300,000
Shares in Lepton plc (W1)		20,800
Cash and chattels		320,000
		1,310,800
Less: outstanding liabilities		(28,900)
Income tax (part (a))		(4,641)
Capital gains tax (W2)		–
Chargeable estate		1,277,259
Nil rate band in February 2014 (see above)	650,000	
Less: gross chargeable transfers since 1.2.07	(35,000)	
Nil rate band remaining		(615,000)
Excess over nil rate band		662,259
Inheritance tax @ 40%		264,904
Less: QSR (W3)		(8,073)
IHT payable *(with QSR in the right place)*		256,831

WORKINGS

(1) **Shares in Lepton plc**
¼ up value = 416 + ¼ (419 − 416) = 416.75p
Mid bargain = (412 + 420)/2 = 416p
Therefore value at the lower: 416 × (5% × 100,000) =
£20,800

(2) **Gift of Baryon Ltd shares**

	£
Deemed proceeds (MV)	41,000
Less: cost	(32,000)
Gain	9,000
Less: annual exempt amount	(10,900)
Capital gain	Nil

(3) **Quick succession relief**

IHT on Stephen's estate	£
Chargeable estate	360,000
Less: nil rate band in July 2011	(325,000)
Excess over nil rate band	35,000
IHT @ 40%	£14,000
Net transfer is £(360,000 − 14,000)	346,000

QSR (2 − 3 years):

$$£14,000 \times \frac{346,000}{360,000} \times 60\% = £8,073$$

Marking guide

		Marks
(a)	Trading income	½
	Rental income	1
	Bank interest	1
	Dividends	1
	Personal age allowance	1½
	Income tax	½
	Tax credits	½
		6
(b)	*June 2013 gift*	
	Value	½
	AEs	1
	Nil rate band	2
	IHT	½
	Death estate	
	Properties	½
	Shares in Lepton plc (W1)	1½
	Cash and chattels	½
	Liabilities	½
	Income tax	1
	CGT	½
	Nil rate band	1
	IHT	½
	QSR (W3)	3
	IHT after QSR in correct place	½
	CGT on gift of shares (W2)	1½
		15
		21

79 Trevor Knott (J11)

(a) (i) **Trading profit: 14 months ended: 28 February 2014**

	£
Sales	77,500
Less:	
Allowable expenses	(32,075)
Client entertaining - disallowed	–
Motor expenses (£1,900 × 30%)	(570)
Capital allowances:	
Car: 8% × £21,000 × 14/12 × 30%	(588)
AIA on computer (not yet VAT registered)	(1,800)
	42,467

(ii) **Trading income assessments**

		£
2012/13	1.1.13 – 5.4.13	
	3/14 × £42,467	9,100
2013/14	12 months ended 28.2.14	36,400
	12/14 × £42,467	
Overlap profit	1/14 × £42,467	3,033
	(£36,400 + £9,100 − £42,467)	

(b) **VAT registration**

Trevor will be required to register for VAT in either of the two following circumstances:

Future prospects test

If at any point Trevor's anticipated taxable turnover in the next 30 days exceeds £79,000, then he will be required to register.

Although the new contract results in anticipated turnover exceeding £79,000 in March 2014, only £10,000 are taxable and the rest are exempt, so the registration threshold is not exceeded.

Historic test

If at the end of any month Trevor's taxable turnover for the previous 12 months exceeds the registration limit of £79,000 then he must notify HMRC of the need to register. Trevor's application to register must be submitted within thirty days from the end of the relevant month.

Cumulative turnover	£
12 months to 31.12.13	62,400
12 months to 31.1.14	65,700
12 months to 28.2.14	69,500
12 months to 31.3.14	74,300
12 months to 30.4.14	79,100

The registration threshold is breached by the end of April 2014.
Therefore the registration deadline is 30 May 2014.

(c) **Partial exemption simplified tests**

Quarter to 31 May 2014	£
Value of standard rated supplies	30,000
Value of exempt supplies	73,000
Value of total supplies	103,000

Test One

Average monthly input tax is £1,500/3 = £500, which is below £625 ✓
However, the value of exempt supplies exceeds 50% of total supplies ie £51,500 ✗
Therefore Test One is failed

Test Two

Total input tax less input tax directly attributable to taxable supplies averages ✓
(£1,500 − £230)/3 = £423 per month, which is below £625
However, the value of exempt supplies still exceeds 50% of total supplies ✗
Therefore Test Two is failed

Marks

(a)	(i)	Sales	½	
		Allowable expenses	½	
		Client entertaining	½	
		Motor expenses	1	
		CAs		
		Car	2	
		Computer	½	
				5
	(ii)	2012/13	1	
		2013/14	1	
		Overlap profit	1	
				3
(b)		Future test	1½	
		Historic test	½	
		Cumulative turnover calculation	½	
		Breach of threshold	1	
		Registration deadline	1	
			4½	
		Max		4
(c)		Value of total supplies	1½	
		Test One	2½	
		Test Two	3	
			7	
		Max		6
				18

80 Bute Traders (M12)

(a) **Agent**

An accountant acts as a client's agent when preparing tax compliance work such as income tax returns or calculating tax liabilities.

The client remains responsible for ensuring that any information given to HMRC is accurate.

Acting as an agent is therefore a low-risk activity which carries lower fees. As such, no specialist assistance is required.

Principal

An accountant acts as a client's principal when giving tax advice such as inheritance tax planning, or tax avoidance schemes.

The accountant takes responsibility for the advice given and may be liable to the client if the advice is incorrect or inappropriate.

Acting as a principal is a high-risk activity which carries higher fees. As such, specialist assistance should be obtained if the accountant is not personally competent in that subject area.

(b) **Bute Traders – year ended 31 December 2013**

	Taxable supplies £	Exempt supplies £	Total supplies £
Wholly attributable input tax:			
Taxable supplies	50,045		50,045
Exempt supplies		5,850	5,850
Non-attributable input tax:			
Recoverable amount % is			
£341,300 / £396,300			
= 87% (rounded up)			
Attributable to taxable supplies:			
87% × £15,000 ie [£12,000 + (£15,000 × 20%)]	13,050		13,050
Attributable to exempt supplies:			
13% × £15,000		1,950	1,950
Input VAT	63,095	7,800	70,895

Tests for *de minimis* limit:

1. Is the monthly average attributable to exempt supplies £625 or less?
   Monthly average is £7,800 / 12 = £650 per month – fails this test

2. Is the proportion of VAT on exempt supplies not more than 50% of input VAT for the year?
   £7,800 / £70,895 = 11% – passes this test

As both tests are not passed, input tax on exempt supplies exceeds *de minimis* limits.

Conclusion

Only input VAT attributable to taxable supplies is recoverable ie £63,095 (ie £60,485 + £2,610 on plant & machinery)

Therefore the annual adjustment is:

£64,570 – £63,095 = £1,475 is payable to HMRC

(c) **Splott plc – VAT on property**

As the first property is a commercial building which is less than three years old, it is a standard rated supply.

VAT due is: £1m × 20% = £0.2 million *(or accept £166,667 depending on how read question).*

As an option to tax has been exercised in respect of the second property, it is a standard rated supply and VAT is due of £2.5m × 20% = £0.5 million *(or accept £416,667 depending on how read question).*

Stamp duty land tax on property

Stamp duty land tax is payable by the purchaser on the VAT inclusive price of the property.

Property 1 = £1,200,000 × 4% = £48,000

Property 2 = £3,000,000 × 4% = £120,000

Marks

(a) Agent
Compliance ½
Example ½
Client responsible ½
Low risk/low fees ½
Principal
Tax advice ½
Example ½
Responsibility ½
Liable ½
High risk/high fees ½
Specialist assistance ½
‾‾
5
Max 4

(b) Wholly attributable tax 1
Recoverable percentage (round up) 1½
Split of non attributable tax 1
Split of input VAT on plant and machinery 1
De minimis test - £625 per month ½
De minimis test - 50% ½
Conclusion re de minimis test ½
Comparison to amount recovered ½
VAT payable 1
‾‾
7½
Max 7

(c) First property
Less than three years old ½
Standard rated ½
VAT ½
Second property
Option to tax ½
Standard rated ½
VAT ½
Stamp duty land tax
Property 1 1
Property 2 1
‾‾
5
‾‾
16

81 Michael Lyon (M13)

(a)

Assessable employment income

	£
Salary £52,000 × 6/12	26,000
Living accommodation (W1)	2,862
Reimbursement of expenses	340
Marginal cost of cookery course (not relevant training)	75
Parking space	nil
Less: entertaining expenses	(340)
mileage allowance shortfall (42p – 45p) × 4,000	(120)
	28,817

WORKINGS

(1) Accommodation

Annual value	12,000
Additional yearly rent £(134,000 – 75,000) × 4%	2,360
Furniture £2,900 × 20%	580
	14,940
Pro rated × 6/12	7,470
Less: rent paid £768 × 6	(4,608)
	2,862

(b) (i)

Adjusted trading profit: Seven months ending 30 April 2014

	£
Net profit	40,202
Add:	
Depreciation	2,870
Expenditure relating to Saffron House	29,400
Parking fine (disallowed as by proprietor)	60
Michael's private fuel £2,520 × 40%	1,008
New hand dryer	630
Catering costs	870
Less:	
Allowable rent = 7/12 × £24,000	(14,000)
Deduction for lease premium (W1)	(396)
Deduction for fees for VAT advice £180 × 120/100	(216)
(Pre-trade expenditure allowable,	
but VAT not recoverable on services >6 months ago so add in the VAT)	
	60,428
Less: capital allowances (W2)	(10,350)
Adjusted trading profit	50,078

WORKINGS

(1) Lease premium

Amount of premium taxed as rent on the landlord

$£5,400 \times \dfrac{50 - 6}{50} = £4,752$

Deduction for Michael: $\dfrac{£4,752}{7} \times 7/12$ £396

(2) Capital allowances

	FYA £	Allowances £
Hand dryers	630	
FYA @ 100%	(630)	630
Low-emission car £13,500 × 120/100	16,200	
FYA @ 100%	(16,200) × 60%	9,720
		10,350

No capital allowances on the paintings

(b) (ii)

Income tax computation: 2013/14

	NSI £	Dividend £
Employment income (part a)	28,817	
Trading income (1.10.13 – 5.4.14)		
£50,078 (part bi) × 6/7	42,924	
Income from REIT (£4,160 × 100/80)	5,200	
Dividend (£2,250 × 100/90)		2,500
Net income	76,941	2,500
Less personal allowance	(9,440)	-
Taxable income	67,501	2,500

Non-savings income		£32,010	× 20%	6,402
Extended BRB		£5,000	× 20%	1,000
		£37,010	(W1)	
Non-savings income		£30,491	× 40%	12,196
Dividend income		£2,500	× 32.5%	813
Income tax liability				20,411

WORKINGS

(1) **Extended basic rate band**

Basic rate band		£32,010
Personal pension contribution	£4,000 × 100/80	£5,000
		£37,010

Marking guide

				Marks
(a)		Salary	½	
		Reimbursement of expenses *(½ each for add back and deduct or 1 for zero if shown)*	1	
		Cookery course	1	
		Parking space	½	
		Mileage allowance	1	
		Accommodation (W1)		
		Annual value	½	
		Additional charge	1	
		Furniture	½	
		Pro rated	½	
		Rent paid	½	
				7
(b)	(i)	Adjustments to net profit (each add back is ½ mark)	3	
		Deduct allowable rent	½	
		Lease premium deduction	½	
		Deduction for VAT advice	1	
		Pre trade expenditure explanation	1	
		Deduct CA's	½	
		No other adjustments	½	
		Lease premium (W1)	2	
		CA's (W2)		
		FYA @ 100% on hand dryers	1	
		Car inclusive of VAT	½	
		FYA @ 100% on car	½	
		Private use adjustment	½	
		No CA's on painting	½	
				12
	(ii)	Employment income	½	
		Trading income	1	
		REIT income	1	
		Dividends	½	
		PA	½	
		Income tax liability	2	
		Extension of BRB band	½	
				6
				25

82 Harry and Zinnia Wormwood (J13)

(a) (i)

Death estate

	£
House (£1,500,000 – £300,000)	1,200,000
Trunchbull plc shares	
Lower of:	
¼ up = ¼ (£6.46 – £6.30) + £6.30 = £6.34	
Average = (£6.32 + £6.43) / 2 = £6.375	
£6.34 × 2,000	12,680
IIP trust created pre April 2006	225,000
Paintings – Related property rules apply	
Value of two of a set of three = [£150 / (£150 + £90)] × £400,000	250,000
Chargeable estate	1,687,680

		£	
Nil rate band in April 2014		£325,000	
Plus 1st spouse's remaining NRB			
NRB @ death of 1st spouse	£285,000		
Less PET within 7 yrs of his death	£55,000		
Less marriage exemption	£(5,000)		
Less annual exemptions current and prior years	£(6,000)		
	£(44,000)		
	£241,000		
NRB available to Zinnia = 241/285 × £325,000		£274,825	
			(599,825)
Excess over the nil rate band			1,087,855
IHT due at 40%			435,142

(ii) IHT is due within six months of the end of the month of death if do not want to pay interest, ie by 31 October 2014.

(iii) Michael and Matilda could elect to pay IHT due on the land in ten equal interest-bearing instalments.

The instalments would be due on 31 October every year, starting on 31 October 2014.

The remaining tax would not qualify for instalments. This IHT is not actually due until the return is due to be filed which is within 12 months of the end of month of death, ie 30 April 2015. However, interest will run from 31 October 2014.

(b) The situation involves the need for ethical conflict resolution and adherence to the fundamental principles of the ICAEW code.

First I need to establish the relevant facts prior to taking any action. I should establish definitively whether there is a particular reason for the approach used by Patricia and whether it was inappropriate.

Then I should consider who is involved – my manager, his wife and a deceased client.

Then I should consider the ethical issues involved – the most obvious issue being the fact that the potential problem concerns the spouse of the person it would be most appropriate to go to in the first instance, ie my manager. In addition whether, now the client is deceased, it is appropriate to bring up this matter.

Then I should consider to which of the fundamental principles the ethical conflict relates:

- My objectivity and my manager's objectivity should not be affected by the fact the potential issue arises because of the actions of my manager's spouse. A potential self-interest threat arises here.

- The firm should have provided a service to the client which offered an appropriate level of professional competence and due care.

- We should behave in a professional way and therefore the fact that the client is now deceased should not impact on our decision whether to investigate this matter.

I should investigate what internal procedures are available, if any, concerning this kind of scenario before deciding on the best course of action.

It would be advisable to document the issue and details of any discussions held or decisions taken concerning the issue.

Marking guide

	Marks

(a) (i)

House less mortgage	1	
Trunchbull plc shares		
Quarter up value	½	
Mid bargains value	½	
Lower value taken	½	
IIP trust	½	
Paintings	2 ½	
Nil rate band		
NRB in April 2014	½	
Considering NRB from spouse	½	
NRB at death of spouse	½	
Value of gift	½	
Deduct marriage exemption	½	
Deduct annual exemptions	½	
Applying percentage unused to NRB in April 2014	1	
IHT at 40%	1	
	10½	
Max		10

(ii) Due date		1
(iii) Elect to pay in instalments	1	
On land	½	
Over ten years	½	
Interest bearing	½	
Due on 31 October each year	½	
Remaining tax not qualify for instalments	½	
IHT due when return due on 30 April 2015	½	
Interest runs from 31 October 2014	½	
	4½	
Max		4

(b)

Establish relevant facts	1	
Consider who is involved	½	
Consider the ethical issues	1½	
Fundamental principles	½	
Objectivity	1	
Self interest threat	1	
Professional competence and due care	½	
Matters even though client is deceased	½	
Internal procedures	½	
Document discussions	½	
	7½	
Max		5
		20

Sample paper 2 exam questions

Assume that the sample paper is being sat in September

1 Abby and Juan

You work as a tax assistant for a firm of chartered accountants. Your manager has left the following information on your desk:

Anti-money laundering procedures

The senior partner recently attended a seminar on money laundering and she is now concerned that our firm is not compliant with current anti-money laundering regulations. Other than having a vague awareness of money laundering I am not sure that we have done anything to ensure compliance with the regulations. I have never had enough time to really look into it but now the senior partner is involved we need to take action fast.

Abby

Abby was a client of our firm for a number of years until her death on 1 January 2014. Abby never married and is survived by her partner, Luka, and their son Joe.

Abby died leaving the following assets in her death estate (all valuations are the market value as at the date of death):

- A property valued at £400,000 with a mortgage secured on it of £200,000.

- A life assurance policy on Luka's life. The policy had a market value of £46,000 on 1 January 2014 and will pay out £123,000 on Luka's death.

- 10,000 units in the Agnew unit trust. On 1 January 2014 the bid price was 180p and the offer price 184p.

- Cash and other personal effects valued at £177,000.

Abby's only lifetime transfer was the gift of a house to a discretionary trust in March 2007. At the time of the gift the house was valued at £420,000. At the time of her death the house was valued at £287,250.

Abby left £25,000 of her death estate to the Purple Party which had ten Members of Parliament elected to the House of Commons at the last general election. The remainder of her death estate was left to her son, Joe, with nothing left to her partner, Luka, although he is still alive.

Juan

Juan is Abby's cousin. He is domiciled in Moldova but moved to the UK on 6 April 2009 and became UK resident from 2009/10. Juan recently became a client of our firm and sent us the following note:

"Now that I have been in the UK for a few years it is my intention to buy a house. So that I have a reasonable deposit for the house I sold the following things in 2013/14. I have translated all amounts into a sterling equivalent where appropriate:

- 30,000 shares in Stiehm plc to my friend George for £45,000. Stiehm plc is an investment company quoted on the London stock exchange with 200,000 issued shares. When I sold the shares they were quoted at 205-210p with marked bargains of 203p, 207p and 209p, and I paid £40,500 for them in March 2010.

- A lease on a UK house for £40,000 with six years left to run at the time of sale. I bought the lease exactly four years before I sold it for £51,000 as a temporary measure shortly after moving to the UK. I lived in the house until its sale.

- A painting was sold at auction for £7,800 and I then paid auctioneer's fees of £468. I bought the painting especially for the house and paid £2,400 for it.

- The remaining three hectares of some land in Moldova for £38,000. I originally bought ten hectares of land in June 1994 for £80,000, but sold the other seven hectares for £60,000 in August 2007. At that time the remaining three hectares were valued at £25,000. I have paid £6,200 of tax in Moldova in respect of the latest disposal.

I have now found my dream home, a freehold property, and I am hoping to complete the purchase of it on 10 October 2014. I have agreed a price of £325,000 which is less than my budget. Therefore I don't expect to need the cash from the sale of the land for my deposit, so I will leave the proceeds in my bank account in Moldova for now".

According to our client files Juan has taxable income for 2013/14 of £27,010. The UK has no Double Tax Treaty with Moldova. Juan is not automatically entitled to the remittance basis and must make a claim if he would like it to apply.

Requirements

(a) Prepare brief notes which set out the anti-money laundering procedures which the firm should implement in order to ensure compliance with anti-money laundering regulations. **(5 marks)**

(b) Calculate the amount of inheritance tax payable as a result of Abby's death on 1 January 2014. **(10 marks)**

(c) Calculate the capital gains tax payable by Juan for 2013/14, showing the amount of any available reliefs, assuming:

    (i)   he does not make a claim for the remittance basis for 2013/14;

    (ii) he makes a claim for the remittance basis for 2013/14. **(14 marks)**

(d) Calculate the amount of stamp duty land tax payable by Juan in relation to the disposal of the lease and the proposed acquisition of the freehold property, and state the date by which it is due. **(2 marks)**

(31 marks)

2   Sharif

(a)   Sharif operated a car maintenance business as a sole trader from 1 May 2003 until he ceased to trade on 30 September 2013. Sharif's tax adjusted trading profits before capital allowances for his final two accounting periods are:

	£
Year ended 30 April 2013	35,813
Five months ended 30 September 2013	8,977

Sharif recorded the following in relation to capital allowances for his final two accounting periods to cessation on 30 September 2013:

- The tax written down values brought forward at 1 May 2012 were:

	£
Main pool	32,145
Special rate pool	950
Expensive car	8,960

- The expensive car was originally purchased in January 2008. Sharif agreed with HMRC that business use of the car was 80%. Sharif sold the car in August 2013 for £7,500.

- Sharif purchased a van in July 2012 for £2,500.

- Sharif installed thermal insulation into his workshop in December 2012 at a cost of £6,500.

- Sharif purchased a car with CO_2 emissions of 200g/km in May 2013 for £8,500. The car was used exclusively for business purposes.

- Sharif purchased new IT equipment in July 2013 for £1,500.

- At 30 September 2013 agreed market values for the following assets were:

	£
Main pool assets	23,500
Special rate pool assets	10,000

When Sharif commenced to trade on 1 May 2003 he drew up his first set of accounts to 30 April 2004. His tax adjusted trading profit for the year ended 30 April 2004 was £15,000.

Requirement

Calculate Sharif's taxable trading income for 2013/14 and state the dates of the basis period. Assume he makes the maximum possible claim for capital allowances in each accounting period. Ignore VAT. **(12 marks)**

(b)   After ceasing to trade Sharif started work for Pericolo Ltd on 6 October 2013 on a salary of £55,000 pa, which is paid monthly, plus the following taxable benefits:

- Company petrol car with a list price of £22,000 and CO_2 emissions of 146g/km. Pericolo Ltd pays for both business and private fuel.

- Pericolo Ltd pays £3,500 pa into a registered occupational pension scheme to which Sharif contributes a further £1,750 pa. Sharif is not contracted out of the State Second Pension.

During 2013/14 Sharif received £2,400 from a real estate investment trust paid out of its tax-exempt property income. Sharif also received interest of £1,500 in 2013/14 relating to a loan he made to a friend. In addition, Sharif received dividends from Table Ltd of £1,800.

Sharif made a donation via Gift Aid of £2,600 in December 2013.

Requirements

Using the information above and your answer to part (a):

(i)   Calculate Sharif's income tax liability for 2013/14, making clear your treatment of each item.
(8 marks)

(ii)   Calculate Sharif's liability to national insurance contributions for 2013/14.   **(5 marks)**

(25 marks)

3   Chair Ltd

Chair Ltd is an unquoted trading company. The company changed its accounting date from 31 March to 31 July by preparing accounts for the sixteen months to 31 July 2014. Its net operating profit for those sixteen months was £2,109,955 after accounting for the following items:

	Note	£
Interest	(1)	5,050
Depreciation		74,500
Rental income	(2)	126,000
Profit on sale of head office	(3)	650,000
Profit on sale of shares	(4)	35,000
Dividends received	(5)	72,000

Notes:

		£
(1)	Interest receivable on cash deposits	17,000
	Interest payable on loan to purchase office units	(8,000)
	Overdraft interest payable	(1,450)
	Interest payable on head office loan	(2,500)
		5,050

The loan used to purchase the head office was repaid on 1 December 2013. All other interest received and paid was accrued evenly over the sixteen month period.

(2)   Chair Ltd has owned an investment property consisting of six office units for many years. The office units have been let out to various unconnected businesses since their acquisition.

(3)   Chair Ltd sold its head office on 1 December 2013 for £1.45 million. The property was originally purchased in January 2007 for £0.8 million.

(4)   Chair Ltd sold its 12% shareholding in Pear Ltd, a trading company, on 2 December 2013 for £122,000. The shares were purchased in January 2001 for £87,000.

(5)   On 10 December 2013 Chair Ltd received a dividend of £72,000 from a 6% shareholding in Armoir plc.

(6)   No account has been taken of a £45,000 interest free loan made to an employee on 6 April 2014 which was still outstanding on 31 July 2014. The employer national insurance contributions relating to the loan have not been accounted for.

(7)   The tax written down value of the main pool on 1 April 2013 was £222,000. In June 2014 Chair Ltd purchased new IT equipment for £100,000 and a new electrically propelled car for £14,500.

Chair Ltd has no associated companies and paid corporation tax at the main rate for the year ended 31 March 2013.

Requirements

(a)   Calculate the corporation tax payable by Chair Ltd in respect of the sixteen months ended 31 July 2014.
(21 marks)

(b)   State, with reasons, the due date(s) for the payment of Chair Ltd's corporation tax liability and the filing of its corporation tax return(s) for the sixteen months ended 31 July 2014.   **(4 marks)**

(25 marks)

Notes: **The RPI in December 2013 was 255.8.**

Ignore VAT.

4 Dhruthi, Komal and Shriya

(a) Dhruthi, Komal and Shriya have been trading in partnership for a number of years. The partnership prepares its accounts to 31 December each year. During the year ended 31 December 2013, the partners changed their profit sharing ratio as follows:

- Until 30 June 2013 the profit sharing agreement stated that Dhruthi received a salary of £7,000 pa; all partners received interest on capital at 6% pa; and the balance of profits was to be shared equally.

- From 1 July 2013 Dhruthi receives a salary of £44,000 pa and Komal and Shriya each receive a salary of £8,000 pa; all partners receive interest on capital at 4.5% pa; and the balance of profits is to be shared equally between Komal and Shriya only.

The partners invested capital of: Dhruthi £400,000; Komal £250,000; and Shriya £100,000.

For the year ended 31 December 2013 the partnership made a tax adjusted trading profit after capital allowances of £40,000.

Requirement

Calculate the taxable trading income for each partner for the year ended 31 December 2013.

(7 marks)

(b) Dhruthi also works for her husband's new company Osprey Ltd, a VAT registered trading company making a mixture of taxable and exempt supplies.

Osprey Ltd voluntarily registered for VAT from 1 June 2014. Dhruthi is just about to prepare the first VAT return for the quarter ended 31 August 2014 using the information set out below:

	£
Supplies	
Taxable supplies (VAT exclusive)	52,000
Exempt supplies	48,000
Total supplies	100,000

	£
Input tax:	
Attributable to taxable supplies	1,100
Attributable to exempt supplies	1,200
Non-attributable	80
	2,380

Dhruthi will initially use the simplified partial exemption tests to determine whether the company will be able to recover all input tax for the quarter ended 31 August 2014.

Requirement

Determine whether Osprey Ltd is able to recover all input tax for the quarter ended 31 August 2014 using:

(i) Simplified partial exemption test one, and / or

(ii) Simplified partial exemption test two.

(5 marks)

(c)   Shriya owns 100% of the shares in Property Traders Ltd which is a VAT registered property development company. Property Traders Ltd has recently carried out the following property transactions:

(1)   Purchased materials from a VAT registered supplier in France (which is a member of the EU).

(2)   Purchased a newly constructed office building in the UK (construction date 1 January 2014) for £2.5 million which it intends to rent out to a number of tenants some of whom run businesses which are exempt from VAT.

(3)   Agreed to supply property management services to a customer in Germany (which is a member of the EU). The customer is in business but is not VAT registered in the UK or in Germany.

Requirement

Explain the UK VAT implications of transactions 1 to 3 above.   **(7 marks)**

Note: Marks are allocated between transactions 1 to 3 as follows:

(1)   1 mark

(2)   5 marks

(3)   1 mark   **(19 marks)**

Sample paper 2
exam answers

1 Abby and Juan

(a) Anti-money laundering procedures

The firm should do the following to ensure compliance with anti-money laundering regulations:

- Register with an appropriate supervisory authority (eg the ICAEW).

- Appoint a Money Laundering Reporting Officer (MLRO).

- Implement internal reporting procedures.

- It should train staff to ensure that they are aware of the relevant legislation, know how to recognise and deal with potential money laundering, how to report suspicions to the MLRO, and how to identify clients

- Establish appropriate internal procedures relating to risk assessment and management to deter and prevent money laundering, and make relevant individuals aware of the procedures

- Carry out customer due diligence on any new client and monitor existing clients to ensure the client is known and establish areas of risk

- Verify the identity of new clients and maintain evidence of identification and records of any transactions undertaken for or with the client

- Report suspicions of money laundering to the Serious Organised Crime Agency (SOCA), using a suspicious activity report (SAR)

(b) Inheritance tax payable as a result of Abby's death

	£	£
CLT – March 2007		
GCT (W1)		446,250
Less fall in value relief (£420,000 – £287,250)		(132,750)
		313,500
Nil rate band at death		(325,000)
Death tax due		Nil
Death estate		
Property		
Value	400,000	
Less mortgage	(200,000)	
		200,000
Life insurance policy		46,000
Agnew unit trust 10,000 × £1.80 *(bid price)*		18,000
Cash & other effects		177,000
		441,000
Less exempt transfer to political party		(25,000)
		416,000
Less nil rate band at death	325,000	
Less GCTs since 1 January 2007 (ignoring FIV relief)	(446,250)	
		(nil)
		416,000
IHT due at 40%		166,400

WORKINGS		
(1) CLT March 2007 gross chargeable transfer		£
MV at date of gift		420,000
Less AE 2006/07 and 2005/06 b/f		(6,000)
Chargeable transfer		414,000
Nil rate band at date of gift		(285,000)
		129,000
Lifetime tax at 20/80		32,250
Gross chargeable transfer = £414,000 + £32,250		446,250

(c) Chargeable gains

	£
Shares in Stiehm plc	
Proceeds (OMV) (W1)	61,800
Less cost	(40,500)
Chargeable gain	21,300

Lease

	£
Proceeds	9,500
Less cost $\dfrac{\%6years}{\%10years} = \dfrac{31.195}{46.695} \times £51,000$	(34,071)
	5,929
Less: PPR - occupation	(5,929)
Chargeable gain	Nil

Painting

	£
Proceeds	7,800
Less costs of disposal	(468)
	7,332
Less cost	(2,400)
Chargeable gain	4,932

Gain cannot exceed 5/3 rule:
(£7,800 - £6,000) × 5/3 = £3,000

	£
Chargeable gain	£3,000

Moldovan land

	£
Proceeds	38,000
Less cost $\dfrac{25,000}{25,000+60,000} \times £80,000$	(23,529)
Chargeable gain	14,471

UK CGT liability

	RB claim £	No RB claim £
Total UK gains = £21,300 + £0 + £3,000	24,300	24,300
Moldovan gain	–	14,471
	24,300	38,771
Less AEA	–	(10,900)
Taxable gains	24,300	27,871
Basic rate band remaining is £5,000		
£5,000 @ 18%	900	900
£19,300/ £22,871 @ 28%	5,404	6,404
Total CGT due	6,304	7,304
Less Double Tax relief		
Lower of:		
UK Tax on overseas gains £0/£14,471 × 28% = £4,052	–	(4,052)
Overseas Tax £6,200		
	6,034	3,252

WORKINGS
(1)   Stiehm plc
Lower of
¼ up = 205 + ¼ × (210-205)   =206.25
Mid bargain $\dfrac{203+209}{2}$ =206

30,000 × £2.06 = £61,800

(d) Stamp duty land tax

SDLT is payable by the purchaser, so there is no SDLT payable on the disposal of the lease.

SDLT of £9,750 (£325,000 x 3%) is payable by Juan on the acquisition of the freehold.

Juan must pay the tax due within 30 days ie by 9 November 2014.

Marks

(a) Register with supervisory authority .... ½
     Appoint MLRO .... ½
     Implement internal reporting procedures .... ½
     Train staff 1½
     Establish internal procedures re risk assessment .... ½
     Customer due diligence 1
     Verify identity of new clients 1
     Report to SOCA using SAR .... <u>1</u>
                                                                                                            6½

                                                   Max   5

(b) *Gift to discretionary trust – lifetime tax*
          Value at gift .... ½
          AE's .... ½
          NRB .... ½
          IHT @ 20/80 .... ½
          GCT .... ½
     Gift to discretionary trust - tax as a result of death
          Transfer value .... ½
          Fall in value relief 1
          NRB .... ½
          IHT .... ½
     Death estate
          House less mortgage .... ½
          Life insurance 1
          Unit trust .... ½
          Cash .... ½
          Exempt transfer to political party .... ½
          NRB at date of death .... ½
          GCT's in previous 7 years 1
          IHT .... <u>½</u>
                                                                                                            10

(c) Gains
     Shares in Stiehm plc
          Gain .... ½
          Working 1 .... 1½
     Lease
          Proceeds .... ½
          Cost 1½
          PPR 1
     Painting
          Costs of disposal .... ½
          Cost .... ½
          5/3 rule calculation using gross proceeds .... ½
          Lower gain taken .... ½
     Moldovan land
          Cost 1½
     CGT
          Total UK gains .... ½
          Treatment of Moldovan gain 1
          Treatment of AEA 1
          CGT @18% .... ½
          CGT @ 28% 1
          DTR .... <u>1½</u>
                                                                                                            14

(d)	Payable by purchaser	½
	Calculation	1
	Due date	½

$$\frac{2}{31}$$

2 Sharif

(a)

Capital allowances

Y/E 30.4.13	Main Pool £	Special Rate Pool £	Expensive Car £	Allowances £
TWDV b/f	32,145	950	8,960	
Additions				
Van	2,500			
AIA	(2,500)			2,500
Insulation		6,500		
AIA		(6,500)		6,500
	32,145	950	8,960	
WDA @ 18%	(5,786)			5,786
Write off of small pool		(950)		950
WDA @ 18%			(1,613) × 80%	1,290
				17,026
TWDV c/f	26,359	Nil	7,347	
P/E 30.9.13				
Additions				
Car emissions >130g/km		8,500		
IT equipment	1,500			
Disposal of expensive car			(7,500)	
	27,859	8,500	(153)	
Balancing charge × 80%			153 × 80%	(122)
Deemed disposals	(23,500)	(10,000)		
Balancing allowance	(4,359)			4,359
Balancing charge		1,500		(1,500)
				2,737
TWDV c/f	Nil	Nil	Nil	

Taxable trading income

	£
Basis period: 1 May 2012 – 30 September 2013	
Y/e 30 April 2013 (£35,813 – £17,026)	18,787
P/e 30 September 2013 (£8,977 – £2,737)	6,240
Less overlap profits from commencement (W1)	(13,750)
Taxable trading income	11,277

WORKINGS

(1) *Overlap profits from commencement*

	£
2003/04 1 May 2003 to 5 April 2004 = 11/12 × £15,000	13,750
2004/05 1 May 2003 to 30 April 2004	15,000
Overlap is therefore £13,750	

ICAEW

(b) (i) **Income tax liability for Sharif for 2013/14**

	Non Savings £	Savings £	Dividend £
Trading income (part (a))	11,277		
Employment income (W1)	31,151		
Property income (£2,400 × 100/80)	3,000		
Interest received gross		1,500	
Dividend (£1,800 × 100/90)			2,000
Net income	45,428	1,500	2,000
Less personal allowance	(9,440)		
Taxable income	35,988	1,500	2,000

Non-savings income	£32,010	× 20%	6,402
Extended BRB (W2)	£3,250	× 20%	650
Non-savings income	£728	× 40%	291
	£35,988		
Savings income	£1,500	× 40%	600
Dividend income	£2,000	× 32.5%	650
Income tax liability			8,593

WORKINGS

(1) Employment income

		£
Salary	£55,000 × 6/12	27,500
Company car	£22,000 × 21% × 6/12	2,310
Fuel benefit	£21,100 × 21% × 6/12	2,216
Employer pension		-
		32,026
Employee pension	£1,750 × 6/12	(875)
		31,151

(2) Extended basic rate band

BRB extended by:	£2,600 × 100/80	£3,250

(ii) **National insurance**

	£
Class 2	
26 weeks at £2.70	70
Class 4	
(£11,277 – £7,755) × 9%	317
Class 1 primary	
Monthly salary = £4,583	
No NIC on benefits	
(£3,454 – £646) × 12% × 6 months	2,022
(£4,583 – £3,454) × 2% × 6 months	135
	2,157

Marks

(a)   *Capital allowances*
       Year ended 30 April 2013
       AIA on van   ½
       AIA on insulation   ½
       WDA on main pool   1
       Write off of small pool   1
       WDA on expensive car @ 80%   ½
       P/e 30 September 2013
       Additions (½ each in correct column)   1
       Disposal of expensive car   ½
       Balancing charge on expensive car   1
       No AIA or WDAs given   ½
       Deemed disposals (½ each)   1
       Balancing allowance on main pool   ½
       Balancing charge on special rate pool   ½
       Taxable trading income
       Basis period   ½
       Year ended 30 April 2013   ½
       P/e 30 September 2013   ½
       Deduction of overlap profits   1
       Overlap profits calculation (W1)   <u>1</u>
                                                                        12

(b)   (i)   Trading income   ½
              Salary pro-rated   ½
              Car benefit   ½
              Fuel benefit   ½
              Employer pension contributions   ½
              Employee pension contributions   ½
              Property income   1
              Interest   ½
              Dividends   ½
              PA   ½
              Income tax liability   2
              Extension of BR band   <u>½</u>
                                                                        8

       (ii)   Class 2   ½
              Class 4   1½
              Class 1 primary   <u>3</u>
                                                                        <u>5</u>
                                                                        <u><u>25</u></u>

3 Chair Ltd

(a) Corporation tax computation for the sixteen months ended 31 July 2014

	Y/e 31 Mar 2014 £	P/e 31 July 2014 £
Adjusted trading profit (£1,292,372 × 12:4 (W1))	969,279	323,093
Less: Capital allowances (W3)	(39,960)	(109,755)
Trading profits	929,319	213,338
Property income (£126,000 × 12:4)	94,500	31,500
Chargeable gain (W4)	434,800	
Non-trading loan relationships (12:4 (W5))	6,750	2,250
Taxable total profits	1,465,369	247,088
FII £72,000 × 100/90	80,000	
Augmented profits	1,545,369	247,088
Corporation tax payable:		
CT @ 23%	337,035	56,830
Less Marginal relief (3/400 × (£500,000 − £247,088))	-	(1,897)
	337,035	54,933

WORKINGS

(1) Adjusted profits

	£
Trading profit	2,109,955
Less:	
Interest receivable	(17,000)
Rental income	(126,000)
Profit on sale of head office	(650,000)
Profit on sale of shares	(35,000)
Dividend received	(72,000)
Class 1A NIC on loan to employee	(83)
Plus:	
Interest re office units	8,000
Depreciation	74,500
	1,292,372

No other adjustments

(2) Class 1A NIC on loan to employee

Taxable benefit = £45,000 × 4%	£1,800
Subject to NIC	
In P/E 31 July 2014 = 4/12 × £1,800 × 13.8%	£83

(3) Capital allowances

	Main pool £	Allowances £
Y/E 31 March 2014		
TWDV b/f	222,000	
WDA @ 18%	(39,960)	39,960
TWDV c/f	182,040	
Total allowances		39,960
P/E 31 July 2014		
Additions		
IT equipment	100,000	
AIA (max £250,000 × 4/12)	(83,333)	83,333
Electric car	14,500	
FYA @ 100%	(14,500)	14,500
	198,707	
WDA @ 18% × 4/12	(11,922)	11,922
TWDV c/f	186,785	
Total allowances		109,755

(4) *Chargeable gain*

	£
Proceeds	1,450,000
Less: Cost	(800,000)
Unindexed gain	650,000
Less: indexation allowance (255.8 – 201.6)/201.6 = 0.269 × £800,000	(215,200)
Gain	434,800

Shares
Gain on shares exempt as SSE applies

(5) Non-trading loan relationships

	£
Interest received	17,000
Less: Interest paid	(8,000)
	9,000

(6) Corporation tax limits

	Y/E 31 March 2014	P/E 31 July 2014
UL	£1,500,000	£500,000
LL	£300,000	£100,000

(b) Payment dates

Year ended 31 March 2014

The company pays corporation tax at the main rate for the year ended 31 March 2014 and also paid corporation tax at the main rate in the previous accounting period. Therefore the payments must be in four equal instalments due by:

14 October 2013
14 January 2014
14 April 2014
14 July 2014

4 months ended 31 July 2014

As the company pays corporation tax at the marginal rate for the period ended 31 July 2014 the tax must be paid by nine months and one day after the end of the accounting period ie by 1 May 2015.

Filing dates

As the period of account is longer than 12 months but does not exceed 18 months the returns for both accounting periods (Year ended 31 March 2014 and four months ended 31 July 2014) must be filed by 12 months after the end of the period of account ie by 31 July 2015.

		Marks
(a)	Adjusted profits (W1)	
	Deductions (½ each)	3
	Interest re office units	½
	Depreciation	½
	Class 1A NIC on loan to employee (W2)	1½
	No other adjustments	½
	CA's (W3)	
	Y/e 31 March 2014	½
	P/e 31 July 2014	
	AIA	1
	FYA	½
	WDA's	1
	Chargeable gain (W4)	
	Unindexed gain	½
	IA	1
	Shares exempt under SSE	1
	NTLR (½ each type of interest) (W5)	1
	CT limits for 4 month accounting period (W6)	1
	Correct chargeable accounting periods stated	1
	Time apportionment of adjusted trading profit 12:4	1
	Deduction of CA's	½
	Property income split 12:4	1
	Chargeable gain in correct AP	½
	NTLR allocated 12:4	½
	FII	1
	CT liability y/e 31 March 2014	½
	CT liability p/e 31 July 2014	1½
		21
(b)	Payment – y/e 31 March 2014	
	Main rate this year and prior year	½
	Instalments	½
	Dates	1
	Payment – 4 m/e 31 July 2014	
	Due date	1
	Filing dates	1
		4
		25

4 Dhruthi, Komal and Shriya

(a)

	Dhruthi £	Komal £	Shriya £	Total £
Six months to 30.6.13				
Salary × 6/12	3,500			3,500
Interest on capital @ 6% × 6/12	12,000	7,500	3,000	22,500
PSR 1:1:1	(2,000)	(2,000)	(2,000)	(6,000)
	13,500	5,500	1,000	20,000
Six months to 31.12.13				
Salary × 6/12	22,000	4,000	4,000	30,000
Interest on capital @ 4.5% × 6/12	9,000	5,625	2,250	16,875
PSR 0:1:1		(13,438)	(13,437)	(26,875)
	31,000	(3,813)	(7,187)	20,000
Total for year to 31.12.13	44,500	1,687	(6,187)	
Reallocate notional loss				
£6,187 × 44,500 : 1,687	(5,961)	(226)	6,187	
Total profits for the year	38,539	1,461	Nil	40,000

(b) **VAT partial exemption**

Test one

Average monthly total input tax must not exceed £625 – not satisfied as monthly total input tax is £793 (£2,380/3).

Exempt supplies must not exceed 50% of total supplies – satisfied as exempt supplies are 48% of total supplies.

Therefore as both parts not satisfied test one does not allow full recovery of input tax.

Test two

Average monthly total input tax less input tax attributable to taxable supplies must not exceed £625 – satisfied as it is £427 ([£2,380 – £1,100]/3).

Exempt supplies must not exceed 50% of total supplies – satisfied as exempt supplies are 48% of total supplies.

Therefore as both parts are satisfied test two does allow full recovery of input tax.

(c)

Transaction 1 – Acquisition from EU

Property Traders Ltd will need to account for output VAT on the purchase of materials.

This input VAT is then recoverable as input VAT provided the materials are used to make taxable supplies.

Transaction 2 – VAT on property

As the property is a commercial building which is less than three years old, it is a standard rated supply.

Property rental is an exempt supply. Therefore Property Traders Ltd will not be able to recover the input tax.

However, if Property Traders Ltd opts to tax the building then:

- VAT must be charged at 20% on rent

- Property Traders Ltd will be able to recover the input tax of £0.5m on the purchase of the building in addition to any other input VAT incurred in relation to the rental of the property

- Any of the tenants who are VAT registered will be able to recover the VAT charged on the rent as input VAT

- However, those tenants who are exempt from VAT will not be able to recover the VAT charged on the rent as input VAT which will make the property rental more expensive for them

- The option to tax is irrevocable for 20 years

- The option to tax can however be revoked during the 'cooling-off' period ie within the first six months after it becomes effective

- A sale of the building within 20 years will therefore be standard rated.

- This potentially makes the sale price of the building higher than other similar buildings if the purchaser cannot recover the VAT as input VAT

Transaction 3 – Supplies of services

This is a provision of services from one business to another. It is irrelevant that the customer is not VAT registered.

VAT is therefore charged where the customer is located, ie in Germany.

Property Traders Ltd therefore does not need to account for any VAT on the supply of its property management services in this case.

Marking guide

		Marks	
(a)	Split periods into 6 m/e 30.6.13 and 6 m/e 31.12.13	½	
	6 m/e 30.6.13		
	Salary	½	
	Interest on capital	1	
	PSR	1	
	6 m/e 31.12.13		
	Salary	½	
	Interest on capital	½	
	PSR	½	
	Reallocation of notional loss using full year figures	½	
	Attempt at reallocating the notional loss	1	
	Correct reallocation of notional loss	1	
			7
(b)	Test one	2½	
	Test two	2½	
			5
(c)	*Transaction 1*	1	
	Transaction 2		
	Standard rated; <3 years old	1	
	Property rental is exempt supply	1	
	Possible OTT	½	
	Effect of OTT (½ per point)	4	
	Transaction 3		
	Provision of services	½	
	VAT charged where customer located	½	
	No need to account for VAT	½	
		9	
	Max		7
			19

September 2013
exam questions

1   Stear Ltd

(a) Stear Ltd is an unquoted trading company. It has always had an accounting date of 31 December, the most recent filed accounts being prepared to 31 December 2013. Stear Ltd has now changed its accounting date, preparing accounts to 31 August 2014. The company has recorded draft profits for the eight months ended 31 August 2014 of £1,660,165, after accounting for the following items:

	Note	£
Depreciation		175,400
Staff costs	(1)	421,624
Research and development (R&D) expenditure	(2)	141,900
Rental income	(3)	96,000
Bank interest receivable		95,300
Interest payable	(4)	55,882
Profit on sale of assets	(5)	66,180
Dividends received	(6)	6,320

The accountant has calculated the capital allowances for the eight months ended 31 August 2014 to be £124,795 before taking account of any adjustments required by notes (1) to (6) below. The Annual Investment Allowance (AIA) has already been fully utilised by the company.

Notes

(1)   Staff costs comprise the following:

	£
Administrative staff	124,300
Pension contributions for directors	80,000
Other staff costs (allowable)	217,324
	421,624

Administrative staff spend 40% of their time working specifically on qualifying R&D projects. The pension contributions of £80,000 payable for the directors include £10,000 accrued at the period end. None of the directors is directly involved in R&D.

(2)   In addition to costs mentioned in note (1), the profit and loss account includes a deduction for the following R&D expenditure:

	£
Research staff working directly on R&D projects	135,000
Consumables	4,100
Machinery	2,800
	141,900

Stear Ltd is a small company for R&D purposes.

(3)   Stear Ltd has its offices in Oyo Towers an office building in North London. In recent years, the company has only used three of the five floors in Oyo Towers and has let the remaining two floors for an annual rental income of £144,000.

(4)   Interest payable comprises:

	£
Bank overdraft interest	6,432
Interest payable on a loan to purchase Oyo Towers	46,500
Interest payable on a loan to purchase shares in Quinny Ltd	2,950
	55,882

(5)   On 20 January 2014 Stear Ltd sold debenture stock for £40,000 which it had acquired for £21,300 on 15 July 2001 as an investment.

The company also sold its 80% shareholding in Quinny Ltd, a UK trading company, on 1 August 2014 for £154,600. The shares had been purchased on 5 September 2013 for £104,000 plus 3% broker's fees.

(6)   In July 2014 Stear Ltd received dividends of £5,600 from Quinny Ltd, and £720 from a 1% holding in Cooke plc. Stear Ltd has no other shareholdings.

Stear Ltd had taxable total profits of £2,465,943 in the year ended 31 December 2013.

Requirements

(i) Calculate Stear Ltd's corporation tax liability for the eight months ended 31 August 2014. Explain your treatment of the dividends received. **(16 marks)**

(ii) State the due date(s) for payment and amount(s) of corporation tax payable by Stear Ltd for the eight months ended 31 August 2014. **(3 marks)**

Note: **Assume RPIs as follows: 253.1 for September 2013; 256.0 for January 2014; 261.2 for August 2014.**

Ignore VAT

(b) Stear Ltd is VAT registered and makes taxable supplies. The company purchased Oyo Towers newly constructed in February 2010 for £270,000 plus VAT at 17.5%. At that time, all five floors were used exclusively by Stear Ltd staff, but from 1 April 2012 the top two floors were let to an unconnected company.

The directors of Stear Ltd have decided that the office building Oyo Towers is now too large for the size of its workforce. Therefore they plan to sell Oyo Towers for £495,000 after deducting all selling costs on 1 November 2014. From that date, Stear Ltd will use smaller, rented premises.

Stear Ltd's VAT year for capital goods scheme purposes runs to 31 March. No option to tax has been exercised.

Requirements

(i) Calculate any stamp duty land tax payable by Stear Ltd on the purchase and disposal of Oyo Towers. **(2 marks)**

(ii) Show, using calculations, the VAT treatment of the building under the capital goods scheme over the period of ownership by Stear Ltd. **(6 marks)**

(27 marks)

2 Joshua

(a) Joshua traded as 'Perfect Patterns' for many years, drawing up accounts to 31 December. The VAT-registered manufacturing business ceased on 31 March 2014 because Joshua was ill.

Recent tax-adjusted trading profits before capital allowances are as follows:

	£
Year ended 31 December 2013	73,696
Three months ended 31 March 2014	10,310

The tax written down value of the main pool at 1 January 2013 was £14,300. Purchases of plant and machinery since then are shown below and are inclusive of VAT at the standard rate:

		£
15 April 2013	Machinery	37,200
24 August 2013	Car (CO_2 emissions 152g/km)	14,130
10 October 2013	Air conditioning units	18,000
23 January 2014	Plant	3,600

Joshua's car, purchased on 24 August 2013, was used 40% of the time for private journeys until 31 March 2014. On cessation he kept the car, which at that time had a market value of £8,600.

All the other items of plant and machinery were sold to a competitor for less than their original cost. Total proceeds including VAT were £21,600, of which £6,000 related to the air conditioning units.

Joshua has unrelieved overlap profits of £3,100.

Requirements

(i) Calculate the tax-adjusted trading profits of Perfect Patterns for the year ended 31 December 2013 and for the three months ended 31 March 2014. **(9 marks)**

(ii) Calculate Joshua's taxable trading income for 2013/14. **(2 marks)**

(b) Joshua, aged 55, is a widower. He has let out a furnished room in his house for £240 a month since December 2012.

On 1 July 2013 Joshua purchased Liberty House, a commercial property. As soon as he had bought the property, he leased it out. The tenant paid a lease premium of £16,400 on the grant of a 10-year lease at an annual rent of £12,000.

During 2013/14 Joshua received interest of £2,400, of which £800 related to an investment in an ISA. Joshua also received trust income of £405, from an interest in possession trust of which he is the life tenant. The trust's only source of income is dividends.

Requirements

(i) Calculate Joshua's property income assessment for 2013/14. **(2 marks)**

(ii) Using the information in parts (a) and (b) calculate Joshua's income tax and national insurance payable for 2013/14. **(7 marks)**

Note: **Ignore VAT**

(c) Since he ceased to trade, Joshua's health has worsened. He is now expected to live for a maximum of four years.

Joshua owns the following assets with current market values as stated:

(1) His home in Wales worth £450,000

(2) A holiday apartment in Spain with a sterling equivalent value of £200,000. On his death overseas death duties equivalent to £53,000 will be payable.

(3) A vintage car valued at £37,000

(4) Personal chattels and cash balances of £24,000

(5) Liberty House, the commercial property, worth £700,000. Joshua is considering giving Liberty House to his son George in November 2014 to reduce the inheritance tax payable on his death.

Joshua is the life tenant of a qualifying interest in possession trust. On his death, the trust assets will pass to his grandchildren. The trust assets comprise 4,000 shares in Challoner plc, an investment company, quoted at 208 – 214p, with marked bargains of 201p, 209p and 219p.

The value of all assets is expected to remain the same for the next four years with the exception of Liberty House and Joshua's home in Wales. These are both expected to stay at the same value for the rest of 2014, but will increase in value by 10% by March 2018.

Joshua was the sole beneficiary of his wife Emily's will when Emily died in August 2011. No lifetime gifts have been made by either Emily or Joshua. On his death, Joshua will leave his free estate to his son George.

Requirements

(i) Assuming that Joshua dies in March 2018 and that he:

- makes the lifetime gift of Liberty House to George in November 2014; or alternatively
- does not make the lifetime gift and still owns Liberty House at his death in March 2018,

calculate the inheritance tax payable as a result of his death in each case, and explain your treatment of the trust assets. Show your death-estate calculations in two columns labelled 'gift' and 'no gift'. **(14 marks)**

(ii) Assuming that Joshua gave Liberty House to George in November 2014, identify who pays the inheritance tax due as a result of Joshua's death in March 2018. (No calculations are required). **(2 marks)**

(36 marks)

3 Isabella Sansom

(a) Your firm of ICAEW Chartered Accountants has been approached by a potential new tax client, Isabella Sansom. Isabella's husband Patrick has been a tax client of the firm for many years. However you have become aware that Patrick and Isabella have recently separated and are considering a divorce.

Requirement

Identify which two of the five fundamental ethical principles are threatened in this situation. List the safeguards that should be considered if your firm wishes to accept Isabella as a new client.

(5 marks)

Note: You are not required to discuss anti-money laundering procedures.

(b) Having put in place appropriate safeguards, your firm is now acting for Isabella.

Isabella inherited a large sum of money several years ago and has substantial investments, which have generated taxable income of £31,000 in 2013/14. During 2013/14 she has made several capital disposals as follows:

- Sale of a Ming vase to her friend Ciara on 20 April 2013 for its market value of £5,700.

  Isabella had purchased a pair of Ming vases in August 2001 for £2,600, and sold one of the vases to Ciara's sister Aoife in January 2013 for £5,000. The other vase subsequently sold to Ciara was valued at £5,300 in January 2013.

- Sale of 5,000 shares in Woodcock plc, a company listed on the London Stock Exchange, on 10 September 2013 for £38,000.

  Isabella had bought 6,000 shares in Woodcock plc in May 1985 for £9,000. In November 1996 she took up her full entitlement of a 1 for 4 rights issue at £3 per share. Isabella subsequently purchased 1,000 more shares in Woodcock plc on 20 September 2013 for £5,000.

- Sale on 31 March 2014 of the lease of a commercial property for £42,000.

  Isabella had purchased the lease with 40 years left to run for £120,000 on 31 March 1980, as an investment. The lease was valued at £103,000 on 31 March 1982.

Requirement

Calculate Isabella's capital gains tax payable for 2013/14. **(14 marks)**

(c) Following her separation from Patrick, Isabella wishes to move overseas. She is planning to leave the UK at the end of November 2014.

Isabella owns the house that she had shared with Patrick, having inherited it on 1 June 2006, on her father's death. She lived in the house until her recent separation and plans to sell it on the open market either while still UK resident or soon after becoming non-resident.

Requirement

Explain Isabella's liability to UK capital gains tax on the sale of the house either

- if she is UK resident, or
- if she is non UK resident

at the time of the sale. **(2 marks)**

(21 marks)

4   Alicia Lilley

(a)   Alicia Lilley accepted an offer to work for Anderton Ltd from 6 April 2013. She received the following remuneration package from Anderton Ltd during 2013/14:

- Salary of £60,000 per annum.

- An interest-free loan of £10,000 on 6 April 2013. Alicia repaid £4,000 of the loan on 5 March 2014. The balance was still outstanding at 5 April 2014.

- A mileage allowance of 50p per mile. During 2013/14 Alicia drove 14,000 business miles in her own car.

- Childcare vouchers of £55 per week for 52 weeks towards the cost of sending her two children to an approved childcare provider.

- Anderton Ltd pays an amount equivalent to 5% of Alicia's salary into the company's occupational pension scheme. Alicia is required to pay an additional 3%.

Requirement

Calculate Alicia's taxable employment income for 2013/14, showing your treatment of each item.

(6 marks)

Note: **Assume an official rate of interest throughout 2013/14 of 4%.**

(b)   The directors of Anderton Ltd have reviewed Alicia's remuneration package and offered her the choice of either additional salary of £7,000 or a company car.

The car has a list price of £30,000 and CO_2 emissions of 163g/km. Anderton Ltd will acquire the car by way of a lease with an annual lease rental of £3,600. The company will pay all running costs, totalling £2,500, including £1,200 for the provision of petrol for both business and private purposes.

Alicia remains a higher-rate taxpayer. Anderton Ltd pays corporation tax at the rate of 23%.

Requirements

(i)   Determine the annual income tax and national insurance cost to Alicia of accepting:

- the additional salary; and alternatively
- the company car arrangement.

(4 marks)

(ii)   Calculate the annual cost to Anderton Ltd of providing:

- the additional salary; and alternatively
- the company car arrangement.

(6 marks)

(16 marks)

Note: **Ignore VAT.**

September 2013
exam answers

1 Stear Ltd

(a) (i)

		£
8 m/e 31 August 2014		
Tax-adjusted trading profit (W1)		1,370,090
Less: capital allowances (£124,795 + £2,800 [FYA])		(127,595)
		1,242,495
Property income		96,000
Non-trading loan relationship (W3)		92,450
Chargeable gain (W4)		44,052
Taxable total profits		1,474,997

Upper limit: £1.5m/2 × 8/12   = £500,000 – main rate company
Lower limit: £300,000/2 × 8/12 = £100,000

Corporation tax liability @ 23%	£339,249

Dividends received from Quinny Ltd are from an associated company and so are not FII
Dividends received from Cooke plc are exempt but are treated as FII of £800 (£720 ×100/90)

WORKINGS

(1) Tax-adjusted trading profit

		£
Profit per accounts		1,660,165
Add:	Depreciation	175,400
	Pension contributions accrued	10,000
	R&D machinery (capex)	2,800
	O'draft interest	–
	Interest on Oyo Towers (£46,500 x 2/5)	18,600
	Interest on Quinny Ltd share purchase	2,950
Less:	R&D expenditure (W2)	(236,025)
	Rental income	(96,000)
	Bank interest received	(95,300)
	Profit on sale of assets	(66,180)
	Dividends received	(6,320)
Tax-adjusted trading profit (before capital allowances)		1,370,090

(2) R&D expenditure

	£
Research staff	135,000
Admin staff (£124,300 × 40%)	49,720
Consumables	4,100
Machinery	–
	188,820
Additional deduction 125% × £188,820	236,025

(3) Non-trading loan relationships

	£
Bank interest receivable	95,300
Debenture stock profit (£40,000 – £21,300)	18,700
Interest payable on Oyo Towers (2/5 × £46,500)	(18,600)
Interest on loan re: Quinny Ltd shares	(2,950)
	92,450

(4) Gain on Quinny Ltd shares

		£
Sale proceeds		154,600
Cost (£104,000 × 103%)	107,120	
Indexation $\dfrac{261.2 - 253.1}{253.1}$ × £107,120	3,428	(110,548)
		44,052

Not SSE as not owned for at least 12 months in the last 2 years

(a) (ii)

		£
First instalment (month 7) – 14 July 2014	3/8 × liability	127,218
Second instalment (+ 3 months) – 14 October 2014	3/8 × liability	127,218
Final instalment (month 4 after AP end) – 14 December 2014	balance	84,813
		339,249

(b) (i)

SDLT payable by Stear Ltd on purchase of the property:
(£270,000 × 117.5%) × 3% = £9,518
There is no SDLT payable by Stear Ltd on the sale of the property (payable by the vendor)

(ii) The building has a 10-year period of adjustment

	£
Y/e 31 March 2010	
Input tax recovered 17.5% × £270,000	47,250
Y/e 31 March 2011 and 2012	
Used 100% for taxable purposes – so adjustment	-
Y/e 31 March 2013	
Used 60% for taxable purposes (3 out of 5 floors)	
Adjustment = repay to HMRC £47,250 × 40% × 1/10	(1,890)
Y/e 31 March 2014	
As for y/e 31 March 2013	(1,890)
Y/e 31 March 2015 – sale during the year	
(1) Normal adjustment as for the two previous years	(1,890)
(2) Disposal 100% exempt – so clawback for remaining 4 periods	
Adjustment = repay to HMRC £47,250 × 1/10 × 4	(18,900)

Marking guide

			Marks
(a)	(i)	Adjustment to profit (W1)	
		Additions	
		Depreciation	½
		Accrued pension costs	½
		R&D machinery	½
		No adjustment for overdraft interest	½
		Interest on Oyo Towers	1
		Interest on Quinny Ltd shares	½
		Deductions (½ mark each)	2 ½
		Deduction of CA's	1
		R&D expenditure (W2)	2½
		Non trading loan relationships (W3)	2
		Gain on Quinny Ltd shares (W4)	1½
		Property income	½
		Limits	1
		CT liability	½
		Dividends from Quinny Ltd not FII	½
		FII – dividends from Cooke plc	½
			16
	(ii)	First instalment	1
		Second instalment	1
		Third instalment	1
			3

(b)	(i)	SDLT payable on purchase	1½	
		No SDLT payable on sale	½	
				2
	(ii)	Recognition that 10-year period of adjustment	½	
		Adjustment for y/e 31 March 2010	1½	
		Adjustment for y/e 31 March 2011 and 2012	1	
		Adjustment for y/e 31 March 2013	1	
		Adjustment for y/e 31 March 2014	½	
		Adjustment for y/e 31 March 2015	½	
		Clawback due to sale	1	
				6
				27

2 Joshua

(a) (i)

Tax-adjusted trading profit	Y/e 31.12.13	3 m/e 31.3.14
	£	£
Profit before capital allowances	73,696	10,310
Capital allowances (W)	(49,252)	634
Tax adjusted trading profit	24,444	10,944

WORKING

Capital allowances

Y/e 31.12.13	Main pool	SRP	PU Car	Allowances
	£	£	£	£
TWDV b/f	14,300			
Additions – AIA				
Machinery (× 5/6)	31,000			
Aircon unit (× 5/6)		15,000		
AIA				
Max £250,000	(31,000)	(15,000)		46,000
	14,300	Nil		
Addition – car			14,130	
WDA @ 18%	(2,574)			2,574
WDA @ 8%			(1,130) ₓ60%	678
				49,252
TWDV c/f	11,726	Nil	13,000	
P/e 31.3.14				
Additions				
Plant (× 5/6)	3,000			
	14,726			
Disposals	(13,000)	(5,000)	(8,600)	
(21,600 – 6,000);6,000 × 5/6				
	1,726		4,400	
Balancing allowance × 60%			(4,400) ₓ60%	2,640
Balancing allowance	(1,726)			1,726
Balancing charge		5,000		(5,000)
	Nil	Nil	Nil	
Capital allowances				(634)

(ii) **Trading income 2013/14**

	£
Y/e 31.12.13	24,444
3 m/e 31.3.14	10,944
	35,388
Less overlap profits	(3,100)
	32,288

(b) (i)

Property income

Liberty House

			£
Premium	$\frac{50-9}{50}$	× £16,400	13,448
Rent	9/12 × £12,000		9,000
			22,448

Rent-a-room

Rent 12 × £240 = £2,880

< £4,250 therefore exempt

			–
			22,448

(ii)

Income tax payable 2013/14

	Total £	Non savings £	Savings £	Dividends £
Trading income (from (a)(ii))	32,288	32,288		
Property income (from (b)(i))	22,448	22,448		
Bank interest (£2,400 – 800) ×100/80	2,000		2,000	
Trust income (IIP dividends)				
£405 × 100/90	450			450
Net income	57,186	54,736	2,000	450
Less Personal allowance	(9,440)	(9,440)		
Taxable income	47,746	45,296	2,000	450

Income tax:

		£	£
Non savings	32,010 × 20%		6,402
	13,286 × 40%		5,314
	45,296		
Savings	2,000 × 40%		800
Dividends	450 × 32.5%		146
			12,662
Less tax credits			
On trust dividend income			(45)
On savings income			(400)
Income tax payable			12,217

National insurance contributions

Class 2	52 × £2.70	140
Class 4	£(32,288 – 7,755) × 9%	2,208
		2,348

(c) (i)

Joshua	Gift £	No gift £
Free estate		
Liberty House (W)		
£700,000 × 110%	–	770,000
Home £450,000 × 110%	495,000	495,000
Holiday home – Spain	200,000	200,000
Car	37,000	37,000
Chattels	24,000	24,000
	756,000	1,526,000

Settled property (Note)
Challoner plc
Lower of:

¼ up	208 + ¼ × (214 – 208)	=209.5
Mid barg	$\frac{201 + 219}{2}$	=210

209.5p × 4,000	8,380	8,380
Total estate	764,380	1,534,380
Less Nil Rate Band		

–Gift	Joshua's	325,000		
	Wife's	325,000		
	Lifetime gift (W)	(694,000)	–	

–No gift		(650,000)
	764,380	884,380
IHT @ 40%	305,752	353,752
Estate rate (IHT payable/ Total estate) × 100	40%	23.06%
Less DTR lower of:		
– UK IHT on overseas asset £200K × 40%/ 23.06%		
£80,000/ £46,110		
– Overseas death duty £53,000	(53,000)	(46,110)
IHT payable	252,752	307,642

As Joshua is the life tenant of a qualifying IIP trust the trust assets are included in his death estate.

WORKING

Lifetime gift – tax on death	£
Liberty House	700,000
Less annual exemptions 2014/15 &2013/14	(6,000)
	694,000
Less Nil Rate Band	
Joshua's	(325,000)
Wife's	(325,000)
	44,000
£44,000 × 40%	17,600
IHT after taper relief (3-4 years) 80% × £17,600	14,080
Total IHT payable on death (£252,752 + £14,080)	£266,832

(ii) IHT is payable on:

- The lifetime gift by George (transferee)
- Free estate within the death estate by the PRs/executors
- Settled property within the death estate by the trustees of the IIP

Marks

(a)	(i)	Deduction of own CA's from profit before CA's	1
		CA's y/e 31.12.13	
		Additions eligible for AIA	1
		AIA	½
		Car	½
		WDA @ 18% on main pool	½
		WDA @ 8% on car, restricted to 60%	1
		CA's 3 m/e 31.3.14	
		Additions	½
		Disposals	2
		BA on PU car	½
		BA on main pool	½
		BC on SRP	½
		No AIA or WDA in this period	½
			9
	(ii)	Trading income	
		Y/e 31.12.13	½
		3 m/e 31.3.14	½
		Overlap	1
			2
(b)	(i)	Property income	
		Premium	1
		Rent	½
		Rent-a room	½
			2
	(ii)	Income tax payable	
		Trading income	½
		Property income	½
		Bank interest	½
		ISA interest exempt	½
		Trust income	1
		PA	½
		Income tax liability	1½
		Less tax credits	½
		National insurance contributions	
		Class 2	½
		Class 4	1
			7
(c)	(i)	Two column approach	½
		Liberty house	1
		Home	1
		Holiday home	½
		Car & chattels	½
		Challoner plc shares	1½
		Nil rate band in no gift column	½
		Nil rate band less lifetime gift in gift column	½
		IHT @ 40%	1
		DTR	2
		Inclusion of settled property in estate	1
		Working	
		Liberty house value	½
		AE's	½
		Nil rate band	1
		IHT @ 40%	½
		Taper relief	1
		Total IHT for gift scenario	½
			14

(ii)	Lifetime gift	1	
	Free estate	½	
	Settled property	½	
			2
			36

3   Isabella Sansom

(a) The two fundamental principles that are threatened by this situation are objectivity and confidentiality.

Safeguards before taking on the client include:

- Notifying both parties that the firm will not be acting exclusively for any one client.

- The firm should obtain consent from both parties to act.

- If consent is refused by either party, or if the accountant concludes that the threat cannot be eliminated/ reduced to an acceptable level, then the firm must not act for both parties.

On accepting the client:

- The firm must issue an engagement letter.

- There will be separate engagement teams for the two clients.

- Procedures will be put in place to prevent access to information, eg secure data filing.

- Clear guidelines will be issued to members of the engagement teams on issues of security and confidentiality.

- Confidentiality agreements will be signed by employees and partners

- A regular review of the application of safeguards will take place by an individual not involved in the two engagements.

(b)

	£
Capital gains tax payable 2013/14	
Ming Dynasty Vase (W1)	4,173
Woodcock plc shares (W2)	25,800
Commercial property (W3)	7,887
	37,860
Less annual exempt amount	(10,900)
	26,960
Tax payable:	
Remaining basic rate band £(32,010 – 31,000) = £1,010 × 18%	182
Remaining gains £(26,960 – 1,010) × 28%	7,266
CGT payable	7,448

WORKINGS

(1)   Ming Dynasty Vase

Set of chattels with total proceeds > £6,000 so 5/3 rule applies
January 2013 disposal

		£	£
Sale proceeds		5,000	
Cost $\frac{5,000}{5,000 + 5,300}$ × £2,600		(1,262)	
			3,738

April 2013 disposal

	£	£
Sale proceeds	5,700	
Cost £(2,600 – 1,262)	(1,338)	4,362
		8,100

	£
Gain cannot exceed 5/3 × £(10,700-6,000) So use £7,833	7,833

Apportioned to April 2013 disposal (2013/14) = $\dfrac{5,700}{5,000+5,700}$ × £7,833   4,173

(2)   Woodcock plc shares

Matching rules	S 104 pool	Next 30 days
May 1985	6,000	
Rights issue (1:4)	1,500	
September 2013		1,000
	7,500	1,000
Disposal	(4,000) [2]	(1,000) [1]
Remaining shares	3,500	-

Next 30 days	£	£
Sale proceeds (1,000/ 5,000) × £38,000	7,600	
Cost	(5,000)	2,600

S104 pool

	No	Cost
May 1985	6,000	9,000
Nov 1996 right issue		
(1:4 @ £3ps)	1,500	4,500
	7,500	13,500
Disposal	(4,000)	(7,200)
	3,500	6,300

Sale proceeds (4,000/5,000) × £38,000	30,400	
Cost	(7,200)	23,200
Total gain on shares		25,800

(3)   Lease – assignment of short lease

Sale proceeds (6 years)		42,000
Cost (using MV 31.3.1982 – 38 years)		
% 6 years $\dfrac{31.195}{94.189}$ × £103,000		(34,113)
%38 years		
		7,887

(c)   If Isabella sells the house while she is still UK resident, she would be liable to UK CGT on any gain. However, any gain arising will be reduced to nil using PPR relief as any short period of absence since separation will be exempt as part of the last three years of ownership.

An individual who is not resident (NR) in the UK is not subject to UK CGT, and so Isabella will also have no liability if she waits until she is NR.

Marks

(a) Fundamental principles   1½
    Safeguards   2
    Accepting the client
    Engagement letter   ½
    Separate engagement teams   ½
    Secure information   ½
    Guidelines   ½
    Confidentiality agreements   ½
    Regular independent review of safeguards   ½
                           Max   6½
                                                                         5

(b) AEA   ½
    CGT payable   1½
    Ming vase
    January 2013 disposal   1½
    April 2013 disposal   1½
    Chattel restriction   1
    Apportionment to April 2013   1
    Woodcock plc shares
    Matching rules   ½
    Gain on shares from next 30 days   1
    Gain on shares from s104 pool
    S104 pool   2½
    Gain   1
    Lease   2
                                                                         14

(c) R subject/NR not subject to CGT   1
    Gain nil due to PPR   1
                                                                                2
                                                                                21

4 Alicia Lilley

(a)

		£
Salary		60,000

Beneficial loan interest
  Average method

$$\frac{10,000 + 6,000}{2} \times 4\% = £320$$

  Strict method
  $(£10,000 \times 4\% \times 11/12) + (£6,000 \times 4\% \times 1/12) = £367 + £20 = £387$

As there is no significant difference between the two methods HMRC are
unlikely to select an option hence Alicia will use the averaging method
                320

Mileage allowance

Received 50p × 14,000		7,000	
Less: 45p × 10,000		(4,500)	
25p × 4,000		(1,000)	1,500

Childcare vouchers
Higher-rate taxpayer so tax-free element is £28pw
  £(55 − 28) × 52   1,404
Employer pension contributions exempt   –
                                     63,224

Less: employee pension contribution
3% × £60,000   (1,800)
Employment income   61,424

(b) (i)

Cost to Alicia
Salary of £7,000

	£
Additional income tax £7,000 × 97% [pension] = £6,790 × 40%	2,716
NIC – 2% × £7,000	140
Total tax & NIC cost	2,856

Company car – 163g/km

	£
Car benefit 24% × £30,000	7,200
Fuel benefit 24% × £21,100	5,064
	12,264
Additional income tax 40% × £12,264	4,906
NIC – no NIC for the employee on benefits	–
Total tax & NIC cost	4,906

(ii)

Cost to Anderton Ltd
Salary

	£
Salary	7,000
Pension costs (employers) £7,000 × 5%	350
Class 1 secondary NIC £7,000 × 13.8%	966
	8,316
Less corporation tax saving	
£8,316 × 23%	(1,913)
Cost to company	6,403

Company car

	£
Lease costs	3,600
Running costs	2,500
	6,100
Class1A NIC £12,264 [part bi] × 13.8%	1,692
	7,792
Less corporation tax saving	
£(7,792 − [£3,600 × 15%]) = £7,252 × 23%	(1,668)
Cost to company	6,124

Marks

(a) Salary .... ½
    Beneficial loan interest 2
    Mileage allowance 1½
    Childcare vouchers 1
    Employer pension contribution .... ½
    Employee pension contribution .... ½
                                                     ___
                                                      6

(b) (i) Cost to Alicia
        Salary
        Additional IT 1
        NIC .... ½
        Company car
        Car benefit 1
        Fuel benefit .... ½
        Additional IT .... ½
        No NIC .... ½
                                                     ___
                                                      4

    (ii)
        Salary
        Salary .... ½
        Employer pension costs 1
        Class 1 secondary NIC 1
        CT saving .... ½
        Company car
        Lease costs .... ½
        Running costs .... ½
        Class 1A NIC 1
        CT saving 1
                                                     ___
                                                      6
                                                     ___
                                                     16

Notes

ICAEW

ICAEW

REVIEW FORM – TAX COMPLIANCE QUESTION BANK

Your ratings, comments and suggestions would be appreciated on the following areas of this Question Bank:

	Very useful	Useful	Not useful
Number of questions/answers	☐	☐	☐
Standard of answers	☐	☐	☐

	Excellent	Good	Adequate	Poor
Overall opinion of this Question Bank	☐	☐	☐	☐

Please add further comments below:

Please return completed form to:

The Learning Team
Learning and Professional Department
ICAEW
Metropolitan House
321 Avebury Boulevard
Milton Keynes
MK9 2FZ
E learning@icaew.com